THE COMPLETE GUIDE TO QUILTING

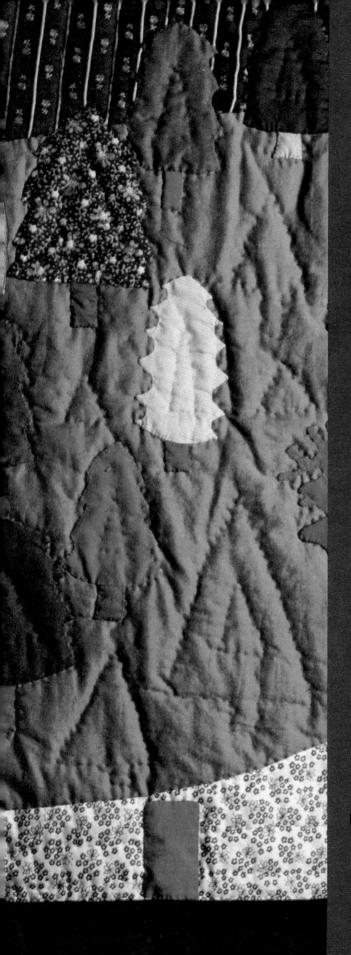

THE COMPLETE GUIDE TO QUILTING

Audrey Heard & Beverly Pryor

CHL CREATIVE HOME LIBRARY®
In Association with Better Homes and Gardens®
Meredith Corporation

Vermont Farm Quilt detail, designed and made by Diane Wilson, collection of Mr. and Mrs. Steven W. Parker.

Designed by Allan Mogel
Artwork by Carol Hines
Photography by John Garetti except for the following:
Marianne Stets, pages 161 and 207 (Noank, Connecticut, children)
Helga Studio, page 176
Ford Hovis, pages 172, 192
New London Day, page 207 (Waterford, Connecticut, children)

Cover:
Vermont Farm Quilt, designed and made by Diane Wilson,
collection of Mr. and Mrs. Steven W. Parker.

CHL CREATIVE HOME LIBRARY®
© 1974 by Meredith Corporation, Des Moines, Iowa
All rights reserved
Printed in the United States of America
Library of Congress Cataloging in Publication Data
Heard, Audrey.
  Complete guide to quilting.

  Bibliography: p.
  1. Quilting. I. Pryor, Beverly, joint author.
II. Title.
TT835.H36   746.4'6   74-14643
ISBN 0-696-25800-5

Noank Wall Hanging, designed by Kathryn Forest, made by Beverly Pryor.

ABOUT THE AUTHORS

It was the graphic quality of quilts that first attracted *Audrey Heard* to them. Fascinated by the art forms and the marvelous colors, she began to collect quilts many years ago. The design complexities of quilt making further stimulated her interest and led to her developing a knowledge of the craft skills involved.

Several years ago, she founded a cottage industry in Noank, Connecticut, making pillows from the salvaged remnants of great old quilts. She became an important influence in the revival of the craft through national distribution of the pillows. This endeavor caught the imagination of people all over the country, leading them to renewed interest in a native heritage.

Born in New York City, Mrs. Heard is a graduate of Ohio State University and the New York School of Interior Design. She was home furnishings coordinator for a New York City department store and a successful interior designer. Today, she owns and runs Hands All Around, an eclectic shop in Mystic, Connecticut. She lives in Noank, Connecticut, with her husband Manning and her sons, Bill and Nick.

After graduating from the Westover School in Middlebury, Connecticut, *Beverly Pryor* spent several years abroad at the University of Geneva, The Sorbonne, and l'Ecole du Louvre as a student of fine arts. Ultimately, she discovered that quilt making could be a very satisfying and expressive medium for working with color and design, and, in recent years, she has developed her own innovative approach to the craft. With a fascination for all forms of American folk art and a healthy respect for the skilled craftsmanship demonstrated by quilt makers of the past, she stresses foremost to her quilting students the value of being original in their work.

Along with teaching quilt making and creating her own quilts, Mrs. Pryor is also a genealogist. For many years, she has worked with local historical groups and has recently co-authored a genealogical work to be published for the Denison Society of Mystic, Connecticut. A native of Haverford, Pennsylvania, she now lives in Mystic with her husband Ed and their four children.

CONTENTS

Preface

We have been interested in quilts for a long time, and, between us, have been involved in all facets of quilt making, collecting, selling, designing, and teaching. We feel that quilt making is a unique and important contribution to the fields of design and art and that it is a singular achievement, solely the domain of women. We feel very close to the nameless women of long ago who gave us the heritage we treasure today.

Quilt making is an art form whose total effect supersedes the excellence of simple craftsmanship. It gives us great pleasure to see quilts hung on walls, serving as decorative focal points in the manner of paintings. Excitement of color and harmony of design should be the goal of every person who puts needle to cloth.

There has been a resurgence of interest in not only quilt making but all the crafts. People are seeking their own identities, fighting the plastic one-world that threatens to drown us in a sea of sameness. We believe that the satisfaction earned in doing something entirely one's own is important. In this book, we try to guide our reader into doing what is hers alone, by giving instruction and, it is to be hoped, inspiration. The disciplines of craftsmanship are soon mastered; perhaps we can provide the impetus to creative thought and deed.

Chapters 1, 2, 3, and 4 deal with the principles and techniques of quilt making. A glossary is included in Chapter 1 to familiarize the reader with a new group of terms. Words used by the quilt maker are often not what they seem to be; they have their own special meanings and connotations, almost like a trade jargon. Besides including many, many patterns for patchwork and appliqué work, we have written at length about the Amish people and the atonal graphic quilts they made. The simple geometric shapes, the stark design, and the peculiar dissonant colors set this group of quilts apart. We have included patterns for quilting taken directly from a collection of Amish quilts. We have also treated Hawaiian quilt making in almost the same depth, again offering patterns and quilting designs.

Chapter 5 deals with needleworked quilts—a very special kind of quilt making. It is here that we discuss the incredible trapunto quilting and *broderie Perse* techniques.

Chapter 6 is about creating original quilts and wall hangings. It tells about some of those pictured in this book, about the people who made them, their thoughts in conceiving them, and the way they realized their designs. Also in Chapter 6, we have discussed quilts made for and by children. One of its features is the wall hanging made by a group of youngsters at the local art school. This project is a wonderful expression of spontaneous accomplishment, in a medium completely new to the participants.

Chapter 7 gives general step-by-step instructions and patterns for creating ten of the quilts shown in this book. Before undertaking any one of these, however, it is important that the techniques given in the first part of the book be familiar.

Chapter 8 is about making quilted things: skirts, pillows and pillowcases, ornaments, upholstery, and other related items. We have designed and made these projects to show the reader the applications of quilt making to other forms besides bedcoverings and wall hangings. Many of the projects are small and quickly completed, enabling the beginner to build skills without having to spend the enormous amount of time needed to make a quilt.

Working on this book has been a great experience for us. Seeing the way in which people can set off chain reactions has been the most exciting of all—the generosity and enthusiasm with which one person leads you to another, the continual evolving of ideas, the paths that people travel on their own to the eventual meeting of all whose interests mesh.

This book is about quilts, but it is also about people. It is about all the women whose work is shown in this book and about all those who share our interest, past, present, and future. The authors wish to express their gratitude to the women who made the quilts and quilted things shown in this book. Most of them are close personal friends who share our passion for this most

The makers of the new quilts and quilted things shown in this book: seated from left to right are Lynn Kent, Barbara McKie, Helen Henry, Rieta Park, Joyce Everett, Sandra Dwyer, Rosemary Buckley, Sue Knisley, Joyce Payer, Sharon McKain, and Diane Wilson; standing from left to right are Carol Hines, Ann Ross, Audrey Heard, Beverly Pryor, and Martha Maxwell.

intriguing art form. Most of them are also from Connecticut. Rosemary Buckley, Ann Ross, Joyce Everett, Helen Henry, and Diane Wilson are all from Mystic. Joyce Payer is from Stonington; Sandy Dwyer and Lynn Kent, from Westerly; Sue Knisley lives in Watch Hill; Sharon McKain, Martha Maxwell, and Rieta Park are from Noank; Barbara McKie is from Ledyard; and Jutta Chapman is from Gales Ferry.

Diane Wilson, who designed and made our cover quilt and whose work appears throughout these pages, more than anyone else, sustained and helped us. She gave us her time and her talent, with joy and brightness and with special, sharp neatness.

We never knew Kathryn "Speedy" Forest, who lived and died in Noank many years ago. She was a well-known artist, whose specialty was batik. We used her designs for the elephant wall hanging and for the Noank wall hanging on the dedication page. She also made the Bates Family Quilt.

Those who lent us their treasured quilts to be photographed have our thanks: Adelaide Hirsche of Mason's Island, Alice Potter of Ledyard, Ruth Palmer of Noank, Mr. and Mrs. Steven W. Parker of Vermont, Patricia Smith of Noank, Mrs. Kenneth Bates of Mystic, Joan Allen Walker of Art Asia, Inc., in New York City, and especially Phyllis Haders of New York and Mystic, who put her own wonderful collection at our disposal and who was most generous in sharing her knowledge with us.

We extend our gratitude to the Women's Auxiliary to the Addison Gilbert Hospital in Gloucester, Massachusetts, for lending us their 350th Anniversary Quilt. These women are Margo New, Helen Lasley, Phyllis Sudbay, Mrs. Manuel Rocha, Betty Jedry, Jean Arthur, Ruth Webber, Gertrude Griffin, Mrs. Paul Lundburg, Eleanor Lee, Mrs. John Sesta, Marion Haskell, Barbara Aparo, Evelyn Noble, Mary French, Ida Corliss and Kay Pine, Mrs. James Rassmusson, Beatrice Dyer, Marion Boudreau, Sally Lusk, Jean Morton, Madeline O'Donnell, Mabel Foster, Janis Stelluto, Gwen David, Helen Powers, Peggy Norton, Lorraine Bishop, Dorothy Norton, Kay Brooks, Nancy D. Gray, Elsie Rocha, Irma Cohen, Margaret Goodnow, and Betty Vye.

We also wish to thank Bill Everett, Tom Eyles, Chet Vail, Mr. and Mrs. Charles T. Berry, Mr. and Mrs. Manning W. Heard, Sr., Helen Grey, Marion Stubing, Lisa Hemond, the late David Kingsbury Fentress, The Mystic Art Association, Lil Maxwell and her art students, and the Great Neck School of Waterford, Connecticut.

The deer, frog, pony, bird, cow, and horse designs in the Animal Quilt, Plate 71, were adapted from *Preschool Big and Little Animals Paint with Water* © 1971 by Western Publishing Company, Inc., used by permission. The owl design in the Owl Quilt, Plate 72, was adapted from *Teddy Bear Color Book* © 1970 by Western Publishing Company, Inc., used by permission.

Our children, Bailey, Julie, Mardy, and Teddy Pryor and Bill and Nick Greenfield, also deserve thanks. They were quiet, cooperative, patient, long-suffering, critical, and generous in their praise and encouragement.

We consider ourselves fortunate to have had Jeanne McClow as our editor. She rearranged parts of our text, but never once did she delete any of our "deathless prose." We are indebted to her for her able editing, for her enthusiasm and encouragement.

Our artist, Carol Hines, has our deepest gratitude, for with her charming, accurate drawings, she brought our book to life.

With this book, we hope that we are helping to keep old traditions alive and that, in some way, we are using them to find new horizons.

Audrey Heard

Beverly Pryor

Mystic, Connecticut
Noank, Connecticut
June 1, 1974

1
About Quilt Making

Orchid Hawaiian Quilt, designed and made by Diane Wilson.

First a craft and then an art, quilt making encompasses many talents, from the simple plying of a needle in fine seaming to the creation of marvelous art forms, splendid in both concept and execution. Basically, quilting is the joining together of three layers of material by means of little stitches in an effort to produce something that can be used for both warmth and protection. The earliest known examples are Chinese; there is evidence that it was prevalent in ancient Egypt, and we know that it was used throughout medieval Europe.

Necessity is a wonderful goad, and because fabrics in early America were in short supply, hard to come by, and expensive, the thrifty housewife salvaged the bits and pieces left over from worn-out clothing and joined them together to make covers for her family's beds. At first, these quilts were just squares of fabrics joined together, but, gradually, remembering the luxuries left behind in the Old World and desiring to embellish their new surroundings, these hardworking women found the time and the skill to make something beautiful out of the rags available to them. The pieces were put together in decorative ways, and the designs were passed from neighbor to neighbor. Names were given to the patterns, and a wonderful legacy of history and of people combined to enrich our lives today.

Before the beginning quilt maker can contribute to that legacy, there are certain basics that must be learned, step-by-step and over and over—the discipline of becoming skillful —before the ultimate artistry can be evident. What good the most dazzling colors, the most cohesive design, if the needlework is poor, the seams are crooked, the interlining is bunchy,

and the backing wrinkled. There are techniques that must be mastered, skills that must be built. Finally, with experience, comes the harmony of perfect craftsmanship and honest expression in pleasing form and color.

This is the way it is for a painter, for a silversmith, for a sculptor. It is only after one has mastered the techniques that he becomes a craftsman, and sometimes an artist. To be either of these, one must learn and practice and become competent. Then one can claim what is uniquely his, in his own way. He has earned his freedom of expression only after learning how to express himself.

That is what this book is about. We will share with you what we know about the techniques of quilt making. After you have learned them, there will be no limit to what you can do.

QUILTING TERMS

To learn to make a quilt, one must first familiarize himself with some new terms and redefine others already in everyday use. Since these terms are used throughout the book, we have collected them for you at the beginning of the book rather than at the end.

Album quilt: A quilt whose individual blocks have been made by different people. Sometimes, the quilt has a theme, but more often the designs and colors of the blocks are unrelated to each other. These are usually quilts made to be presented to an individual as a testimonial of the group's esteem.

Amish quilting: A style of quilting indigenous to the Amish people. The quilts are usually of pieced patchwork arranged in a simple geometric design, and they are always extraordinary in atonal color combinations.

Appliqué: The laying of one piece of fabric upon another and the securing of the top piece by stitching. An appliqué design is usually made up of many pieces, which are stitched in planned sequence to a foundation. Whether the forms are naturalistic or realistic, they are all part of a cohesive scheme.

Autograph quilt: A quilt made up of either pieced or appliquéd blocks, each of which contains one or more signatures of friends, inscribed in India ink. Occasionally, they have been embroidered over the ink. At one time, it was not uncommon for a noted person to receive a quilt block in the mail accompanied by a request for him to autograph it. In one instance, an autograph quilt specialized in famous musicians; another featured statesmen. Lost links in genealogical research have often been found by studying these quilts.

Backing: The bottom layer of a quilt. It is usually made up of either plain or printed fabric, lengths of which are joined to be the same size as the quilt top.

Batting: A Dacron or cotton filler that is used as an interlining between the quilt top and the backing. It is sold both by the bag and in sheet form. There are various grades available, which are usually classified according to trade names. Experiment to find one with the most resiliency and the least tendency to shift and lump. Those in sheet form are preferable for quilt making.

Bias: A diagonal across the weave of a fabric. The maximum stretch of a fabric is on the bias; when a fabric is cut on the bias, the fabric will accommodate to curved lines to be sewn.

Binding: The method used to finish the raw edges of a quilt. To make the binding, the backing is sometimes trimmed just larger than the quilt top and is brought forward, to be turned under and hemmed to the quilt top. Or the quilt top and the backing can be turned inward to each other and stitched together. Another method is to sew a strip of either matching or contrasting fabric around the quilt. Commercial bindings and tape are often used for this.

Block: A complete design unit or pattern. It can be one of many square or varied-shaped units composing a quilt, or it may be the entire quilt top. Usually, a quilt top is made up of many blocks, sewn together side by side or separated by strips of fabric called lattices; sometimes patterned blocks are sewn between.

Border: A frame of fabric completing or enhancing the central element of a quilt. It can be plain strips of fabric, or it can be pieced or appliquéd; often it is quilted in a handsome design.

Broderie Perse ("Persian embroidery"): An early form of quilt making, in which scraps of precious chintz or other picture prints were appliquéd to a foundation fabric in a decorative manner. This was a substitute for the richly embroidered silk coverlets being brought from the Orient, for the technique gave the effect of lavish embroidery.

Counterpane: An old term meaning "bedspread."

Coverlet: A quilt that covers only the top of the bed, but not the pillows, and that extends over the sides just far enough to cover the mattress. It is the most popular size for a quilt.

Crazy quilt: A quilt composed of irregularly

shaped pieces, randomly joined, of seemingly unrelated fabrics. The form is an old one, dating back to colonial days, when it was born of necessity. It culminated in Victorian times, in a frenzy of color, pattern, and stitchery.

Diversified design: A term describing a quilt top that is composed of disparate sizes of blocks or that has unrelated design and color elements.

Friendship quilt: A quilt put together by a group of friends for someone else as a token of friendship. Each block is the work of a different person, and all are set together and quilted communally; the completed quilt is presented to the recipient as a gift.

Hawaiian quilting: A style of quilt making that was developed in the Hawaiian Islands. It is characterized by a large design that has been cut from one piece of fabric and that is then appliquéd to a foundation fabric. After the quilt has been interlined and backed, it is quilted in waves, outlining the design. Usually, the quilts are of two colors only and the designs are taken from nature.

Hemming: The folding under and the sewing down of the edge of a fabric, using small stitches. This not only holds the fabric in place but prevents fraying of the edges.

Hexagonal quilt: A pieced quilt made entirely of hexagons. Patterns emerge through color arrangement.

Interlining: The middle layer of a quilt. Sandwiched between the quilt top and the backing, it provides warmth, or body and thickness.

Usually cotton or Dacron batting is used, though an old blanket or a flannel sheet will serve.

Lattice strips: Narrow, equally sized strips of fabric, which are used to join and frame the blocks of a quilt top. These form a grid, which hold together the blocks; the intersections of the grid can be done in a contrasting-color square.

Log cabin quilt: A type of quilt made up entirely of blocks of even size and design, each containing strips of fabric of even width and arranged in color sequence, as diagonals or as opposites. The overall design is developed by arranging the light and dark areas of the blocks to a prescribed effect, as in Barn Raising (Plate 11 on page 93), Straight Furrow (Plate 12 on page 93), or Courthouse Steps (Diagram 3-74 on page 92.)

Marking: The drawing of the quilting design on the quilt top or backing preparatory to quilting. Usually, it is done by perforating a pattern with a sharp pencil or by using powdered chalk. Sometimes, templates or the outlines of other objects, such as cups or saucers, are traced to produce the design.

Marriage quilt: Traditionally, the thirteenth quilt made by a young woman for her hope chest. Supposedly, the thirteenth was the apex of her abilities; into it, she put the finest materials she could afford and the best of her work. When the quilt top was finished, her friends would quilt it for her, and it became a prized possession to be exhibited on special occasions. Many of these employed hearts as part of the design motif.

Miter: A method used to turn a 90-degree corner with a straight strip of fabric. To do it, a 45-degree miter is made that goes through the bias of the grain line of the fabric. This is the most desirable way to finish the four outside corners of a quilt.

Mock quilt: See **Tied quilt.**

Mola: The name given to the quilt blocks sewn in reverse appliqué by the San Blas Indians of Panama and other South American natives.

Needlework quilts: Quilts whose primary decorative quality depends on ornate stitchery. Crewel, trapunto, whitework, and Turkey red quilting fall into this category.

Patch: To place one piece of fabric over another and fasten them together by hemming the turned-in edges of the top piece to the bottom. Technically, it means to appliqué, but the term is often used as a misnomer for pieced patchwork.

Piece: *noun:* A unit of cloth used in making up a quilt block.
verb: To join units of fabric together to form a block.

Putting in: The procedure of mounting a quilt on a quilting frame by securing it to two muslin-covered poles. The quilt is rolled on the poles, leaving open the area to be quilted.

Quilt: *noun:* A bedcovering made up of a quilt top, interlining, and backing and joined together either by stitching in patterns or by tying through the layers.
verb: To secure the three layers of a quilt together by means of small running stitches, either by hand or by machine.

Quilt top: The top layer of the quilt. It can be pieced, appliquéd, embroidered, or decorated in whatever way the quilt maker wishes.

Quilting frame: A wooden stretcher that holds the quilt taut while it is being quilted.

Repeat design: A quilt top containing blocks of identical size and pattern. Different colors, however, may be used in the blocks.

Reverse appliqué: An appliqué technique in which several layers of fabric—each a different color—are basted together. Designs are cut through from the top, revealing the layer beneath. The edges of the opening are turned under and hemmed. The next layer is handled in like manner. Fabric is removed, rather than added, to create designs.

Running stitch: The most commonly used stitch for basting, piecing, and quilting. The needle is inserted through all layers, in and out several times, before being pulled through. Quilting stitches should be very small and uniform in size and spacing for best effect.

Scale: To adjust the size of a pattern or design to fit required measurements. Any pattern or design can be enlarged or reduced by the use of one of several devices, among them graph paper or a pantograph.

Scrap quilt: A quilt made up of bits and pieces of leftover fabric, usually joined in random fashion, although blocks can be made, each varying in fabric and color. Scrap quilts are appealing because they are spontaneous; they are also economical because they utilize what fabrics are available.

Setting together: The joining together of finished blocks to make a completed quilt top. This can be done either by sewing the blocks to each other or by separating them with lattice strips or plain blocks. Sometimes, the blocks are set diagonally.

Stuffed or puffed quilt: A quilt made up of individual units that have been stuffed with batting before being joined together. Sometimes, a quilt interlined with a thick layer of cotton or Dacron is called a puff quilt.

Template: A rigid, full-scale pattern made of cardboard, plastic, tin. The pattern shapes, as well as the quilting outlines, are made into templates, the outlines of which are then traced directly onto the fabrics being used.

Tied quilt (also called mock quilt): A quilt that has had its three layers joined by a stitch of yarn or string, the loose ends of which are then tied together in a square knot. The stitches are taken at regular intervals and, if desired, tufts are left. If the tufts, or knots, are not wanted, the knot is made on the back of the quilt. Tying is used when time is limited or when the fill is too thick to be quilted.

Trapunto quilting (also called Italian quilting): A method of quilting in which double rows of stitching form channels, or pockets, which are later filled from the back, throwing the design into high relief. Only two layers—the quilt top and the backing—are used.

Whitework quilt: A quilt made up of two sheets of white fabric, with a thin interlining between. The entire quilt is decorated with fine stitches done in white thread to create ornate picture patterns. Whitework quilting is the most skilled, most tedious, method of quilting.

ABOUT PATTERNS AND COLOR SCHEMES

We feel that any woman can learn to be original, to do something that is truly her own. If you are an inexperienced quilt maker, go on to read the following chapters and then select a pattern that appeals to you (for patchwork patterns, see pages 56 to 84; for appliqué, see pages 132 to 145). Don't, however, choose an exceedingly difficult pattern with curved lines for your first project. Nor should you select a pattern that has too many pieces in it, for it can be discouraging to leap into a project that is beyond your abilities. There are many easy and moderately easy patterns with which to begin. Like the rich getting richer, success attracts success, so try something simple and within your range of accomplishment. Remember that your first attempts represent a learning process, not an endurance contest. Quilt making should be fun and relaxing, and the results will improve as your techniques evolve.

It does not matter whether you choose patchwork or appliqué for your first quilt. The former, which is called "pieced work," involves the piecing together of small, usually geometric, shapes to form a patterned block. Appliqué is the placing of one fabric on top of another and securing it by stitching to form a pictorial representation. Patchwork tends to be graphic and tight and is done by machine for the most part; appliqué is freer and more pictorial and is best, we feel, when done by hand. Do whichever appeals to you.

After a while, you will be able to design your own patterns. This is the goal—to create and manufacture an object that is an expression of your own taste and ability. You will then be truly giving of yourself, and you will be making a personal statement. In any book picturing old quilts, those that have the most charm and character are those that are individual and that say something about their makers. Don't expect to accomplish this in a day or a month or even half a year. You must first master the techniques and learn the ground rules. Pattern, color, and fabric impose limitations. You must learn to live within them. The important thing is to learn the skills of the craft, to be neat, and to be accurate.

It takes a certain amount of skill to coordinate a pattern and a color scheme. Some people are born with a knack for it; others must acquire the ability through training and experience. Color schemes are enormously personal; you like certain colors and not others. Choose the colors you like and learn to work with them. Follow the basic rules of color harmony—or willfully flaunt them for a striking effect. If you are a novice at color work, limit your palette at the beginning. Too many colors can drown out a pattern. Look at quilts whenever you get a chance. Note what makes some work and others not so effective. (A further discussion of color is contained in Chapter 6.)

A great quilt is seen in its maker's mind as a painting is seen in an artist's. Both the painter and the quilt maker see the finished work in its entirety, with respect to both design and color, before a stroke is put to canvas or a stitch is put to cloth.

ABOUT SETTING A QUILT

Once you have thought about a pattern and a color scheme, you must consider how you want to "set"—join the blocks of—your quilt. There are many ways in which to do this. The simplest

Diagram 1-1

method is to place the blocks side by side and then sew them. A variation is to place pieced blocks between plain blocks (Diagram 1-1) and then quilt the plain blocks later with a quilting pattern. Blocks can also be separated by lattice strips, as shown in Diagram 1-2. The blocks are then joined in rows by one strip being sewn vertically between each block in the row. Then the rows are joined by sewing one long horizontal strip between each row. Or blocks can be framed (Diagram 1-3), as described in Chapter 3. Another method is to join the blocks on a diagonal (Diagram 1-4), which is a more difficult method than some of the others, partly because the quilt must be finished with half-squares on the sides. Another possibility is to set the blocks in a mélange of rectangles and squares (Diagram 1-5). This effect can be achieved by alternating plain blocks with pieced blocks (see Plate 59 on page 186) or by using all

Diagram 1-3

Diagram 1-2

worked blocks, which represents a lot of sewing.

When rectangles and squares are cut for this kind of quilt, the measurements must be based on multiples of the same number. For example, if a multiple factor of 4 inches is chosen, then squares may be 4 by 4 inches, 8 by 8 inches, 12 by 12 inches, and rectangles, 4 by 8 inches, 4 by 12 inches, etc. A rectangle involving another set of factors, such as 3 by 9 inches, wouldn't fit. But if the multiple factor were 3 inches, then any combination of 3 inches, 6 inches, 9 inches, etc., would work.

The Hines Marriage quilt, (see Plate 60 on page 186) illustrates an interesting method of setting a quilt. Here large, irregularly sized blocks are joined together. Careful figuring, of course, is required in order to ensure coming within the desired overall finished quilt size.

Whatever method you choose for setting your quilt, the overall dimensions must be planned ahead. Again, this should be done at the very beginning, in the layout stage of a quilt.

Diagram 1-5

Diagram 1-4

ABOUT BORDERS

The border of a quilt serves as a frame. It should enhance the central designs or motif and should never be so strong as to overpower the body of the quilt. It may echo the design, reflecting its colors and details in subtle counterpoint, or it may contrast or complement. It may be patterned or plain. A series of borders, concentrically placed, can reflect the colors of the quilt. They can be light or dark, narrow or wide.

The main consideration in planning a border, both in relation to color and size, is scale. The border must complement the quilt body. If it is too large, it will overwhelm the quilt body. If it is too small, it will be useless. Think of the border and the quilt body in terms of a frame surrounding a picture.

Borders fall into three classifications: pieced, appliquéd, and plain. Pieced borders usually work best on pieced quilts, appliquéd on appliquéd quilts. This is not a hard-and-fast rule, though, and the two are often mixed with success. Many quilts combine patchwork and appliqué, using color to tie the two forms together. Plain borders are usually used on highly geometric quilt designs, such as the Amish type, and are then ornately quilted.

The pattern of the quilt will suggest the best pattern for the border. For instance, almost every pieced quilt is based upon a particular geometric unit, either triangles, squares, or rectangles, which can be echoed in the border design. In arranging these units, you can duplicate an entire segment of the pattern or you can use just one unit. For example, two triangles can be sewn together to form a square; by changing the direction of the colors used in the quilt body, you can create even more design interest. Sometimes you can take inspiration from the border designs printed in quilting books. However, when a quilt is very busy, like a crazy quilt, do not use a decorative border. Finish it, instead, with a simple plain border strip (see Diagram 1-2).

ABOUT FABRICS

It is mainly with fabrics that quilting concerns itself. The perennial favorites are calico, 100-percent cotton broadcloth, cotton percale, chintz, gingham, satin, velvet, corduroy, cotton satin, cotton taffeta, and felt. Lightweight sailcloth, Kettle Cloth, and cotton Indian Head are heavy, but they can be used. The 65-percent Dacron 35-percent cotton broadcloth, which comes in marvelous colors, is also suitable for our use, even though it does not have the quality and texture of 100-percent cotton broadcloth. As a general rule, the higher the ratio of Dacron or polyester to cotton, the less desirable the fabric becomes to the quilt maker. It does not have the "hand" of pure cotton. Feel the fabrics. You'll be able to tell.

Avoid fabrics that shred or are loosely woven; such as burlap. Sailcloth, denim, and canvas are heavy and difficult to sew through. Polyester knits and acrylics are too stretchy, and linen wrinkles too easily.

We love the East Indian prints and the wax-resist batiks and the subtle colors of madras; however, beautiful as they are, these can be used only with extreme caution because the dyes run, which precludes washing them. If we know that they will be dry-cleaned only, we will use them. Sometimes we use wools, knowing that they too must be dry-cleaned.

When choosing a palette of fabrics for a quilt, consider varying the weights and textures. However, you must do this harmoniously. For example, satin shrieks at Kettle Cloth, while calico accepts it graciously. Use your eye and your sense of touch to determine what goes well with what.

Fabrics are available from many sources. There are fabric stores, mill outlets, remnant counters, and discount shops. Large fabric houses and dressmaking establishments often sell their scraps by the pound. Friends and relatives will have castoffs, remainders of their own sewing projects or outgrown clothing that is not soiled or frayed.

A quilter must have a scrap bag. Most quilters develop the acquisitive instincts of manic pack rats, and the bag soon becomes a trunk, then a closet, and then a room. It's difficult to live in a house with an active quilter; very little space is left.

Try to build an intelligent scrap bag. Vary the assortment of colors, both in prints and solids. When you see a great bargain in a fabulous fabric, buy enough of it. You'll soon learn basic yardage requirements, but don't pass up bits and pieces either. You never know when you'll need them. Antique shops and auctions are good places to find unusual fabrics, and thrift shops and other people's attics are treasure troves.

Interlining: The interlining, which is sandwiched between the quilt top and the backing, serves a dual purpose. It provides warmth, and it gives the quilt thickness and body, enhancing the beauty of the stitching. The variety of linings that can be used is wide, ranging from lightweight blankets through flannel to thin, worn-out old quilts. You can, of course, buy cotton or Dacron batts, which are available in a range of sizes and thicknesses. We like Dacron batt better than cotton because it does not shift and lump when washed. It also has good resiliency and wears well.

Backing: The backing is the bottom layer of the quilt sandwich. Usually, an inexpensive fabric, such as muslin, is used for it. Unless you plan to do a reversible quilt, the color is unimportant. Whatever you use, it must be made the same overall size as the quilt top. Generally, you will need to join two or three lengths of fabric to make your backing large enough. Sometimes, it is possible to use a sheet, again if it is large enough.

ABOUT TOOLS

A quilt maker does not need a great many tools and implements, but those that are required should be kept together and, as is true for working in any other craft, should be of as good quality as can be procured.

Needles: We find #7 or #8 sharps the most satisfactory needles for general sewing, as well as for quilting. Number 8 embroidery needles are good, too, as they have a larger eye than sharps. They can be used for regular sewing and are excellent, of course, with embroidery thread or crewel yarn. The larger eye makes a bigger hole in the fabric, so that the passage of heavier thread is eased. A yarn needle is required for tied, or mock, quilts (discussed in Chapter 2).

Use the right needle for the right job; it makes sewing simpler. How frustrating it can be to try to thread a needle whose eye is too small for the thread!

Thread: We like mercerized, boil-proof cotton threads, heavy-duty cotton threads, and cotton-covered Dacrons. Avoid old or poor-quality threads sometimes put on sale in fabric stores. They are not bargains! They knot and tangle when sewn by hand and break easily when sewn by machine.

As a general rule, for joining patchwork we use either regular or heavy-duty thread. We prefer heavy-duty thread for appliqué. For doing the actual quilting, buy thread in a color to match the background of the quilt. Averaging ten to fourteen stitches to the inch, counting top and bottom stitches, we find that six to eight small spools are needed to quilt the entire top. This does not include the number of spools needed to join the pieced patchwork or to do the appliqué work. Thread used for this purpose does not have to match the background since it does not show. We find the best thread length for quilting is 30 inches; for appliqué, 20 inches. If the thread is too long, it will tangle, knot, and break.

Embroidery work calls for a durable soft thread; we like silk floss for its luminous texture and its workability. Crewel yarns can also be used. Because those made of wool will shrink when machine-washed, we recommend Orlon yarn.

Shears and scissors: Shears are big, heavy, and cumbersome when you are not used to them. Professionals use them, however, and they are the most efficient for general cutting. The best-quality large-size scissors you can buy will be the best investment you can make. Before purchasing them, though, test them to be sure they fit your hand. (Left-handed scissors are also available.) Test the points of the scissor blades to be certain that they are sharp. A good pair of scissors should be sharp enough to cut a clean line without shredding the material; the blades should not jam, and they should be well balanced. Use them only for cutting fabrics, and hide them from your family! Use another pair for cutting thread, paper patterns, and the like.

Thimble: Whether to use a thimble or not is a matter of individual taste. For some, it is a necessary adjunct—in fact, we know quilters who wear two thimbles, one on the thumb and one on the third finger. For others, it is a nuisance. These persons will prefer calloused fingers and punctured nails to the clumsiness of a thimble. If you have the opportunity, watch a dextrous quilter as she deftly scoots her needle through the thicknesses of the quilt with tiny, exactly spaced stitches. Watch the knowing way that her left hand feels ahead, guiding her needle.

Quilters build up callouses where the needle touches the left forefinger as it emerges from the fabric. In some circles, the formation of this callous is hastened by the forefinger being passed through the flame of a candle. We don't recommend this, however, preferring to let nature take her course.

In her booklet, *Pennsylvania German Quilts*, Marie Knorr Graeff instructs brightly: "The quilter places the forefinger of the left hand over the spot where the needle should come through the cloth. With her right hand she pushes the needle from underneath, through the three layers of material, until the needle touches the tip of the forefinger of the left hand. Experienced quilters develop callouses of their bold forefinger. As the tip of the needle emerges, it is drawn through the three layers of cloth; the thread is drawn to its full length and then plunged downward again. One stitch has been made."

Most modern quilters don't quilt by sewing one stitch at a time. The needle is pushed in and out of the three layers, taking half a dozen stitches at a time, before the thread is pulled through. Quilting is much quicker when sewn in this way, but thimbles, callouses, and "bold" forefingers are just as relevant as they ever were.

Cardboard: We use cardboard for making our patterns, or templates, as they are sometimes called. Many years ago, they were made of tin, cut out by considerate husbands or itinerant tinsmiths. We find a light- or medium-weight cardboard adequate for this purpose. A few shirt cardboards will usually be sufficient to make all the templates you will need for a quilt.

Tracing paper, graph paper, and drawing paper: These are invaluable aids to the quilter; keep a stock of them at all times.

Pins, yardstick, and pencils: For general use, #17 steel dressmaker pins are the best pins to use. It's cheapest to buy them by the pound, but when you spill them by the pound, it's quite a performance to pick them up. Because the pins must go through three layers, many European quilters use needles instead. Your yardstick should be made of steel preferably and have its markings incised for permanency and accuracy. A wooden yardstick can be used, but always use the same one as the markings may vary from yardstick to yardstick. Never use a dressmaker's tape. These are stretchy and, consequently, unreliable. Soft pencils are fine for general use.

Miscellaneous: It is helpful, too, although not essential, to have on hand a ruler; a compass; an engineer's scale rule if you know how to use one; protractors; plastic and metal templates (available from quilting supply companies), which can be used instead of cardboard ones; drafting triangles; and colored pencils. These items are all helpful in planning and drawing out your quilt design. The colored pencils are also good for tracing patterns onto dark or "busy" fabrics.

To keep your pattern pieces together, use large manila envelopes that are marked and catalogued for future reference. A stitch ripper and masking tape are also good to have on hand.

ABOUT QUILTING HOOPS AND FRAMES

The quilting hoop or frame is used once you are ready to assemble the three layers of the quilt. Although both are optional equipment— quilting can be done without them—there are several advantages to using them. First, they serve as a stretcher, keeping the three layers of the quilt taut and free of wrinkles. They also enable your stitches to acquire a precision and neatness unsurpassed by any other method. Last, they are far more comfortable to sew over than the dining room table or in your lap.

The **quilting hoop** is available through large department stores. It works on the same principle as the embroidery hoop. It is a double wooden circle, about 22 inches in diameter, and is mounted on a stand or attached to a table by a self-contained clamp. You do your quilting in sections, and if your quilt is properly basted and marked, it works quite well. It's also extremely useful for quilting small articles, such as a pillow, a bag, or even a skirt.

A **quilting frame** is even more efficient, particularly for quilting large items. Its main disadvantage, however, is its size. Even though it can be dismantled and put away, it is an object to contend with when it is in use. If you decide that you have enough room to use a quilting frame, you can buy one, find one in an attic or antique store, or make one. It's really quite easy and relatively inexpensive to build your own.

Instructions for building two types of frames follow:

Chair-mounted frame: To build a frame designed to be mounted on four low-backed chairs of even height, four strips of wood are needed. Two should measure 1 inch by 2 inches and be as long as the width of your quilt plus 12 inches, or up to 10 feet. The other two should be 1 inch by 2 inches by 4 feet. The two shorter strips hold the longer ones in place by means of C clamps, which are available at local hardware stores (Diagram 1-6). Cover the long strips with muslin, as shown. The quilt will be basted to these covered strips when it is mounted in the frame.

Sawhorse frame: The notched sawhorse frame eliminates the use of chairs and C clamps. The notched sawhorses (Diagram 1-7) become the anchoring supports. Only two strips of wood, covered with muslin, are needed. These should measure 1½ inches by 1½ inches and be as long as the width of the quilt plus 12 inches.

A collapsible sawhorse frame can easily be made at home; it can be dismantled quickly and stored in a closet. To make it, you will need:

8 pieces of lumber, each 2×4×28 inches, for legs
2 pieces of lumber, each 2×4×36 inches, to hold sawhorses together
2 pairs sawhorse brackets (medium-duty)
2 pieces stock lumber, each 1½ inches ×1½ inches×10 feet
16 nails

Follow Diagram 1-7 to assemble.

ABOUT THE SEWING MACHINE

The sewing machine has been used by quilters since it was invented in the middle of the nineteenth century. It was used for piecing and for binding, as we do today, and its use in no way negates the philosophy of handwork and craftsmanship. A sewing machine is a tool, an adjunct, like a needle or a pair of scissors or a ruler. You must learn its functions and make it work for you. It saves hours of time, and it makes up for the years not spent learning to sew a fine

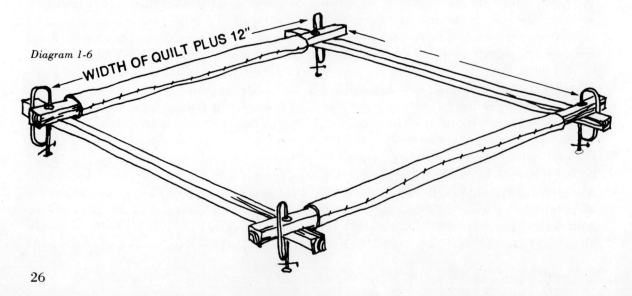

Diagram 1-6

WIDTH OF QUILT PLUS 12"

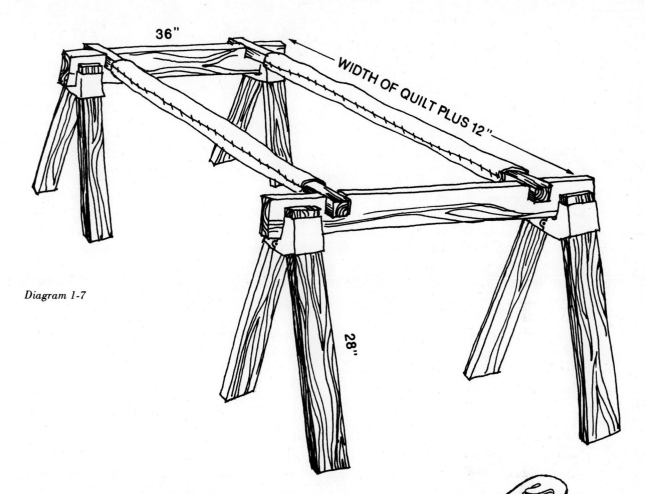

36"

WIDTH OF QUILT PLUS 12"

28"

Diagram 1-7

seam. It is important to the modern quilter. Although some of us enjoy piecing a patchwork top by hand with tiny running stitches, we appreciate the speed and accuracy of a well-handled machine.

It's nice to have a brand new machine, but it is not necessary. A vintage "clunker" will piece a quilt top as well as its modern counterpart, as long as it goes forward and in reverse. You must know it thoroughly, though—its mechanics, its principle parts, and how they work. Read the instruction book carefully, and examine the machine. Try it out, step-by-step, and experiment with it. Learn about the gadgets if you have them. They can be very helpful, especially the seam guide and the quilting foot. The seam guide (Diagram 1-8) is invaluable for accurate piecing of patchwork, for it enables you to sew a seam of an exact width and perfect straightness; the quilting foot (Diagram 1-9) is a must for

Diagram 1-8

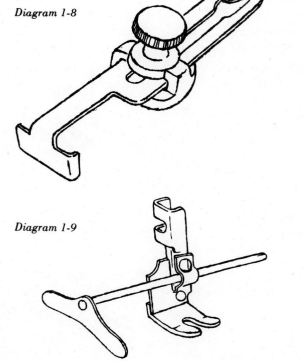

Diagram 1-9

27

machine-quilting. If your machine will take them, they're inexpensive to buy and worth learning how to use.

If you wish to use your machine to best advantage, you should be able to do the following: (1) thread the machine, (2) adjust the stitch length,

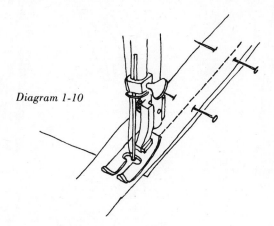

Diagram 1-10

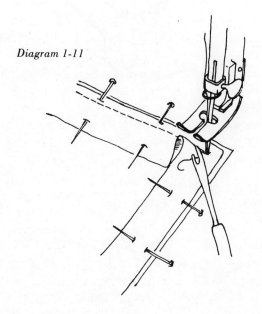

Diagram 1-11

(3) sew forward and in reverse, (4) regulate the needle thread tension, (5) regulate the bobbin thread tension, (6) turn a square corner, (7) sew a straight seam, (8) change the needle, (9) thread the bobbin.

Knowing how to turn a corner is also a basic prerequisite (Diagrams 1-10 and 1-11). It is useful not only in piecing but in binding and in making pillows and other things. If you use bias tape or any other kind of binding to finish off a raw edge, you must be able to turn a clean corner without catching the fabric or the binding in the process. In Diagram 1-10, we show how the bias tape has been pinned and, particularly, how it has been folded at the corner. The dotted line shows where the machine-stitching is to go. When the machine reaches the corner, stop; be sure that the needle is buried in the fabric, then lift the pressure foot and turn the fabric 90 degrees (Diagram 1-11). The underneath folds in the bias tape must be free so that they are not sewn down accidentally. Sometimes, it is helpful to unpin the tape as you approach the corner and, proceeding slowly, turn the wheel by hand to sew stitch by stitch until the very apex of the corner is reached.

Bias tape or any other kind of binding should not be started or ended at a corner of the quilt. Also, it should be applied a little off the edge of the fabric to be certain that there is a healthy seam.

In summary, you must learn to use your sewing machine with precision. It makes the difference between a good quilt and a bad one. When seams are crooked, the whole quilt is out of alignment and its sections will not match up.

Time-saving hints: There are several ways in which to save time when you are sewing by

machine. Since most piecing involves many, many small bits of material, each sewn to the other, it makes sense to assemble these as in an assembly line. When done in this way, you will spend less time per block and be able to do many blocks in only a little more time than it would have taken to do one. As you cut the pieces for the quilt blocks, sort them into piles according to color and shape. Then feed them through the machine one right after the other. Time-study experts have found that this sort of repetition of process cuts the time required for a given job to a minimum.

For example, look at the Churn Dash Quilt shown in Plate 1. Twelve blocks make up the quilt top. After cutting the material for all the blocks, sew together the triangles that make up the corner squares. There are four identical corner squares in the block, though each is turned in a different direction. Sew four triangle squares for each block, one right after the other. Then separate them, and press them flat. Next, sew one white square to the left side of the center patterned square. Repeat this for each of the blocks. Continue to do this until you have used each piece in every block and they are all sewn. Then, instead of only one block being complete, they will all be complete.

Another time-saver is to wind a number of bobbins ahead of time, since bobbins are always running out of thread. If your machine has zig-zag attachments, you'll find them helpful for fancy sewing, especially for appliqué. The techniques for doing patchwork and appliqué by using the sewing machine are discussed in detail in the following chapters of this book.

2
Basics of Quilting

Birds in Air Quilt detail.

Once you have in mind a general plan for your quilt, including a pattern, a basic color choice, and a basic fabric choice, you are ready to learn the ten basic steps (plus one that is optional) in quilt making. These steps apply to any quilt whether it is to be pieced patchwork or appliqué. They are:

1.
Drafting the overall quilt-top pattern.

2.
Estimating the yardage.

3.
Making and using the templates.

4.
Cutting and piecing or cutting and appliquéing the blocks and borders.

5.
Setting the quilt.

6.
Assembling the borders.

7.
Marking the quilting pattern.

8.
Preparing the quilt for quilting.

9.
Mounting the quilt in the frame (optional).

10.
Quilting or tying the quilt.

11.
Finishing the quilt.

After you have familiarized yourself with the basic procedures given in this chapter, go on to read the following chapters for specific instructions in preparing various kinds of quilt tops.

1 | DRAFTING THE OVERALL QUILT-TOP PATTERN

Assuming that you have by now decided upon the block pattern you are going to use, you must next decide upon what size the individual block will be. (A block usually measures from 8 to 18 inches on a side, but this is your decision. Of course, if you have chosen a pattern featured in this book, the size will already have been determined for you.) Then, on graph paper, allowing so many squares to equal a block, draw a diagram of your overall quilt-top design (see "The Mechanics" in Chapter 6 for further discussion of this process.) Show the design detail within each block, and use colored pencils to show color detail.

2 | ESTIMATING THE YARDAGE

Determining how much fabric is needed for the quilt you plan to make is a matter of simple measuring. Following is a table of standard bed measurements, which will serve as a guide for you. However, since some beds, particularly the old ones, will vary from the standard sizes, you need to know how to measure. Always measure your bed with the bedding (mattress and spring) and bedclothes (sheets, blankets, pillows) in place. Include the length, width, depth of mattress and of spring exposed, and, assuming there are no bed rails, the height from the top of the mattress to the floor. (If the quilt is to be used on a bed without a footboard or as a bedspread, it will have to be longer since it will have to cover the foot of the bed or the pillows.)

BED SIZES*

Type of Bed	Size (in inches)
Crib	27 × 52
Cot	27 × 75
Daybed	30–33 × 75
Single	36 × 75
Twin	39 × 75
Three-quarter	48 × 75
Double	54 × 75
Queen	60 × 75–80
King	78–80 × 80

*Inches shown are actual bed measurements. The bedding (mattress and spring) size is usually less to allow for clearance and bedclothes. There is some uncertainty among bedding manufacturers as to the standard length in the queen- and king-size widths. We consider a normal length to be 75 inches; 80 inches or longer is considered oversize. (Beckley Bedding Co., New York City.)

There is no such thing as a standard quilt size. The variations in measurements are endless, and it all comes down to a matter of personal choice. When a quilt is made to cover only the mattress top and sides, it is called by some a coverlet. When it covers the mattress top and the sides almost to the floor and also covers the pillows, it is called a bedspread. Originally, quilts were used as blankets; in our opinion, they look best when they are smaller and more contained. Because of their bulk, they do not lend themselves to draping and excessive fullness.

With the exception of the crib quilt and the cot quilt, we usually add 17 inches to either side of the mattress, a total of 34 inches, and 9 inches to the foot if there is a footboard. If not, we add 17 inches. Some quilt makers make their quilts to the size of the inexpensive lightweight blankets that they buy for interlining. These measure 68 by 90 inches for a twin bed, 80 by 90 inches for a double bed, and 108 by 90 inches for a queen- or king-size bed. If you decide to use prepacked Dacron batts for the interlining, they come in the following sizes: 45 by 60 inches, 72 by 96 inches, 81 by 96 inches, and 90 by 108 inches.

It is not necessary, though, to limit your quilt to any given size. You can adjust the interlining to fit your quilt top by joining it with more interlining to make it larger or by trimming it. We are purposely vague about these measurements, as there is no set rule for the size of your quilt. However, if you are a literal recipe follower, the following measurements for the common bedclothing sizes should be helpful.

BEDCLOTHING SIZES
(in inches)

Type of Bed	Size	Coverlet	Bedspread
Crib	27 × 52 . .	40 × 60 . .	
Cot	27 × 75 . .	40 × 80 . .	60 × 84
Twin	39 × 75 . .	72 × 84 . .	72 × 108
Double . .	54 × 75 . .	84 × 84 . .	90 × 108
Queen . . .	60 × 80 . .	94 × 90 . .	96 × 120
King	80 × 80 . .	112 × 90 . .	120 × 120

Interlining: The interlining or batt should be the same size as the quilt top, and, often, it is helpful to have it and the backing a bit larger. This ensures complete coverage. *Do not trim away the excess interlining or backing before the quilt has been quilted.*

Backing: Fabrics usually come in widths of 36 or 45 inches. To back any quilt other than a crib quilt, which takes only one length, you need two or more lengths of fabric just longer than the quilt top. These are sewn together to provide the needed width. For instance, a twin-size quilt measuring 72 by 84 inches requires two lengths of fabric, each 2½ yards long, sewn together. One 94 by 90 inches needs three lengths of material, each 3 yards long.

Quilt top: It is more difficult to estimate the yardage needed for the quilt top, since it depends on the block pattern being used. Even though the top is to be the same size as the backing and interlining, it requires more fabric because each component piece is sewn all around with a seam allowance of ¼ inch. The best way to estimate yardage is to examine the pattern and measure the pieces, making notes as to the quantity and color of each piece in one block. Add ¼ inch to all sides of each piece in one block. Multiply this by the number of blocks in the quilt to arrive at the first figure. The lattice work or dividers around each block should also be measured and ¼ inch added to each side. Then multiply that figure by the number of lattices to get the second figure. For the borders, you need a length of fabric longer than the longest border. How wide to make the border depends on the design of the quilt; experiment to find what width looks best with it. Also, any adjusting that you must do to make the completed quilt top a standard size should be done with the borders by either increasing or decreasing their width. When you have arrived at the amount needed for the borders, add that figure to the first two to get the total amount of fabric required.

You will learn with experience to "guesstimate" fabric requirements. At the beginning, overestimate. This protects you from running out of material and is ensurance against mistakes. Any leftover fabric can always be added to the ubiquitous scrap bag.

3 | MAKING AND USING THE TEMPLATES

A template is a pattern that can be used over and over for both the blocks of the quilt and for the overall quilting designs. Plastic or metal templates in all sizes and shapes can be bought from quilting-supply houses or they can be made of cardboard at home. Shirt cardboards are excellent for this purpose. Usually, we make several of each one required because, as they are used, the edges wear and become ragged. When this happens, the template must be discarded because the pattern is no longer true. Great care must be used in tracing and in cutting them. Accuracy is primary; lack of it can throw a quilt off.

To make a template, enlarge on graph paper the lines either from one of the full-scale patterns pictured in this book or from a full-scale drawing that you've made of your own original pattern. Cover a piece of cardboard with carbon paper, face down, and place your tracing over the carbon. Trace over the pattern lines; the imprint will appear on the cardboard. Cut out the templates—one for each different shape—using either a sharp knife or scissors. (It will save time if you will note on each template how many pieces of each color your pattern requires to be cut from that template. It will eliminate the need for constant reference to the master design while you are tracing onto fabric.)

Then lay out the fabric, making sure that it is wrinkle-free. If the quilt is to be pieced, lay the

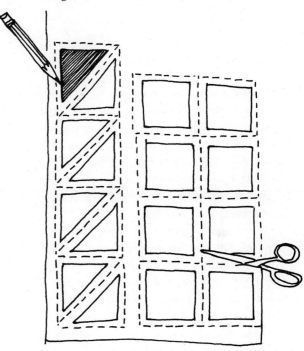

Diagram 2-1

fabric out so that the wrong side is up; if it is to be appliquéd, have the right side of the fabric up so that you can see exactly where the hems of the pieces are to be turned under for stitching. Then lay on one of the templates, making certain that it is laid on the grain of the fabric, and trace around it with a soft pencil. Then do the same for a second shape, placing it about ½ inch from the first, and so on until all the shapes for the entire quilt top have been cut.

Note that the pencil line on the fabric *always* represents the line for sewing. It is *not* the cutting line. Margins of ¼ inch must be added on all sides of the traced pattern for seam allowances. Study Diagram 2-1; note the tracing line and the dotted cutting line. You will also see that the material is being used with as little waste as possible.

Some people prefer to cut the templates with the ¼-inch seam allowance already added. Although this takes more time initially, it is useful in high-production sewing. However, since most patterns in pattern books are designed without the seam allowances added, it is best to get used to having to remember to add the ¼ inch on all sides of every piece in the pattern.

Full-scale patterns are available, but they may not be the exact size you wish to use. Therefore, it is often necessary to enlarge or reduce the patterns. There is a comprehensive discussion of this under "The Mechanics" in Chapter 6.

4 | CUTTING AND PIECING OR CUTTING AND APPLIQUEING THE BLOCKS

Although patchwork and appliqué are entirely different from each other, they both require pre-cision and neatness in tracing and cutting the forms. All cutting should be done with the finest scissors or shears available to you. They should be kept sharp, with sharp points as well. *Cut with precision*. A careless cutting job produces a quilt of poor quality. For instance, never cut a pattern directly from a template without tracing it on the fabric first. Some women hold the template and fabric together and cut. This is a sloppy way of doing things. Haphazard methods show up in the final results; accurate cutting makes sewing easier and truer.

Be economical in your cutting—do not waste fabric. Cut the borders first, each in one continuous strip, unless the borders are to be pieced, as shown in the Owl Quilt, Plate 72 on page 196 In that case, of course, it doesn't matter whether you have enough material to cut one continuous piece. Again, be certain to cut the borders ¼ inch larger all around to allow for seaming. Then go on to cut the pieces that will make up the individual blocks. These should be

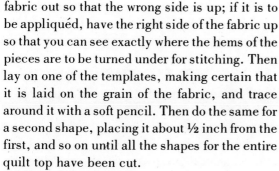

cut individually, one at a time. Don't double up and cut through two or more layers at once. The underneath layers will slip and be a little off size. The one exception to this rule occurs when you are cutting long strips of nonslippery fabric, such as 100-percent cotton. It is then possible, and often helpful, to pin two layers together and to cut them in that way.

As you cut, remember to keep the pieces separated according to color and shape. Now you are ready to piece (or appliqué) a block. Sew the pieces together, following your full-scale block pattern. Keep a hot iron available to press the seams each time a step is completed. Seams should be pressed to one side except when three or more are joined, as in a corner. Then the seams are pressed open. Continue sewing and pressing until you have completed the number of blocks that your overall quilt pattern designates.

5 | SETTING THE QUILT

When all the individual blocks for the quilt top have been completed and whatever fancy stitchery desired has been done, as for the crazy quilt discussed in Chapter 3, then it is time to set the quilt (join together the blocks). (See "About Setting a Quilt" in Chapter 1 for further discussion of ways in which to join the blocks.) Whatever way you choose, place the pieces to be joined with right sides together and sew them together with a ¼-inch seam allowance. Continue setting in the same way until a row is completed. The blocks are then joined row by row and, finally, are joined row to row.

Again, it is very important, when setting your quilt, to be certain that all the blocks are exactly the same size and that all the corners meet where they are supposed to. A wavy vertical or horizon-tal line or blocks that are not square and true represent sloppy craftsmanship and destroy the final result.

6 | ASSEMBLING THE BORDERS

Borders are sewn to the completed quilt top in one of two ways, according to the way in which you wish to finish the corners. If you are going to overlap them, as shown in Diagram 2-2, simply pin the lengthwise strips to the quilt, right sides together, and then machine-sew across, ¼ inch in. Then do the same for the widthwise strips.

If you choose to miter the corners, first pin, with right sides together, the lengthwise border strips to the quilt, allowing the ends to extend a little more than the width of the strip (Diagram 2-3); machine-sew ¼ inch in. Then, again with right sides together, pin the widthwise strips to the quilt top only, not to the lengthwise strips (Diagram 2-4). These should also be longer by the width of the border. Machine-sew only the width of the quilt top. Referring to Diagrams 2-5 and 2-6, fold back the widthwise border so that it is face down, fold its extension up at a 45-degree angle, turn the widthwise border back so that it faces up, and hand-stitch the diagonal fold in place. Repeat the procedure for the other three corners. Although mitered corners are more difficult to do than overlapped, the extra effort required will add greatly to the quality of the quilt.

Pieced borders: Pieced borders are made in the same way as pieced blocks, but making the corners presents special problems. Rarely, even with perfect measuring, do the pattern seams match when they reach the corners (Diagram 2-7 shows a poor corner). The only solution is to camouflage the defect so that it becomes less

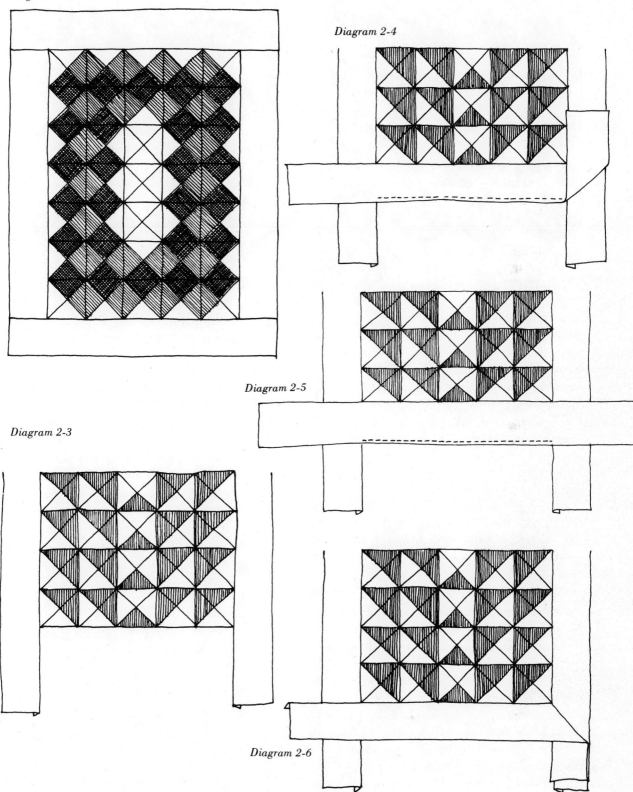

Diagram 2-2

Diagram 2-4

Diagram 2-5

Diagram 2-3

Diagram 2-6

37

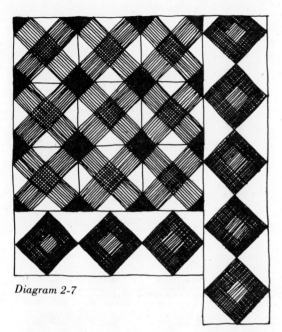

Diagram 2-7

Diagram 2-8

obtrusive. This can be done by placing the flow of the design away from the corner or by placing a plain or a pieced block at each corner, as shown in Diagram 2-8. The eye is drawn to something positive, and the defect or flaw is less noticeable.

Appliquéd borders: To be most effective, appliqué borders must relate to the body of the quilt both in color and in design. In addition, the appliquéd designs must be centered on the border strip and round each corner smoothly without losing their flow. Careful designing and measuring are required to ensure this. (To find the center of the border, fold it in half lengthwise and press a crease down the center.)

Many quilters like to use a running vine pattern (Diagram 2-9) on their appliquéd borders. The vine can be applied either in a straight line, encircling the quilt, or, in a more lifelike manner, in a winding design. Bias tape, which stretches to take in the meanderings of the curves, is good to use for the vine, or you can cut it out of fabric on the bias. Leaves, flowers, fruit, birds' nests, or whatever else you fancy are then cut from fabrics of your choice and appliquéd around the vine.

Scalloping the edges is a popular way to finish appliquéd borders. (Pieced borders are too complicated in design for this treatment. Plain borders are sometimes scalloped if the design of the quilt top is not too geometric.) The scallops, however, must be planned to be in scale with the rest of the quilt, and their corners must be carefully measured so that the finished border has no incomplete scallops (Diagrams 2-10A and B). To ensure your coming out even, the size of the scallop you choose must divide evenly into both the length and the width of the quilt. If, for instance, the quilt is 84 inches long, 4-inch,

Diagram 2-9

Diagram 2-10 A *Poor scalloped corners*

Diagram 2-10B *Good scalloped corners*

6-inch, 7-inch, 12-inch, or 14-inch scallops may be used. Choosing which of these to use depends on the size of the design of the quilt—if it is small, use small scallops', and vice versa.

Plain borders: Plain borders are noteworthy, for, when they have been quilted, they can transform a Plain Jane quilt into something very elegant. There are many quilting designs that can be used, many of which are beautifully illustrated in the Amish quilts pictured in Chapter 3. In fact, we include in that chapter full-scale quilting patterns taken directly from Amish quilts.

7 | MARKING THE QUILTING PATTERN

When the quilt top has been finished, it is time to choose and mark on the quilt top a quilting pattern. The next paragraphs explain how to mark the pattern you choose, and the following paragraphs describe the three most commonly used patterns. Others may be found throughout this book, or you may make up your own.

To begin, make a test of the pattern you plan to use. Draw a segment of the design on tracing paper or any other transparent paper. Lay it on top of the quilt. Study it; if you don't like it, do

something else. (By laying out an entire section in this way, you can tell whether it pleases you or not. If corrections are needed, it's a simple thing to do on paper.) When the design is satisfactory, carefully place the paper over the area to be quilted and transfer the design to the fabric by punching holes through the paper with a sharp pencil. When these holes are punched at the same interval as the length of stitch you plan to use, you will have left a trail of tiny pencil dots to guide your quilting stitches.

In the old days, templates were often made for quilting patterns. Sometimes they were made of tin, or sometimes kitchen implements, such as cups, bowls, and potato mashers, were used. If you are using templates, lay them on the fabric and carefully dot around them with a pencil. The tiny dots will usually be covered by the stitching and the ugly residue of a solid penciled line is avoided. The three traditional patterns used for quilting are the outline, the diagonal, and the curved line. Read the following descriptions of these types and test them on your quilt top to see whether one of them is suitable to your design.

Outline quilting: Pieced patchwork is often delineated by outline quilting. To do this, stitches

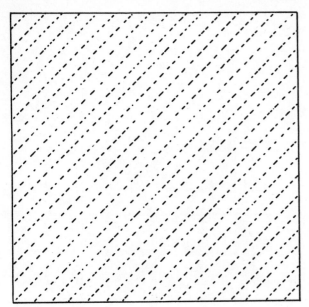

Diagram 2-11

are taken ⅜ inch inside the seam line of each patch so that each patch is outlined. This not only secures the layers to each other but gives new dimensions to the quilt. Use thread that is close to the overall color scheme, usually white on a light quilt, black or navy on a dark one, or match it to the background of the piece you are sewing.

Diagonal quilting: For diagonal quilting, diagonal lines are stitched at regularly spaced intervals across the quilt top, or a section of it (Diagram 2-11). If you stitch on the opposite diagonal as well, diamond shapes will be formed. The thread used usually matches the background color. Since pencils may leave an unattractive line, we prefer to use other methods of marking the lines to be stitched. One way is to use the carpenter's chalk line. To make this, run a cord across a piece of chalk so that it is saturated with chalk dust; then stretch the cord over the area to be marked and snap the line with your fingers, which will leave a clear stitching guide. We recommend using dressmaker's chalk for this, though, and not the blue powder sold in hardware stores, which is often indelible. A straight edge can also be used to mark diagonals, as can a rowel, which is a serrated wheel used over dressmaker's carbons to leave

an impression. A needle buried in a cork will scratch the surface of fabrics but, unfortunately, the line made disappears quickly.

We have found that the *best* way to mark diagonals is with masking tape, though. (It can be bought in ½-inch, 1-inch, and 1½-inch widths, to match the spacing of your diagonals.) Stretch it across the diagonal of the quilt and lightly press down on it with your fingertip. Following the line of the tape, sew up one side and down the other. Then move the tape over one width, and sew another line. Continue in this fashion until all lines are sewn. It is important to use fresh, good-quality masking tape so that a gummy residue won't be left on the quilt top when the tape is removed. Do not leave it on for any length of time either. Adhesive tape and transparent tape are not recommended for this method.

Curved line, or circular, quilting: Circular quilting can be marked by first tying a long piece of string to a pencil so as to make a compass of sorts (Diagram 2-12). Your finger, holding the string, acts as the needle of the compass, and the pencil describes the arc. The next arc is described by releasing the string a measured interval, and so forth. The pencil must be held perpendicular to the cloth, and the line described should be dotted.

Circular quilting can also be marked by tracing around circular shapes. Our ancestors used teacups to mark the clamshell pattern shown in Diagram 2-13. However, it takes a lot of sewing to quilt around all those teacups. Larger objects, such as salad or dinner plates, will work just as well. The lid of a skillet is good, and the cover of an oval soup tureen has great design possibilities when you are developing the overall quilting pattern.

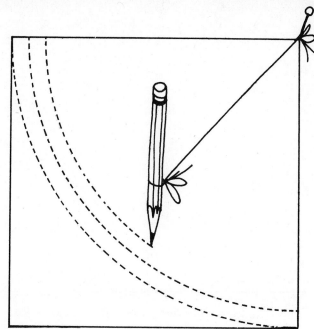

Diagram 2-12

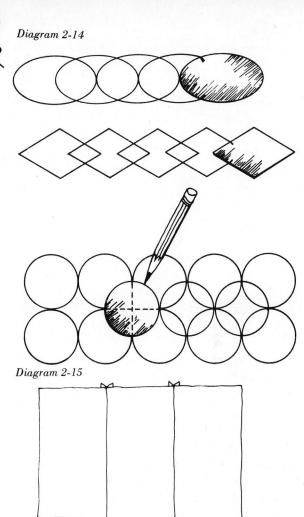

Diagram 2-14

Diagram 2-15

Diagram 2-13

are using the lid to your great-grandmother's tureen, for instance, mark the point of intersection with two tiny dots of nail polish, which can be peeled off when you are finished, or make a cardboard template from the lid and then notch the template at the proper places.

8 | PREPARING THE QUILT FOR QUILTING

When the quilt top has been completed and marked for quilting, you must next make the backing. To make the back, join together the number of lengths of fabric necessary to achieve the proper width by seaming them together as has been shown in Diagram 2-15. Or, for an interesting effect, fabrics in different colors can be joined in random widths.

Since the quilting pattern will appear on the backing as well as on the quilt top when the

When large circles or ovals are overlapped, the linear intricacies are magnified so that large unquilted areas are not left open. (Eight square inches is the maximum space that should be left unquilted—the closer the quilting, the more exciting the quilt and the better its wearability.) When overlapping shapes of any sort, mark the object being used so that the patterns will be evenly spaced, as shown in Diagram 2-14. If you

41

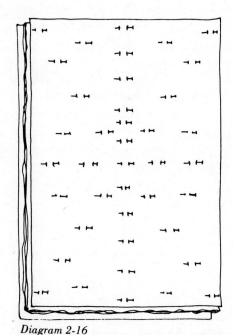
Diagram 2-16

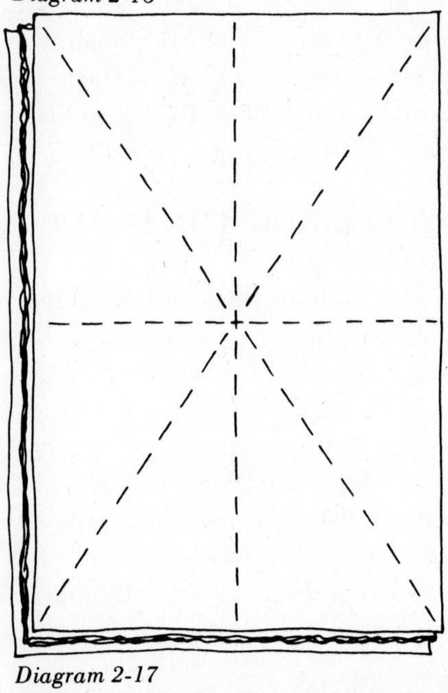

Diagram 2-17

layers have been sewn together, consider how the quilting stitches will look on that side; often, the stitches will be more fascinating when seen from the back side, especially when the thread used for the quilting is darker in color than the fabric and the backing is not patterned.

Quilting with a quilting frame: Before using a quilting frame, you must assemble the three layers of the quilt together. These are the backing, the interlining or batt, and the quilt top, which has been marked for quilting. The back is laid face down on the floor and smoothed out until it is perfectly flat. Then the batt or blanket is placed on top of the backing. It is smoothed out until there are no wrinkles or lumps. The quilt top, pressed and wrinkle-free, is placed on top of the batt and backing and smoothed out. The three layers are first pinned, as shown in Diagram 2-16, and then basted together, as shown in Diagram 2-17. The pins are inserted through all three layers, starting in the center and going in all directions from there. The pins are spaced about 8 inches apart, and care must be taken to smooth wrinkles and lumps ahead of you as you work toward the outer edges.

To baste the quilt, start at the center and sew a running stitch on all diagonals, through all three layers of the quilt, as shown in Diagram 2-17. The quilt *must* be basted if you are using a quilting frame.

Quilting without a quilting frame: If you are not using a quilting frame, the procedure for joining the three layers is slightly different. First, be sure, of course, that each of the layers is flat and wrinkle-free. Then if you are using an old blanket or flannel for the interlining (if not, read following paragraph), lay it on the floor and smooth it out until it is flat. Place the backing on top, face up; baste or pin the two together, starting in the center and working out to the sides, as shown earlier in Diagrams 2-16 and 2-17. Turn the two layers over so that the backing is on the floor and the interlining on top. Again, smooth it out. Then place the ironed quilt top face up over the interlining and the backing. Check the four corners to be sure that the three layers are lined up. Pin or baste through all three layers, starting in the center and working out toward the edges.

If you are using cotton or Dacron batts for interlining, first place the backing, face down, on the floor. Then spread the batt evenly over the top of it and baste it to the backing, using diagonal stitches. The finished quilt top is then placed over the batt, and the three layers are pinned or basted together. The extra step of securing the interlining to the backing is necessary so that the interlining will not shift.

9 | MOUNTING THE QUILT IN THE FRAME (optional)

The next step for those who are using a quilting frame is to mount the quilt. Regardless of the type of quilting frame you are using, the two longest strips (muslin-covered) are the ones that will hold the quilt taut. As each section of the quilt is finished, it will be rolled from one of these strips to the other, in the same way that film in a camera passes from one roller to the other. To mount, or "put in," the quilt, first baste one end of the quilt through all three layers to one muslin-covered strip. Then roll the quilt snugly onto this strip, rolling toward yourself. When it is evenly rolled, stretch several feet of the quilt free. This is to be attached to the other muslin-covered strip.

If a C-clamp frame is being used, secure the rolled end to the two shorter side strips (see Diagram 1-6 on page 26) with two C clamps. If a notched sawhorse frame is being used, secure the rolled strip in the notch at one end of each sawhorse, as shown in Diagram 2-18. Now attach the bottom end of the quilt by basting it to the second muslin-covered strip. Secure the second strip as you did the first, either with C clamps or in the notches of the two sawhorses. Recheck both ends to be sure that the quilt is taut and wrinkle-free.

Bias tape, ribbon, or strips of material can be run zigzag on either side of the frame and secured with safety pins, as shown in Diagram

Diagram 2-18

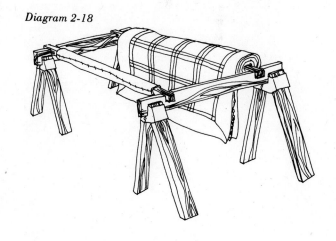

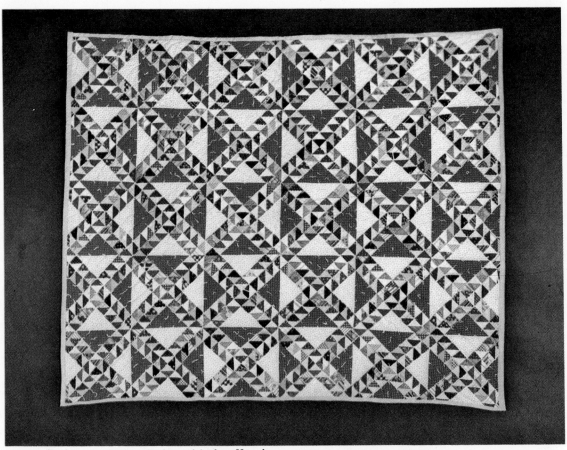

PLATE 2: *Birds in Air Quilt*, collection of Audrey Heard.

PLATE 3: *Birds in Air Quilt* detail.

44

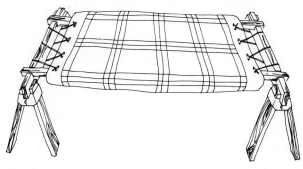

Diagram 2-19

2-19, to support the sides of the quilt. These zigzag fastenings must be unpinned, of course, each time a new section of the quilt is unrolled. It is important to maintain an easy, even tension all over the mounted quilt. If it is too tight, it will be difficult to sew, and if it is too loose, it may wrinkle or be lumpy.

After the quilt is "put in" and adjusted to your satisfaction, the quilting can begin. As each section of the quilt is finished, unfasten the clamps or notches of the rolled end and unroll the next section to be worked on, taking up the finished portion on the other muslin-covered strip. With each unrolling, check the tension of your work.

10 | QUILTING OR TYING THE QUILT

Quilting the quilt: Now that the three layers have been securely fastened together, the quilt is ready to be quilted. Do not trim the interlining or the backing until the quilt is quilted because, as mentioned earlier, the layers may shift slightly during the quilting process. You may also decide later to use the excess backing as a binding to finish off the quilt.

When quilting, always start in the center of the section being worked on and sew toward the edges. If you do this, errant wrinkles will be worked out as you go. Use either a #7 or #8 sharp needle and a single thread, about 30 inches long. Make a small knot in the end of

your thread, and insert the needle from the back to the front, coming out at the point where you plan to sew. Gently tug enough on the thread to pull the knot through the backing to the interlining, where it will be buried. Take two or three or half a dozen stitches at a time, holding them on your needle as you penetrate all three layers with each stitch. Push the needle through and pull the length of the thread out. Continue until you come to the end of the thread. Then, penetrating only the quilt top and the interlining, run the thread through the interlining for an inch or so and out through the quilt top. Cut the thread as close to the fabric as possible without cutting the fabric. The end of the thread will then recede into the lining, and you will never see where your threads begin or end.

Small, uniform stitches are the goal of quilters. The gauge to aim for is 14 stitches to the inch (7 on top; 7 on bottom).

Tying the quilt: A mock, or tied, quilt is one in which the three layers are tied together instead of being quilted together (Plate 2 shows an example of a tied quilt). String, yarn, or embroidery thread is inserted through the three layers and out in the opposite direction to be tied and knotted at regular intervals over the body of the quilt. This locks the interlining in place and prevents it from shifting. However, do not use for interlining cotton batt or lumpy fillers like corn husks or chicken feathers. Our ancestors did, but these fascinating materials make lumpy relics. Dacron batt is great; an old blanket, even better.

For this type of quilt, the backing, interlining, and quilt top are pinned and/or basted together with the same care as was described earlier in this chapter. It can then be "put in"

Diagram 2-20

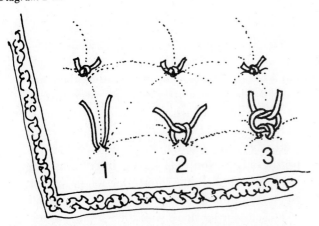

the quilting frame, or it can be worked on the dining room table. Mark the quilt at intervals of from 3 inches to 8 inches, across and down. If the quilt top is made of patchwork blocks, mark the four corners and the center of each block (see Plate 3 for tied quilt detail).

Use an embroidery needle with a large eye to accommodate the string, yarn, or floss, which can either match or contrast with the quilt top. These can be single strand or doubled, depending on the effect you want. Start at the center of the quilt and work to the edges. Push the needle through the layers and out the back. Reenter from the back, through the layers, emerging on the front, 1/8 of an inch from the point of entry. Allow 2 inches of thread at either end of the stitch, and cut. Tie the ends in a square knot —right over left, then left over right, as shown in Diagram 2-20. Trim the ends. Go on to the next tie.

If you do not wish the ties to show on the front of the quilt, enter, end on the back, and tie. No tufts or ties will show on the quilt top, and the tiny stitch will be almost invisible if a thread to match the top is used.

To tie a quilt takes about one afternoon as compared to weeks or months necessary to quilt by hand.

Tufting is a more elaborate method of tying, as it is decorative in its own right. It is done by stitching a design on the surface of the quilt with candlewick, a soft cotton yarn, to form small puffs. The effect is stronger than quilting, for the decoration is more dimensional.

Plain muslin sheeting was originally used as the foundation for tufted quilts. The design was then drawn on the muslin and delineated by a series of long and short running stitches. These stitches were made with the candlewicking yarn threaded into either a darning needle or a special notched tufting needle. When the design was completely sewn, the long stitches were cut to leave puffs.

Although this is a quick way to create a decorated surface, we do not feel that it is a necessary skill for a quilter. Machine-made chenille spreads have taken the place of hand-tufted work.

11 | FINISHING THE QUILT

Trimming and binding: Either bias tape or fabric used in the quilt top or in the backing can be used for binding the quilt. If you are using bias tape, pin the tape to the quilt top, right sides together, starting in the middle of a side. Then sew it around the entire perimeter of the quilt. You can use your sewing machine to do this, but try to keep the corners square. Trim the excess fabric, fold the tape to the back, and blindstitch it by hand, as shown in Diagram 2-21.

To make your own binding, cut fabric into 2-inch-wide strips and join them in a long strip equaling the measurement of the quilt perimeter

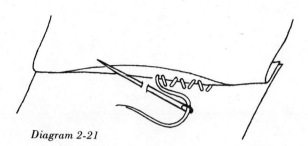

Diagram 2-21

plus an inch or two. You can cut the fabric either with the grain or on the bias. If the quilt edge is scalloped or cut in jagged zigzags, we recommend cutting it on the bias so that it will stretch to accommodate the curves. You attach it in the same way as the bias tape.

If the backing of the quilt is large enough, it can be used as a binding. Trim the interlining to the quilt-top size. Then trim the back so that it is 1½ inches to 2 inches larger than the quilt top on all sides. Bring the backing forward and pin it to the top. Fold under ⅜ inch as you go, and blindstitch it to the quilt top. This process can be reversed, using the quilt top as the binding.

Be sure that your blindstitches are really blind and are invisible on both sides of the quilt.

Sign it, date it, place it: When the quilt is finished, sign it, date it, and place it. Find an empty space in a corner and in it embroider your name, the date, your hometown, and state. We all make footprints on the sands of time, and it's reassuring to have it in writing.

Addenda
You will make mistakes; sometimes they can be repaired or eradicated. Sometimes not. For those of us who can see the sunshine through the clouds, this can be a good learning experience. Mistakes in appliqué can rarely be fixed without

doing the piece over. When you spot an error, try to locate the cause. If the problem is faulty sewing, it can be remedied, but if it's faulty tracing or cutting, rip it out and do another piece.

Patchwork mistakes are easier to correct. If the squares and triangles don't match up at the corners, rip the seams out and tighten the corners until they are right. A faulty seam can also be tightened by careful hand-sewing from the back.

Running out of material can be a horror! It happens even with the best of planning. You are seven-eighths of the way through a quilt top, and there is no more of a key fabric. Not one inch, anyplace. Not in town, or in the next town, or the nearest big city. This is indeed a quilter's nightmare.

Many old quilts have a disconcerting way of turning up short a fabric. If the maker ran out of fabric, she ran out; she simply substituted something else. This, incidentally, was sometimes done intentionally, by those people who believed that only God could make a perfect thing. They willfully mismatched one patch in deference, fearful of offending Him.

But we are not concerned here with an intentional shortage. If you run out of fabric, use ingenuity and make the lack work for you. Look over the quilt top and see what the possibilities are. It might be feasible to use a new fabric in the four corners or perhaps down the sides. Change the design a little; it often makes for a more interesting composition.

Accuracy and neatness are the passwords to the quilter's hall of fame. In piecing, cutting, tracing, and sewing, neatness and accuracy are terribly important. The finished quilt is only as good as its craftsmanship.

Pieced
Patchwork

Victorian Crazy Quilt, collection of Alice Potter.

In the very early days of this country, fabrics were scarce and highly prized. Some chintz and calico was being imported by the East India Trading Company, but England, desirous of being the sole exporter of fabrics to the colonies, soon put an end to that by placing an embargo on the company, forbidding the direct import to America. Consequently, the colonists became dependent on what England saw fit to export —silk, wool, muslin, gingham, cotton, and linen. Of course, some bootlegged fabrics seeped into the colonies, but the harsh penalties England levied on the bootleggers kept the quantities available extremely limited and costly. And, of course, some enterprising—and daring—colonists began to manufacture their own cloth as early as 1712, but since its production was strictly forbidden, the amounts available were again small. Cloth could also be produced at home, but the tasks of weaving and spinning were so long and arduous that the average colonial housewife found herself with barely enough to clothe her family, which was the vital concern in those days.

Understandably, then, every precious scrap of cloth was utilized. When clothing became too worn for further patching, the scraps were salvaged and pieced into blankets. Survival and warmth were the goals—it was to be a long time before the memory of Old World luxuries would become so strong that the colonists would again begin to devote some of their precious time and resources to decorating the home. So, for warmth and for survival, the pieced patchwork came into being. The earliest examples show simply scraps of fabric joined together at random to form new units large enough to serve as bedcoverings and clothing. Shaping the scraps into geometric components and then laying them out according to a planned sequence of color and form to make a design was a somewhat later development that reached its apex in mid- to late-nineteenth-century America. Of course, all sewing was done by hand, so that skillful needlework was a necessary accomplishment.

The majority of the patchwork quilts in existence today date from the mid-nineteenth century, and the number of them, especially in the Midwest, is staggering. It is amazing, too, how many of them are truly superb, not only in workmanship but in design. Although the women who made them regarded themselves as expert craftsmen, they did not consider themselves artists. How pleased they would be to know that their creations hang in museums around the world as examples of original, highly gifted folk art.

Many of their designs depict the life and trials of the early settlers, and the names of their patterns, passed down from generation to generation, are a record of the history of this country. Log Cabin, Bear's Paw, Mohawk Trail, Pine Tree, Burgoyne Surrounded, Lafayette's Orange Peel, Indian Trail, Corn and Beans, Dolly Madison's Star, Free Trade Block, and Martha Washington's Star commemorate events that were part and parcel of daily life; patterns like Ohio Star, Road to Oklahoma, California Star, Missouri Puzzle, 54-40 or Fight, Star of LeMoyne, Kansas Trouble, and Indian Hatchet record the settlement of the West.

Throughout the colonial, revolutionary, pioneer, Civil War, and centennial eras, hundreds of patchwork patterns evolved. Sometimes they were passed down to succeeding generations intact; often they were altered or amended by the recipient to become a new form. The favorites—the stars, the medallions, the hexagons, the baskets, the wedding rings, the log cabins, and the triangles—are seen over and over again.

The intricacies of piecing are shown in the Lone Star Quilt (Plate 4) and in the Basket Quilt (Plate 5). Both of these represent pinnacles of sewing abilities, for the fitting and joining is flawless.

These and all other patchwork patterns can be categorized according to the number of units, or patches—one, two, three, four, five, seven, or nine—used to compose a block. For instance, the repetition of a one-unit pattern is called a one-patch pattern. This will be the only shape used throughout the quilt, and it can take the form of a square, a rectangle, a rhomboid, a hexagon, a triangle, or a design like the clamshell (see Diagram 2-13 on page 41). Starting on page 56, there is a compilation of patchwork patterns. Refer to these as you read the following paragraphs.

Examples of one-patch patterns are all-over designs in blocks, such as is shown in Hit or Miss (Diagram 3-1), Roman Stripe (Diagram 3-2), and Brick Wall (Diagram 3-3). Sunburst (Diagram 3-63) is composed of rhomboids, while hexagons are the basis for Honeycomb (Diagram 3-54) and the various mosaic patterns. Triangles make up Thousand Pyramids (Diagram 3-9) and Streak of Lightning (Diagram 3-10). Crazy quilts and medallion quilts, which employ many borders to build outward from a center motif, are also one-patch designs.

Plate 6 shows a Central Medallion Quilt made in the 1930s. Thousands of squares, whose fabrics are reminiscent of the housedresses of Depression times, are framed within borders for striking effect.

Two-patch can be done in one of two ways.

PLATE 4: *Lone Star Quilt*, collection of Alice Potter.

Some are pieced in lengthwise strips, as shown in Hill and Valley (Diagram 3-52), but others show the basic square or rectangle being used cut in half, one half of which is pieced and the other half of which is either plain or appliquéd. Pinwheel (Diagram 3-4), Maryland Beauty (Diagram 3-28), and the many basket quilts fall into this category.

Three-, five-, and seven-patch are uncommon. The best example of three-patch is the Roman Square Variation (Diagram 3-8). Five-patch patterns are Queen Charlotte's Crown (Diagram 3-59) and David and Goliath (Diagram 3-21). Double Irish Chain (Diagram 3-42) is also a five-patch and shows clearly the composition of the block. There are five squares down and five across, or twenty-five in all. In the seven-patch, there are seven squares down and seven across, making a total of forty-nine. Storm at Sea (Diagram 3-29) and Autumn Leaf (Diagram 3-35) illustrate this.

More than half of all patchwork patterns are either four- or nine-patch. In the four-patch, the block is divided into four equal parts. These four

51

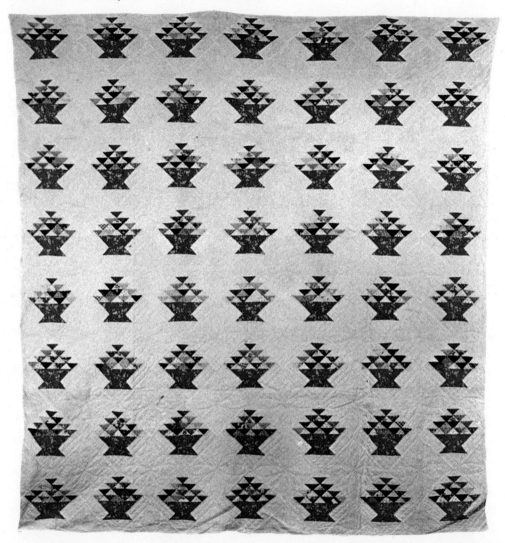

parts can be divided into even more geometric segments as long as the new segments repeat the divisions exactly from center to corners. Lafayette's Orange Peel (Diagram 3-46), Night and Day (Diagram 3-60), Pieced Star (Diagram 3-22), and Virginia Star (Diagram 3-58) are examples.

The nine-patch can be made up in one of three ways. In one method, the block is simply divided into nine equal parts, as shown in Robbing Peter to Pay Paul (Diagram 3-48), Missouri Puzzle (Diagram 3-32), and Shoo-Fly (Diagram 3-5). In another, the block is divided into nine

unequal parts, as shown in Bear's Paw (Diagram 3-25) and Corn and Beans (Diagram 3-38). In the third method, each of the nine divisions is divided in half, forming a double nine-patch. Save All (Diagram 3-49) illustrates this.

Modern-day quilters adapt the traditional patchwork to their own design concepts. For instance, two or more patterns can be combined to make an overall design (see Plate 64 on page 189 or the pattern for one block can be enlarged to the dimensions of the full quilt (see Plate 61 on pages 212-13. The possibilities for original thought are infinite; by changing, re-

PLATE 6: *Central Medallion Quilt*, collection of Audrey Heard.

PLATE 7: *Block Island Puzzle Quilt*, collection of Ruth Palmer.

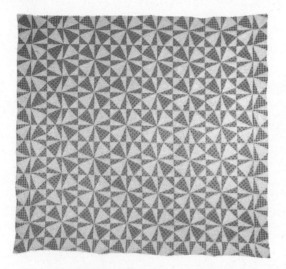

versing, and adapting the old patterns into something new and pleasing, the possible variations are never-ending.

The hard, clear harmony of geometric design fascinates us, children of the computer age; but it fascinated the ancients, too.

> . . . . . Euclid alone
> Has looked on Beauty bare. Fortunate they
> Who, though once only and then but far
>   away,
> Have heard her massive sandal set on
>   stone.
>
> Edna St. Vincent Millay

The geometric traditions of design predate the later florid, larger-than-life realism of the rococo and baroque periods. The work of the early Egyptians, the lost near-Eastern civilizations, the Oriental and Indian artifacts from long ago, bear testimony to the prevalence of geometry in art. Their ceramics, their weavings, the decorations of their buildings—all illustrate with a sharp beauty that is delineated in lines, curves, and angles and that is interpretive rather than realistic, decorative rather than naturalistic.

This, then, is the charm of pieced patchwork, and the wonder of it is that it reached its highest development during the overblown, overripe Victorian era. The simplicity and the precision of patchwork, the sophistication of the simple forms, the atonality of the colors used, are accomplishments out of keeping with the times that produced them. They are far more suited to the eclectic approach of today's thinking. We are today ready to accept patchwork, to appreciate its design qualities, and to accord it its place as an art form. The time is right.

In addition to the cerebral acceptance, our generation, pampered beyond belief by "conveniences," is experiencing a rebirth of rugged individualism, a rebellion against sterile mass production, and an almost overwhelming urge to create with one's own hands what one sees and feels in his or her own mind.

Patchwork is captivating in its intricacy. Its colors bring it to life, accenting the structural elements. Simply by varying the arrangement of color, one can alter the force of a design, subduing or intensifying as one wishes. Color can create optical illusions, or it can provide dimensional effect. The quilt shown in Plate 7, called Block Island Puzzle, illustrates well how simple forms can continually reform as you look at them. The crazy quilt (Plates 14 and 15 on pages 48-49 and 95), composed of random shapes and fabrics, illustrates the importance of color relationships. When the choice is right, the quilt sings. When not, the colors are dull and antagonistic.

Many of the Victorian quilts, crazy patches in somber colors, lavishly embroidered, are suffocatingly dull. The moroseness of dark green

PLATE 8: *Old Maid's Puzzle Quilt*, designed and made by Beverly Pryor.

adjoining dark maroon next to sludge brown on top of grim ochre chills the soul. Of course, these were the colors that were available readily and, therefore, frequently used. It took a rare adventuress to spike the composition with vermilion or brightest yellow, to sliver brilliant turquoise between the expanses of mud. Color is ultimately important; its use or misuse determines the success of the project.

Conversely, today's quilter often has trouble finding colors that have been grayed enough to produce the low-keyed, subtle effect a quilt should have. Most modern fabrics are bright and tinged with neon excitement. Even the traditional calico patterns have been upped in color value. Plate 8, called Old Maid's Puzzle, shows a quilt in which this problem was encountered. The quilt maker wanted it to look antique but was unable to find appropriate fabrics. Finally,

in desperation, she bought out the stock of old ties and shirts at the local thrift shop. Though they were as conservative as tea at Buckingham Palace, the effect is far from subdued.

MAKING A PIECED PATCHWORK QUILT TOP

Making your own patchwork quilt top is not difficult. Although the first quilt will take longer than any successive ones, this is only because doing it is a new experience. It takes time to learn to work automatically and to organize one's self into using time-saving methods. Starting here is the compilation of traditional patchwork patterns. The easiest ones are given first, and the more advanced ones are shown on the following pages. So that you can gain confidence while building your skills, choose your first quilt from among the easy patterns. Squares, rectangles, and triangles are the easiest forms to handle. Rhomboids, pentagons, clamshells, and irregular shapes take more time and ability than most beginners have.

If you will look at the following designs, you will see that most of them are based on a combination of squares and triangles. The squares are often subdivided into smaller squares or triangles; the more intricate patterns will be subdivided several times. The intricate designs are not harder to do; they just require more cutting and piecing.

PATCHWORK PATTERNS
EASY

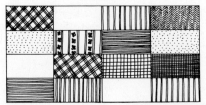

Diagram 3-1/Hit or Miss (one-patch)

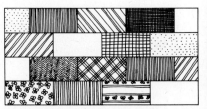

Diagram 3-3/Brick Wall (one-patch

Diagram 3-2/Roman Stripe (one-patch)

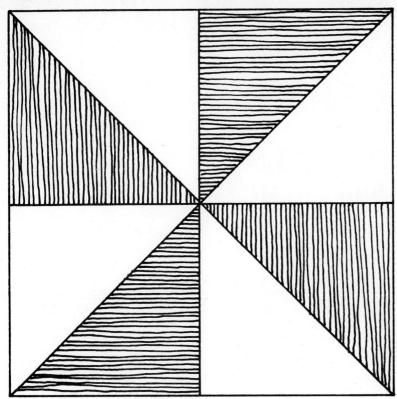

Diagram 3-4/Pinwheel (two-patch)

Diagram 3-5/Shoo-Fly (nine-patch)

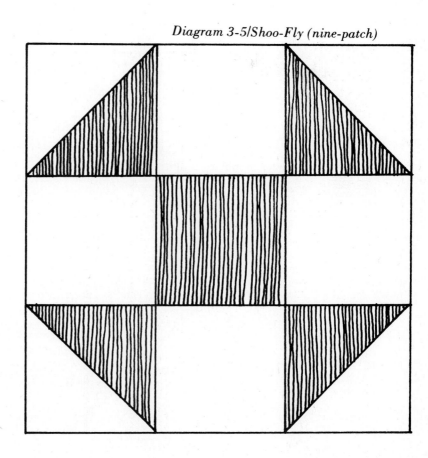

57

Diagram 3-6/Churn Dash (nine-patch)

Diagram 3-7/Wrench (nine-patch)

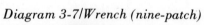

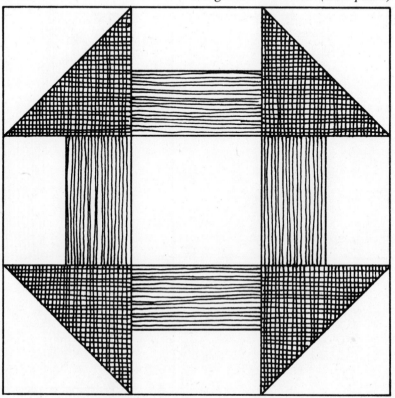

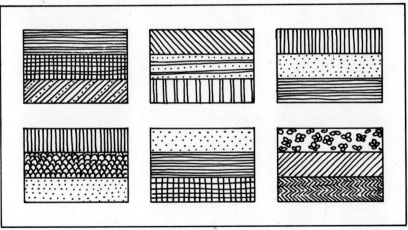

Diagram 3-8/Roman Square Variation (three-patch)

Diagram 3-9/Thousand Pyramids (one-patch)

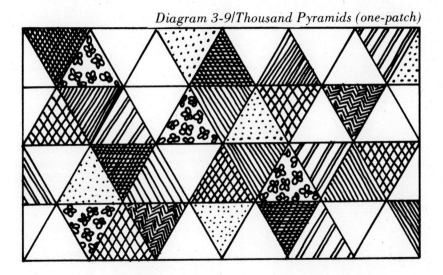

Diagram 3-10/Streak of Lightning (one-patch)

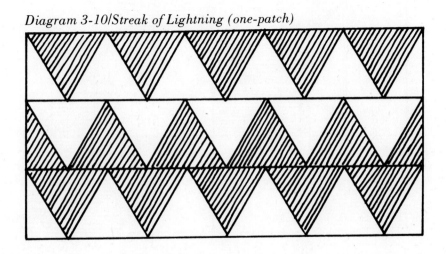

Diagram 3-11/Ohio Star (nine-patch)

Diagram 3-12/Road to Oklahoma (four-patch)

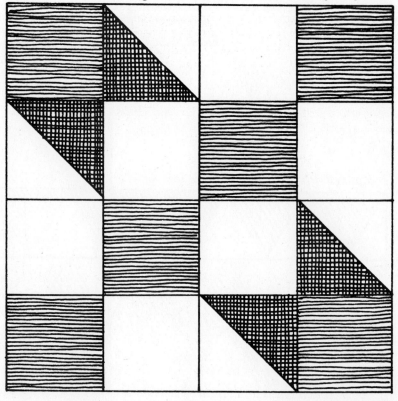

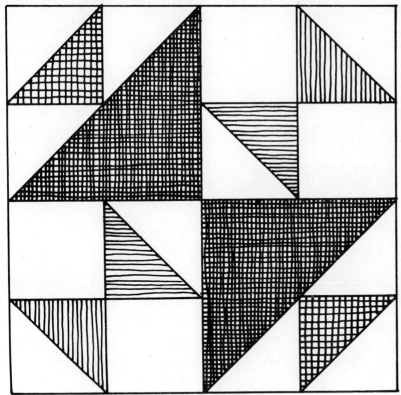

Diagram 3-13/Old Maid's Puzzle (four-patch)

Diagram 3-14/Jacob's Ladder (nine-patch)

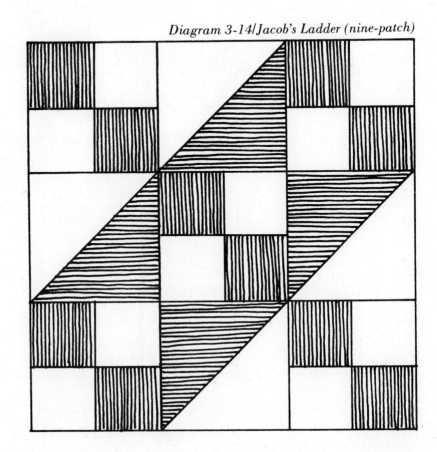

Diagram 3-15/Jack-in-the-Box (nine-patch)

Diagram 3-16/Indian Hatchet (four-patch)

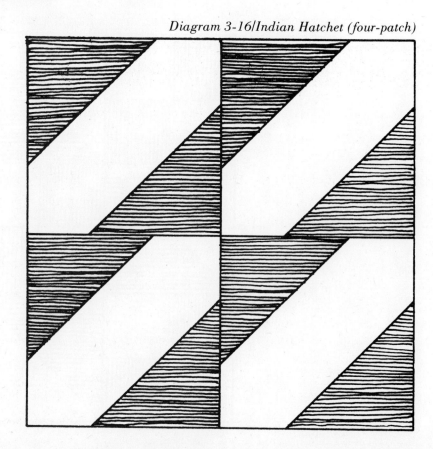

Diagram 3-17/Rolling Stone (nine-patch)

Diagram 3-18/Tippecanoe (four-patch)

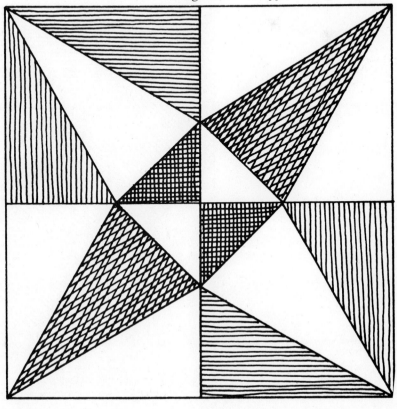

63

Diagram 3-19/Little Red School House (five- patch)

Diagram 3-20/King's Crown (five-patch)

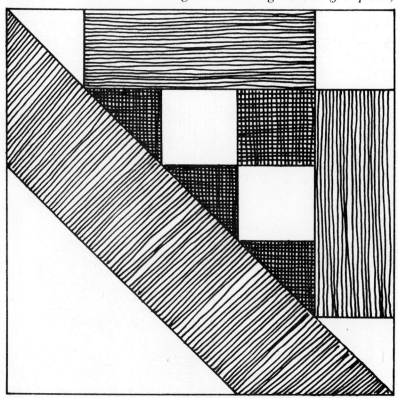

64

Diagram 3-21/David and Goliath (five-patch)

Diagram 3-22/Pieced Star (four-patch)

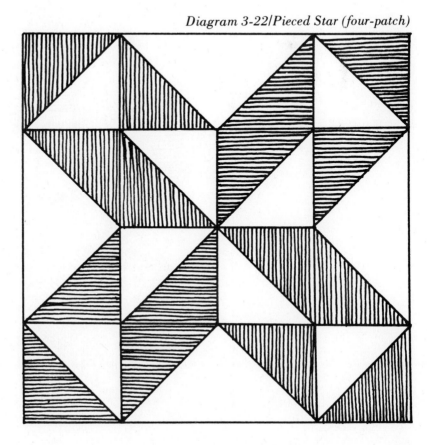

65

Diagram 3-23/Jackknife (nine-patch)

Diagram 3-24/Martha Washington's Star (four-patch)

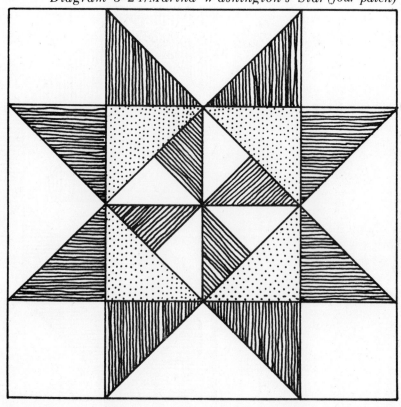

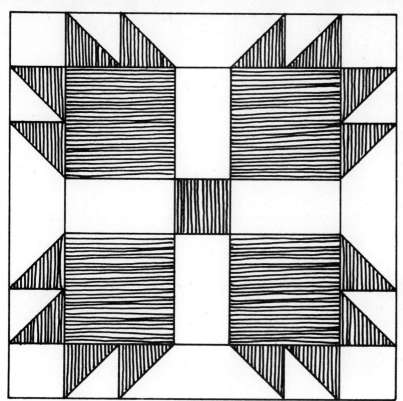

Diagram 3-25/Bear's Paw (nine-patch)

Diagram 3-26/Pine Tree (two-patch)

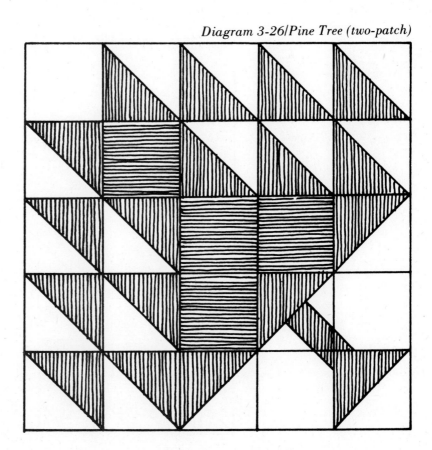

67

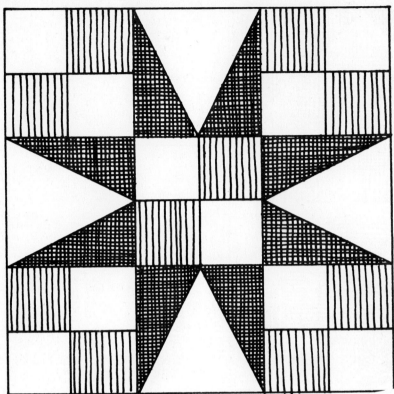

Diagram 3-27/54-40 or Fight (nine-patch)

Diagram 3-28/Maryland Beauty (two-patch)

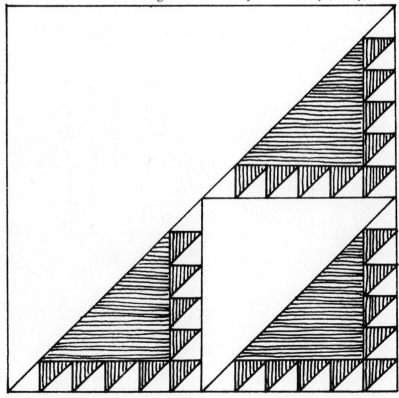

Diagram 3-29/Storm at Sea (seven-patch)

Diagram 3-30/Goose in the Pond (nine-patch)

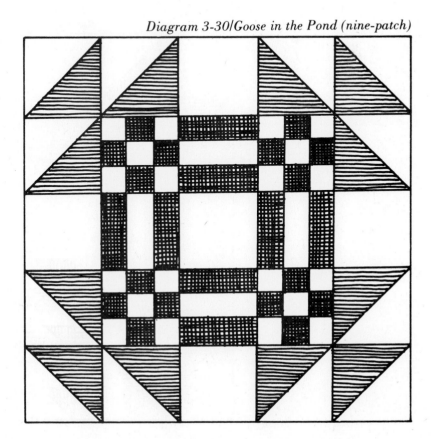

Diagram 3-31/Joseph's Coat (nine-patch)

Diagram 3-32/Missouri Puzzle (nine-patch)

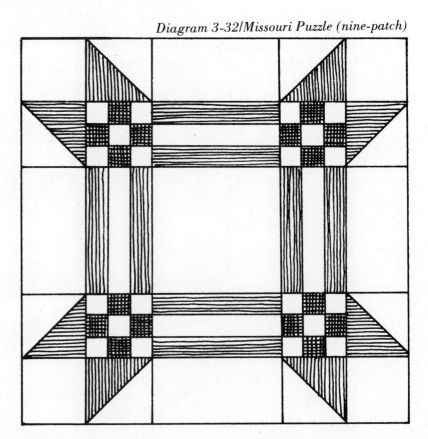

Diagram 3-33/Abe Lincoln's Platform (nine-patch)

Diagram 3-34/Georgetown Circles (four-patch)

71

Diagram 3-35/Autumn Leaf (seven-patch)

Diagram 3-36/Crazy Ann (four-patch)

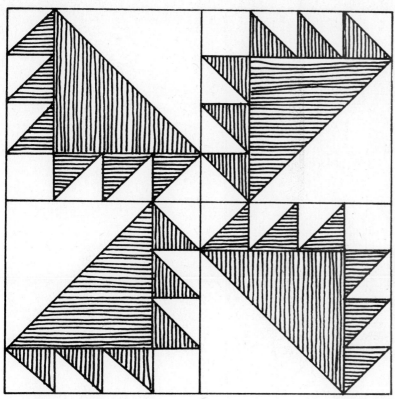

Diagram 3-37/Kansas Trouble (four-patch)

Diagram 3-38/Corn and Beans (four-patch)

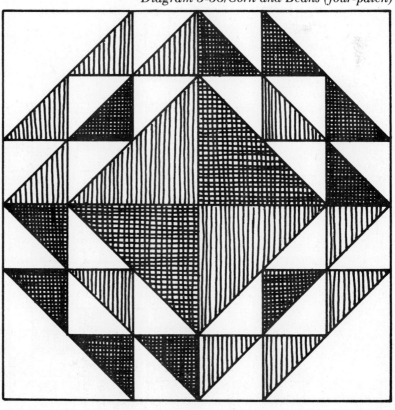

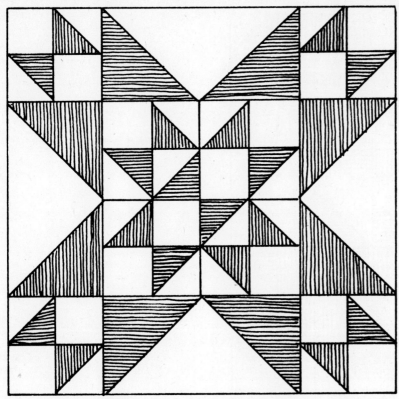

Diagram 3-39/Free Trade Block (four-patch)

Diagram 3-40/Burgoyne Surrounded (one-patch)

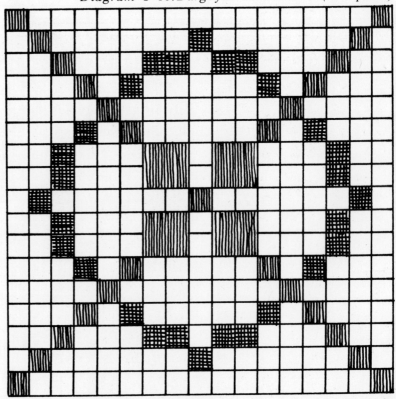

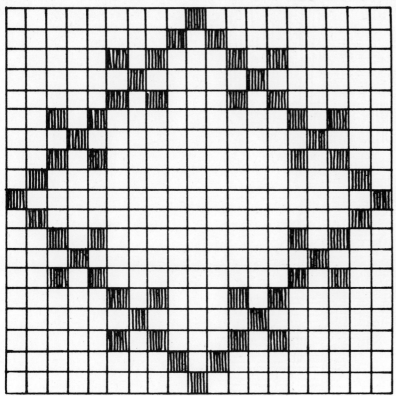

Diagram 3-41/Single Irish Chain (one-patch)

Diagram 3-42/Double Irish Chain (five-patch)

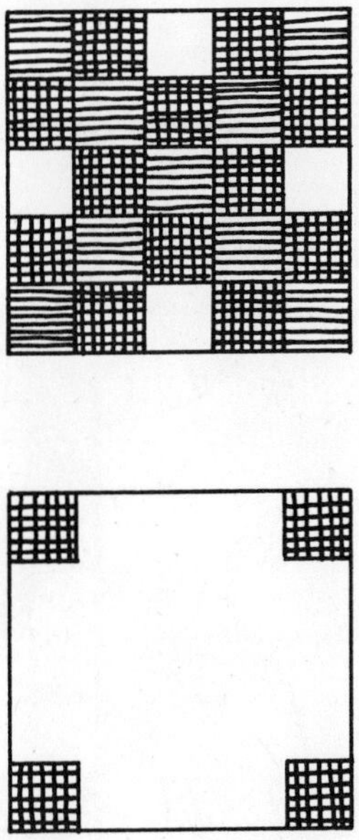

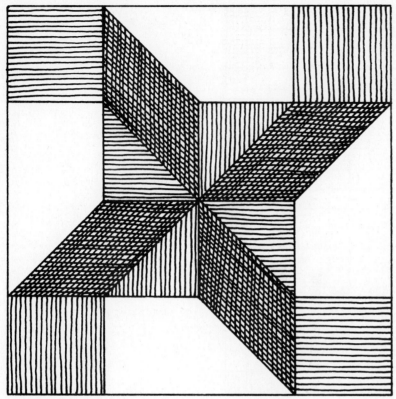

Diagram 3-43/Clay's Choice (four-patch)

Diagram 3-44/Mohawk Trail (four-patch)

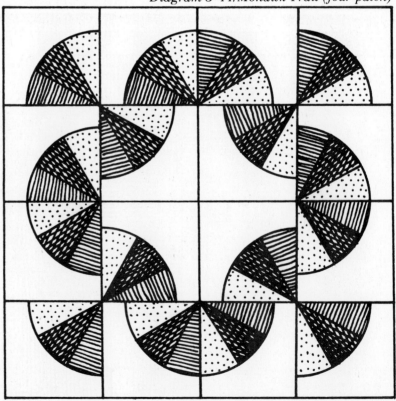

76

Diagram 3-45/Drunkard's Path (four-patch)

Diagram 3-46/Lafayette's Orange Peel (four-patch)

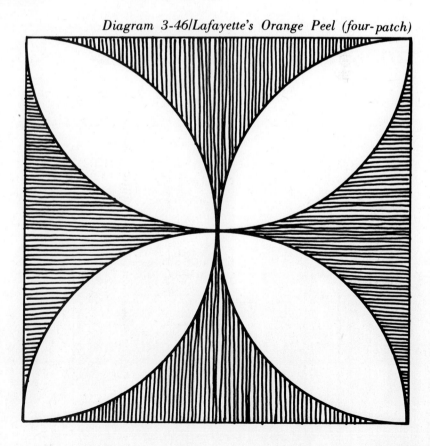

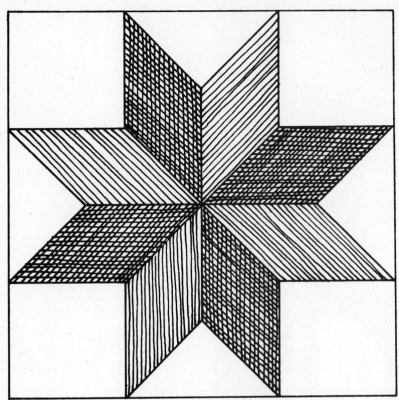

Diagram 3-47/Star of LeMoyne (four-patch)

Diagram 3-48/Robbing Peter to Pay Paul (four-patch)

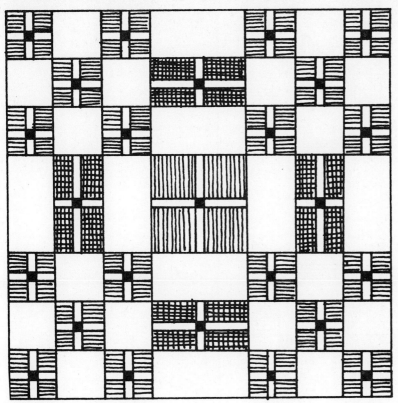

Diagram 3-49/Save All (nine-patch)

Diagram 3-50/Kaleidoscope (four-patch)

DIFFICULT

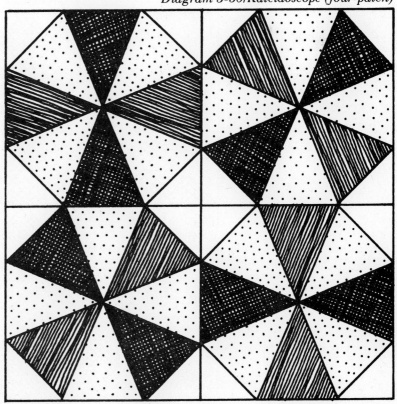

79

Diagram 3-51/Christmas Star (nine-patch)

Diagram 3-52/Hill and Valley (two-patch)

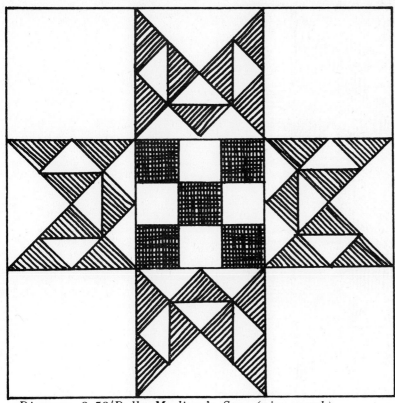

Diagram 3-53/Dolly Madison's Star (nine- patch)

Diagram 3-54/Honeycomb (one-patch)

Diagram 3-55/North Umberland Star (four-patch)

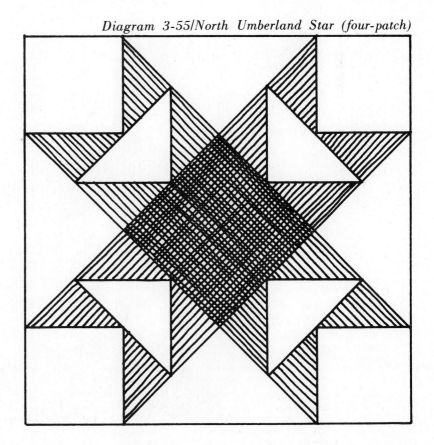

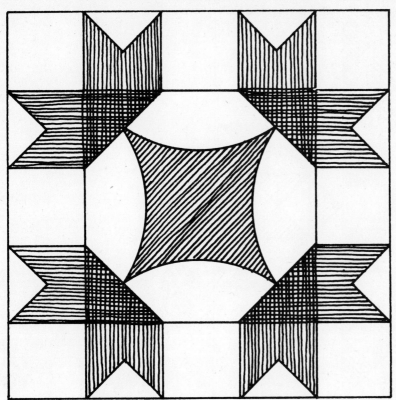

Diagram 3-56/Hands All Around (five-patch)

Diagram 3-57/Baby Blocks (two-patch)

Diagram 3-58/Virginia Star (four-patch)

Diagram 3-59/Queen Charlotte's Crown (five-patch)

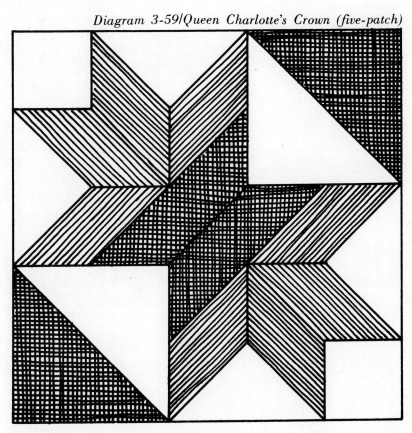

Diagram 3-60/Night and Day (four-patch)

Diagram 3-61/Electric Fans (four-patch)

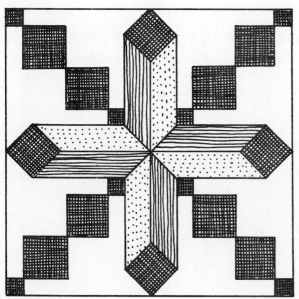

Diagram 3-62/Century of Progress (four-patch)

Diagram 3-63/Sunburst (one-patch)

Because rhomboids, pentagons, hexagons, and other irregularly shaped pieces are cut so that two or more sides are on the bias of the fabric and because they do not come together at right angles, problems in joining them are encountered. Since machine-sewing them is extremely difficult, we recommend doing these shapes by hand unless you are an expert. Curves, convex and concave, as shown in Lafayette's Orange Peel (Diagram 3-46), are beyond the capability of the beginner and should be avoided.

After you have decided on the pattern, colors, and overall plan for your quilt, draft the pattern and prepare the templates as described in the general directions in Chapter 2. Be accurate in tracing and cutting, remember to leave 1/4-inch margins all around the piece being cut, and be sure that you have laid out the designs with the grain of the fabric. This will give the individual pieces stability and prevent their stretching out of shape as you work with them. After the pieces are cut, lay them out in orderly stacks, in any way that makes sense to you, so that when you are sewing quickly, you will have joined the correct sides of the pieces.

Before starting to sew, pin together your pieces, right sides together, to be sure that they line up perfectly. If they do, then sew, joining the patches in sections and then joining the sections to form the whole. *Press as you work*. Ironing is important; unless the individual pieces lie flat, you cannot tell whether the corners match up perfectly. It is much easier to undo one or two pieces than it is to rip out a completed block.

The following section describes how to work with forms commonly used in pieced patchwork.

Hexagons: One of the earliest patterns known is the six-sided, or hexagon, pattern. Depending on the size of the unit used and its color arrangement, it can become Mosaic or Honeycomb, as shown in Plate 9, or Grandmother's Flower Garden (Plate 10). It can also be used to surround a large six-sided center medallion. It is an ingenious one-patch design, and the design possibilities are unlimited.

If rows of hexagons are simply sewn together, one next to the other, the second row to the first, and so on, the pattern is Mosaic or Honeycomb. The size of the hexagons can be small or large, and the colors can be worked out beforehand on graph paper to form diagonals, verticals, horizontals, or even pictorial representations of objects, people, or landscapes. Of course, if you keep the hexagons small in size, there will be more chance to use subtle gradings of color and to get more detail in the picture (Diagram 3-64). The important first step in doing this kind of design is to work out carefully the design beforehand and then to follow it exactly. It's almost like painting by number. It is worth the extra effort because as the quilt keeps getting bigger and bigger and heavier to hold, the effect becomes more and more marvelous, like the old Byzantine walls and floors.

Grandmother's Flower Garden evolved from the Mosaic for convenience in handling. To make it more manageable, the hexagons were grouped into rings, which were later joined together. As shown in Diagram 3-65, each section became a flower, and the hexagons between, paths. It is a simple thing to form these flowers: A mid-tone hexagon is used for the center, which is then surrounded by a ring of flower-colored prints or solids, a ring of green for

Diagram 3-64

PLATE 9: *Honeycomb Quilt*, collection of Audrey Heard.

PLATE 10: *Grandmother's Flower Garden Quilt,* collection of Audrey Heard.

Diagram 3-65

88

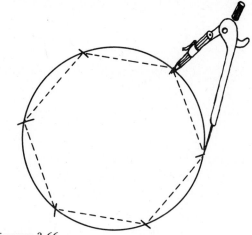

Diagram 3-66

foliage, and finally a ring of white, which represents the paths.

Several years ago, a lovely lady from New Orleans gave us the unfinished Grandmother's Flower Garden shown in Plate 10. It had been made by one of her ancestors from silks brought back in the days of the China Trade. It is a beautiful thing and we wish we could remember her name to acknowledge properly her gift. The bold, clear colors and the perfect sewing make this top museum quality, even though the silks are beginning to fray with age. We wish two things—that she read this book and write us and, second, that some museum will ask to own it, as a gift in the name of the lady from New Orleans. This is one Grandmother's Flower Garden worth preserving.

Following are step-by-step instructions for making a quilt based on the hexagon shape.

1. To make a hexagon pattern (see Diagram 3-66), first use a compass to describe on paper a circle the exact size you wish your finished hexagon to be. Then place the compass point at any spot on the circumference and the pencil point on the center of the circle. Holding the compass in this position, describe an arc that begins at the center point and ends at the circumference. Lift the compass point and place it on the point at which the arc you just drew meets the circumference. Then describe another arc. Continue in the same way around the circle until you have six equidistant points on the circum-

ference. Using a ruler, draw a continuous straight line from one point to the next and you will have formed a hexagon. Make your template from this pattern.

2. Old-time quilt makers always lined their hexagons with paper hexagons. This held the six points sharply and firmly while the quilt was worked, and, very often, they were not removed. Our New Orleans quilt top has the papers still sewn into it. Therefore, the second step in making a hexagon quilt is to cut paper patterns the exact size of the cardboard template you have just made. Then place the template on the straight grain of the material and cut around it so that the fabric is ¼ inch larger all around. Use a ruler and pencil to mark off the ¼ inch if you cannot yet trust your eye. Cut very carefully and uniformly since the points must be sharp and clean. Then, as you cut them, stack the hexagons in groups according to color.

3. The next step is to place a paper pattern on the wrong side of a fabric hexagon. Fold under the margins and baste.

Diagram 3-67

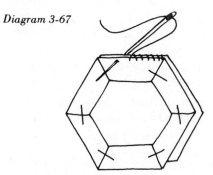

Diagram 3-69

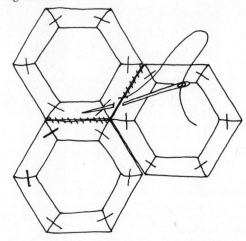

Diagrams 3-67 and **3-68** show the method of joining the patches. Begin by placing them with the right sides together, corners matching corners, and then sew them from one end of the place to be joined to the other. Do not sew through the paper, which serves only to guide the stitching and to eliminate sagging and stretching where the fabric is cut on the bias.

Diagram 3-68

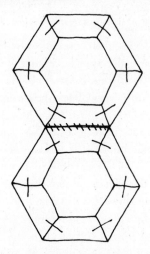

Then, open the joined seams, press them flat, and continue in this way.

The third patch must be joined on two sides (Diagram 3-69). Make certain that both sides and the center point meet exactly. Hexagons can be combined with diamonds for interesting effect.

Diamonds: By joining every other point marked on the circumference of the circle to the center point, you can divide a hexagon into three identical diamonds with angles of 60 and 120 degrees, as shown in Diagram 3-70. These shapes can then be arranged to make a six-pointed star or zigzag and trellis patterns.

Stars: Stars are either six-pointed, having angles

of 60 and 120 degrees, as is shown in Diagram 3-71, or eight-pointed, having angles of 45 and 135 degrees, as shown in Diagram 3-72.

To make an eight-pointed star, make eight diamonds having angles of 45 degrees and 135 degrees (Diagram 3-72) and join on their base lines.

Irregular shapes: Irregular shapes are fun to work with, but they do present problems because of their curves and odd angles. Draw the pattern out on paper first, of course, and then, when tracing it onto the fabric, uniformly follow the grain of the fabric, even though it means you must use more material (Diagram 3-73).

Diagram 3-70

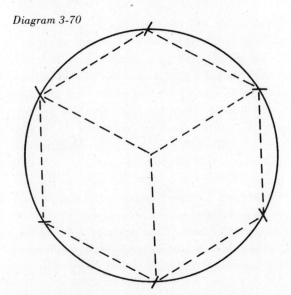

Diagram 3-71

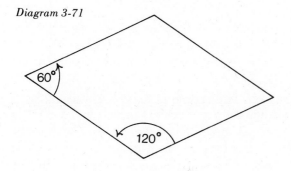

Diagram 3-72

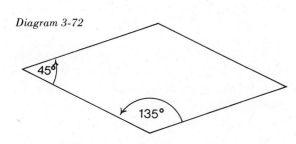

Diagram 3-73

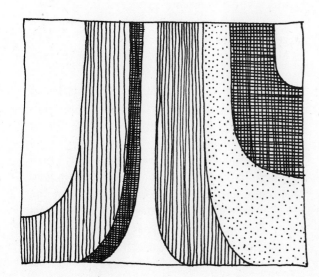

MAKING A LOG CABIN QUILT TOP

Log Cabin quilt blocks are made with light and dark rectangular strips sewn around a central square. These strips can be arranged either on diagonals or as opposites to create different effects. When the blocks are completed, they in turn are arranged for all-over composition.

There are two basic ways in which to make up a Log Cabin block. In the first, the light and dark strips are arranged as opposites (Diagram 3-74). This pattern is known as Court House Steps.

To make it, start with a light-colored 1-inch center square; two dark-colored 1-inch squares are then sewn left and right of the center square. Next, sew on two light 1- by 3-inch strips, one to the top of the three squares and one to the bottom. Then, two dark 1- by 3-inch strips are sewn left and right, followed by two light 1- by 5-inch strips sewn top and bottom and two dark 1-inch by 5-inch strips sewn left and right. Continue in this way until the block reaches 13 to 15 inches in size. Most of the old Log Cabins were made of smaller blocks, 8 to 10 inches, and if you wish to do this, simply decrease the width of the strips. Again, as in all piecing operations, *press as you go*.

When all the blocks are finished, they can be set together with all light sides facing from top to bottom and all dark sides facing from right to left, or the lights and darks can be mixed.

The second method of making up a Log Cabin block is with diagonals of light and dark (Diagram 3-75). This forms the patterns Barn Raising (Plate 11) and Straight Furrow (Plate 12). Pineapple (Plate 13) represents another Log Cabin type of quilt.

Diagram 3-74

Diagram 3-75

Referring to Diagram 3-75, notice that the block is constructed by starting with a light 1-inch center square. To the left is sewn a dark 1-inch square, and to the right, a light 1-inch square. Next a dark 1- by 3-inch strip is sewn to the top of the center and a light 1- by 3-inch strip to the bottom. Then a dark 1- by 3-inch to the left, and a light 1- by 3-inch to the right. Next comes a dark 1- by 5-inch strip sewn to the top, and a light 1- by 5-inch, to the bottom; a dark 1- by 5-inch to the left, and a light 1- by 5-inch to the right, and so forth until the block measures the desired size.

When all the blocks are finished, they can be arranged in any one of several ways to form an overall pattern. Barn Raising is done by placing four light corners together to make up a center square (see Plate 11). This is then surrounded by twelve blocks, each with the dark sides facing toward the center square except for the four corner blocks. As you can see, a diamond-shaped pattern is beginning to emerge. Then, twenty more blocks are arranged in the same manner, with the light and dark sides forming a larger diamond.

In Straight Furrow, all the dark corners face in the same direction (see Plate 12).

Either printed or plain fabrics or a mixture of the two can be used for a Log Cabin quilt, but they should always be arranged so that the lightest shades are toward the center, working out to the darker shades. This means that the colors of the dark half of the block should be arranged from dark to darkest and the light half of the block should go from lightest outward to least light. The blocks can be machine-sewn, using the techniques of pieced patchwork, or the center square and the successive strips can be

PLATE 11: *Barn Raising* (a Log Cabin quilt), collection of Manning Heard.

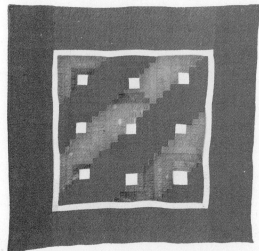

PLATE 12: *Straight Furrow* (a Log Cabin quilt), collection of
Phyllis Haders.

PLATE 13: *Pineapple* (a Log Cabin quilt), collection of Alice Potter.

hand-sewn to a muslin foundation, like the crazy quilts are done (see following section).

Borders may be used on Log Cabins or not. If used, they should be very simple and of a solid color. The quilts can be quilted by outlining each piece, or they can be tied, as described in Chapter 2.

MAKING A CRAZY QUILT TOP

Although we today consider the crazy quilt a type of quilt all its own, it was in actuality the very first form of pieced patchwork. Born of necessity, it was made of scraps and rags that had been salvaged and then joined together without regard to color or pattern. Out of this came intricately designed pieced patchwork; it was not until Victorian times that crazy quilting once again preoccupied the sewing time of American women. These quilts were not made to be practical coverings but were, instead, ornamental, to be used in the parlor as couch and chair throws. They were small in size and aggressively decorative.

Crazy quilts were made of the lush, formal fabrics of the era—soft velvets, luminous silks and satins, taffetas, brocades, and dressy picture prints—elegant scraps representative of an overdressed time. Delicate embroidery garnished each piece, using a sampler's technique of displaying many stitches in one quilt. Colors—dark, for the most part—were mixed together to form a collage of texture and hue.

The quilts were usually made in units of 12- to 15-inch blocks sewn together and then framed in a wide border of plain velvet, silk, or satin. Embroidered flowers, spider webs, butterflies, and other fancies were lavishly scattered on the quilt. Sometimes, miniature pictures were painted on the surface of the blocks, with a thin

PLATE 14: *Victorian Crazy Quilt*, made in 1884 by eleven-year-old Nancy Brown Morgan, collection of Adelaide Hirsche.

PLATE 15: For *Victorian Crazy Quilt*, see pages 48-49.

oil-based paint. The completed quilt became a complex composition, made up of many busy parts. There is so much going on in a Victorian crazy quilt of any merit that meticulous attention must be paid each block individually if the various skills and thoughts of the creator are to be recognized (see Plates 14 and 15).

Modern crazy quilts use the same technique of miscellaneous assortment. The fabrics are brighter, and the composition of the whole is considered above the composition of the individual blocks. The colorful Scrap-Bag-Cleanup Quilt, shown in Plate 16, is an exuberant mod-

PLATE 16: *Scrap-Bag-Cleanup Crazy Quilt*, designed and
made by Sharon McKain.

Diagram 3-76

ern crazy quilt. It seems random, but if you
study it, you will see the planned design and
form relationships.

To make a crazy quilt, you must first provide a
foundation block—a piece of muslin or
sheeting—the size of the block you plan to
make. You then baste scraps of material to this
block in any way you please, overlapping, un-
derlaying, until you find a relationship of shapes
and colors that pleases you. When this is done,
you embroider the edges of the pieces; this not
only decorates the surface of the quilt but secures the scraps to the foundation. When the
blocks have been assembled, you frame them
with a border, provide an interlining and a backing, and finish the quilt by tying through the
three layers.

Step-by-step directions for making a crazy
quilt follow:

1. Cut a foundation block of muslin or sheeting
the size you wish your block to be. Twelve to
fifteen inches is customary, but this is not man-
datory.

2. Select the scraps you want to use and then
arrange them in a pleasing way on the muslin
foundation. They should overlap by at least ½
inch. If the shapes are not pleasing, cut them to
suit—the charm of a crazy quilt lies in its random placement of color and form, whether
studied or casual. To begin, place a scrap either
in the center or in one corner and baste it with
running stitches to the foundation block. Place
the second scrap over the first, right sides together, and baste down one side, sewing through
all layers (Diagram 3-76). Open this second
piece to its right side, and add the third scrap in
the same manner. Continue until the foundation
block is covered. Trim the edges where they
overhang the muslin.

3. Decorating the blocks with embroidery, if
desired, can be done before or after the blocks
are set together. For ease of handling, the best
way, of course, is to decorate each block individually, doing everything but the outside

96

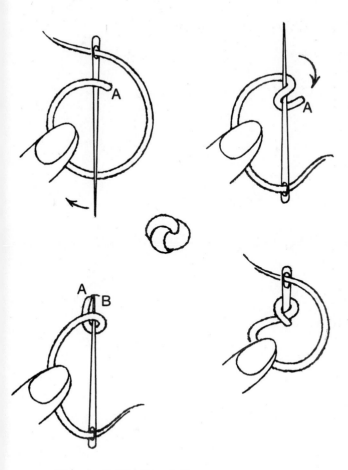

Diagram 3-77 / French Knot

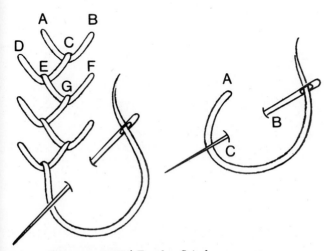

Diagram 3-78 / Feather Stitch

edges. When the quilt top is finished and all the blocks joined to each other, then the seams can be covered with embroidery. Not only is this decorative, but it strengthens the joining.

There are so many embroidery stitches that can be used that we can show only the most popular ones (Diagrams 3-77 to 3-84). The stitchery adds a great deal to a crazy quilt, enlivening it and adding interest. Designs can also be painted on the patches, using fabric paints.

4. Setting the crazy quilt blocks is the same procedure as that described in Chapters 1 and 2. Sew the blocks together in rows, and then sew the rows together. Be sure that the corners match up and that the alignment is perfect. Add the borders, using either square or mitered corners, as described in Chapter 2.

5. When the quilt top is finished, cut the interlining and backing a little larger than the dimensions of the quilt top. Lay the quilt top on the floor, face down, and cover it first with the interlining and then with the backing. Pin the three layers together, being sure that all are wrinkle-free and that the corners line up.

The three layers will not be quilted but will be tied instead because of the bulkiness of the top. So many overlappings of fabric have been used that it is difficult, if not impossible, to quilt through them. To tie it, use a large yarn or embroidery needle threaded with either yarn, fine string, or strong floss; insert the needle from the back of the quilt through the interlining and quilt top, and go back through about an eighth of an inch from where you came up Tie off the stitch at the back, using a square knot (see Chapter 2 for further instructions).

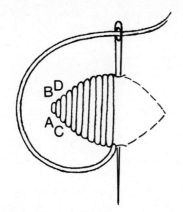

Diagram 3-79 / Satin Stitch

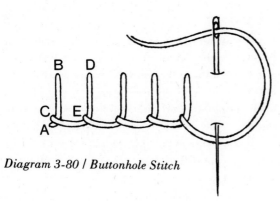

Diagram 3-80 / Buttonhole Stitch

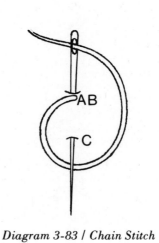

Diagram 3-83 / Chain Stitch

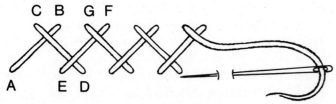

Diagram 3-81 / Herringbone Stitch

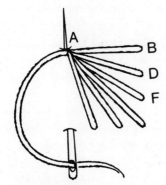

Diagram 3-82 / Fan Stitch

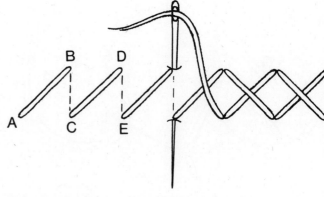

Diagram 3-84 / Cross Stitch

6. Crazy quilts are rarely finished off with bias; usually, either the backing is brought onto the top and blindstitched or the edges of both the backing and the quilt top are folded to the inside and the two are stitched together. See Chapter 2 for details on these techniques.

Crazy quilts can be made easily by using the sewing machine not only for joining the pieces but for doing the embroidery as well. It is not necessary to turn under the edges of the pieces used when sewing by machine. It is enough to pin the scraps in the way you want them to appear. Then use the zigzag stitch to appliqué the pieces to the foundation. Use a stitch length of from six to eight stitches to the inch. Reset the stitch length to ten to twenty stitches to the inch, and go over it again. The satin stitch can be used over the zigzag to create interesting bars. The many disks included with the new machines provide numerous other stitches that can be used decoratively.

Even though the work goes quickly when you sew by machine, in this particular type of quilt we feel that the quality of the work is lessened. It will not have the softness or the subtlety of one done by hand. We are purists, though, and if time is limited and you like to use your machine, go right ahead.

The Scrap-Bag-Cleanup Quilt (see Plate 16) breaks all the rules. To begin, the quilter turned her scrap bag upside down on the floor and gathered huge piles of fabrics that appealed to her. Using a unit size of about two feet by two feet, she sewed her scraps at random, but with an eye to color and design. She did not use a muslin foundation but sewed the pieces to each other, instead, in the manner of pieced patch-work. When she had completed the requisite number of squares, she joined them together. If she thought an extra fillip of color or a correction in design flow was needed, she appliquéd a patch. The border was added, and the letters on it were appliquéd by hand. A lightweight blanket was used for the interlining, and the border fabric was used for the backing. Because she had not overlapped her pieces, she was able to quilt the pieces in outline, using the sewing machine. She used a strip of bias material for the binding and machine-sewed it in place. This quilt is a personal celebration by a very talented artist turned quilter.

MAKING A PRESTUFFED QUILT

A prestuffed quilt is composed of modular units, each of which is completed individually and is then joined to its counterparts to form a quilt. The size of the individual modules must be based on a common denominator of the total measurement of the proposed quilt. For example, if the quilt size is to be 84 by 84 inches, a common denominator could be 4, in which case the modules could measure 4 by 4 inches, 8 by 8 inches, 12 by 12 inches, 4 by 8 inches, or 4 by 12 inches. If the common denominator were 3, the units could measure 3 by 3 inches, 6 by 6 inches, 9 by 9 inches, 3 by 6 inches, etc. Whatever size you choose, the sum of the totals must add up to a given total that is divisible by all of them. For example, two 4- by 4-inch units could be used next to one 4- by 8-inch unit to form a square measuring 8 by 8 inches.

There are two methods of making a prestuffed quilt. With the first, one piece of fabric, twice the size of the planned module plus a ¼-inch seam allowance on three sides, is folded so that

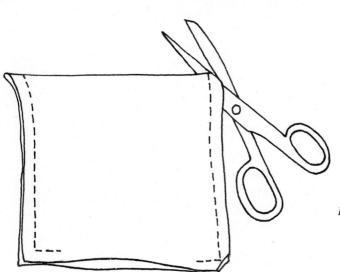

Diagram 3-85

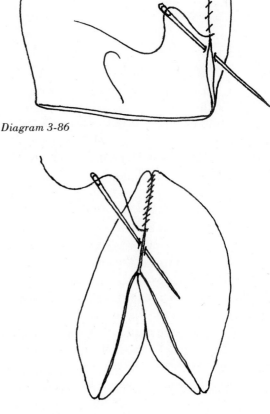

Diagram 3-86

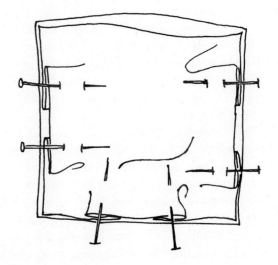

Diagram 3-87

the right sides are together; two of the sides plus part of the third are then sewn together, as shown in Diagram 3-85.

The piece is then turned right-side out, pressed, and stuffed with cotton or Dacron batt. The batt can be bought either by the bag or in sheets. Sheet batt is easier to use because it can be cut to the exact size required, and it can be made thicker by doubling it up. It should be cut a little larger than the area it is to fill. After the module is stuffed, the hems of the open edges are turned in and slip-stitched together (Diagram 3-86). The modules are then joined to each other by slip stitches, sewed first across the top and then across the back, as shown in Diagram 3-87. When all of them have been attached and the quilt has reached full size, it is tied to prevent the stuffing from shifting (see Chapter 2 for instructions). If the units are very small, this is not always necessary.

The second method requires two pieces of fabric cut to two different sizes; one, the foundation block, does not show and so can be of unbleached muslin. The top piece is "for show" and should be chosen to be part of your overall color scheme. This piece, the top, is sewn on three sides to the foundation block and then

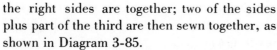

Diagram 3-88

Diagram 3-89

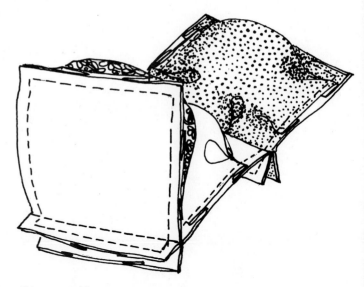

Diagram 3-91

Diagram 3-90

stuffed. To construct this type of quilt, the size of the foundation block must first be determined, as described earlier in this section. For example, if the finished module is to measure 5 by 5 inches, the foundation block must be cut to measure 5½ by 5½ inches, which allows for a ¼-inch seam allowance all around. The top should be larger by 1½ inches—in this case, it would measure 7 inches square—to allow for space for stuffing. With wrong sides together, the top is then pinned to the foundation block,

with two equally spaced tucks taken on each of the three sides to be sewn (Diagram 3-88).

The three sides are then sewn and stuffed through the open side, as shown in Diagram 3-89. When the stuffing is pleasingly plump but not fat, take two tucks in the fourth side and sew it closed, as shown in Diagram 3-90.

The modules are joined by placing two of them, right sides together, so that their corners meet exactly. They are then sewn on the seam line, as shown in Diagram 3-91, row by row, until the quilt is finished.

If you like, the tops can be appliquéd before being joined to the foundation block. For instance, toys or animals can enliven a crib quilt greatly when done in this way. Unless a border is being added, it is not necessary to interline this type of quilt. The backing is attached in the regular way, and the quilt is tied. Bias tape is used to bind the edges.

You are not limited to using squares and rectangles in making the prestuffed quilt. Triangles, circles, and rhomboids can all be used as long as they meet and match perfectly at their joinings.

The Bow Tie Quilt, shown in Plate 17, shows the prestuffed technique. Step-by-step instructions for making this quilt are in Chapter 7.

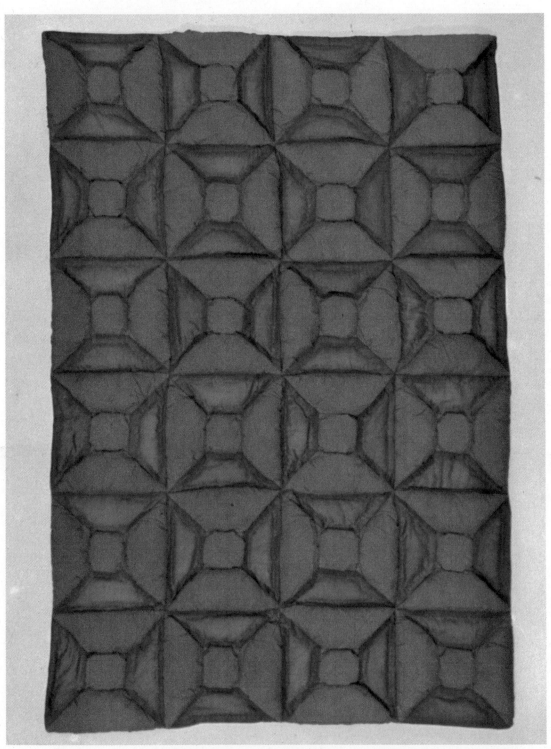

PLATE 17: *Bow Tie Quilt*, designed by Audrey Heard, made
by Barbara McKie.

Amish Quilts

Amish quilts belong within the broad category of pieced patchwork, but because they are uniquely different and completely homogeneous, we feel that they merit special attention. To understand the peculiar and outstanding differences between Amish and other American quilts, it is necessary to know about the Amish people, their origins, their ways, even their philosophy.

Although Amish quilts represent a point in time that happened several hundred years ago, they are—in terms of design, color, and feeling—the most contemporary of all quilts. And nothing in the Amish tradition completely validates the artistic sophistication of these quilts. Perhaps these people have stood still, and we have gone full circle, returning to a point once known and now remembered.

We have visited the Amish communities in Pennsylvania and in Ohio and have read much about them. The deeper we delve into the lives and history of the Amish, or Plain People as they are often called, the more fascinated we are.

Leave Philadelphia and travel west toward Lancaster. If you take the back roads, you will soon come to an area of rolling hills and peaceful farms. You are struck by the absence of telephone poles and electric wires overhead. Immaculately painted black buggies, driven by high-stepping trotters, pass you on the roads. You will notice groups of women standing together, their heads covered by small white caps or with black bonnets shading their faces, wearing long dresses partially concealed by aprons; sometimes they wear black, but often the colors are gay—pink, purple, blue, green, and orange, always unpatterned. The men and boys wear black trousers, wide-legged and baggy, and blue or white shirts crossed by suspenders.

Wide-brimmed hats with high crowns, black felt in winter, straw in summer, cover their heads. The younger men are clean-shaven, for it is the custom not to grow a beard until after marriage.

These are the Plain People, descendants of the followers of Jacob Amman and at one time connected with the Mennonites. Their ancestors came to Pennsylvania about 1725, seeking religious freedom and a place in which to contain their customs and way of life.

Both the Mennonites and the Amish practice adult baptism, nonresistance, and refusal to bear arms. However, the Mennonites have adapted more easily to a changing world in both their thinking and way of living. The Amish are easily identified by their plain dress and extreme simplicity of life-style. All is for the land and for God, as is set down in the Bible.

They live rigidly but not starkly, for they are fine farmers and builders: Their homes and barns are clean, warm, and sturdy and their fields are laid out in neat geometry. Although they are quiet and sober in their personal relationships, they are a generous and friendly people, and their family-unit solidarity is strong. They reject social security, for they take care of their own. They use power machinery only when their own arms and backs, or the strength of their animals, are not adequate. Many do not use electricity or telephones, and mechanization and industrialization come slowly. Yet they are not backward; their farming methods have always been among the most productive and efficient in the country and they are good businessmen, shrewd and careful.

The position of the women in the Amish community is an old-fashioned one. The prescribed pattern of their existence calls for them to be part of a team, a willing and responsible member but one deprived of the creature joys enjoyed by females in other groups. Their lives are uniformly spare, and it is only in their quilt making that the passionate surge of personal expression becomes apparent. Their homes are clean, functional, and comfortable, but there is no decoration, no paintings, no happy fabrics with which to enliven the drab rooms.

Quilts, then, have always been very important to these women, for they represented the only opportunity available to them for decorating their homes with color. Even though the forms of the quilts, and the spectrum used, were almost uniform within the group, the total concept of this kind of artistic thought is exciting. This is not individual creativity, but a conformity of group effort, for the traditions of quilt making among the Amish is as prescribed as everything else in their lives. Rather than each quilt being the personal song of the woman who makes it, it becomes the interpretation of an ethnic method. This is the puzzle and the enchantment of the Amish quilts, for they could have flowered only in the peculiar circumstances surrounding these people.

A great number of these quilts in existence today were made by Amish mothers for their children. Many were made years in advance, to be ready when the child left the household to set up his own home. Bride's quilts were special, for they are the only ones in which hearts were used in the quilting patterns.

Weddings were, of course, important to the Amish community, for they represented continuity in the faith and the old customs. Although courtship was secretive, it was, in reality, again a highly prescribed, moralistic procedure, culminating in public announcement and an elaborate wedding, held on either Tuesday or Thursday in November or December—the time when the workload on the farms was the lightest. At this time, many gifts of a practical nature would be given to the young couple. These would include utensils for the kitchen, farm implements, and the like. Usually, a number of quilts and comforters would also be given to them by both mothers.

It was customary, in Amish homes, to pile the guestroom bed high with prized quilts. When a guest was shown to his room, the quilts would be removed one by one in order of their excellence. The guest was, of course, expected to admire them until, finally, the warm ones under which he would sleep were the only ones left on the bed. Imagine how it would have felt to witness this performance on a freezing winter night in a drafty farm bedroom by the dim light of kerosene lamps!

The earliest of the Amish quilts were made of wool and designed in geometric patterns. The colors· used and the simple perfection of the design work are the two factors that set these quilts apart from other pieced patchwork.

The Amish choice of color is a thought-provoking subject. Every age and every stage of civilization has had its identifying colors. To our knowledge, however, there has never been a range of color values and combinations comparable to that of the Amish. From the earliest examples of Amish quilting on, the colors have been exactly the same in tonality, in value, in combination.

These colors were drawn from the palette of creation—the wild, untamed pinks of the rising sun emerging from the shaded purples of night, the black of the forest before the light has come,

PLATE 18: *Amish Ocean Waves Quilt,* collection of Audrey Heard.

the rusty reds and muted greens of sleeping fields, the blues of ponds struck by the icy light of false dawn. Their colors are lit by the late-waning moon, giving them an eerie vibrancy, evoking worlds unknown and galaxies unfound. The colors are sometimes somber, one by one, but put together, they have a luminosity that is the result of an unerring color sense, a sure juxtaposition of tonal value.

Late Amish quilts tend to look more like those generally seen in the outside world. Synthetic fabrics and crepe have taken the place of wool, but where the traditions are constant, the shimmering effectiveness of the strange colors and geometric patterns is still exciting.

The quilts pictured in Plates 18 and 19 are unusual in both pattern and color. Plate 18 is Ocean Waves, but the colors make it totally unlike its New England predecessors. Plate 19 shows a quilt of unidentified pattern. The colors are grayed as much as possible, but they retain a mysterious vibrancy, showing the strain of darkness that runs through the Amish consciousness.

Even the baby quilt (Plate 20), which is pink and blue and white, is not simply pink and blue and white. Somehow, it achieves a melancholy dissonance. The Amish women have given us a beautiful design heritage, and it is fortunate that contemporary taste has come full cycle so that it can understand and appreciate it.

Assisted by a local weaver and dyer, we have examined the fabrics and speculated about the kind of dyes the Amish used. We are now very sure that the early Amish used natural dyes —indigo for the blues, cochineal for the reds, perhaps madder for the oranges, possibly fustic for the yellows, but, more probably, goldenrod,

PLATE 19: *Unidentified Pattern Amish Quilt*, collection of Audrey Heard.

for it was plentiful and free and they were a thrifty people. (The fact that most of the early quilts were made of wool accounts for their brilliance. Animal fibers are the most vibrant of all when dyed, far more so than cotton and linen fibers, which, of course, come from plants.) Many of the quilts made around the time of World War I were also home-dyed. The reason for this was that the best commercial dyes came from Germany; when this import was stopped, there was a revival of natural dyeing.

From the colors listed above, the Amish were able to get the variations of the color wheel. For example, bright green is indigo mixed with yellow, purple is cochineal with indigo. The Amish liked their colors saturated, full strength, and then subtly grayed. Not for them the primary values we have long associated with the folk art of the Pennsylvania Dutch or the pallid shades so popular in the South and in conservative New England.

106

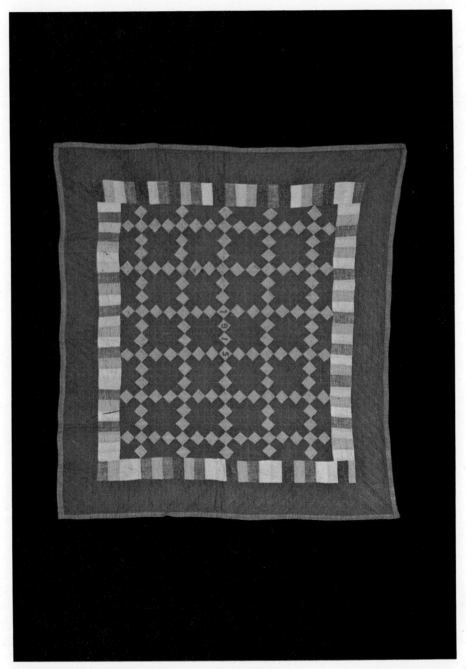

PLATE 20: *Amish Baby Quilt,* collection of Audrey Heard.

PLATE 21: *Amish Squares Quilt*, collection of Phyllis Haders.

PLATE 22: *Amish Diamond Quilt*, collection of Phyllis Haders.

The main body of Amish quilts available to us dates from mid-nineteenth century to about 1920. This, of course, was the heyday of pieced patchwork, and it is interesting to note how well the Amish women met contemporary trends yet maintained their own artistic integrity.

In pattern, the Amish quilts divide into several broad categories. The earliest form shows simply a square of plain fabric set into a broad border of contrasting color. Plate 21 is an example. Made of wool, about 1865, in Lancaster County, Pennsylvania, it is simple perfection. The large center square is set into a strong border and is then framed by a larger border. It is very plain and very powerful.

This centered square eventually evolved into the Amish Diamond (Plate 22), the design probably inspired by the Central Medallion quilts of European memory. The diamond is set into a square, which is then surrounded by a narrow border, then by a wider border, and finally by a thin outer border in strong contrast to the others. This particular quilt is unbelievable in its accomplishment of form and color. Quilting details for it are shown here in Plates 23 and 24. Quilting Diagrams 7-9 and 7-10 are given for it in Chapter 7.

Bars (Plate 25) is another concept uniquely Amish. Here, narrow bands of contrasting fabric are set into a bordered center and flanked by a wider border. The four corner blocks are typically Amish, as is the narrow outer border of contrasting color.

The Nine-Patch (Plate 26) is popular and quite sensational when done with the Amish eye. The blocks are handled as diamonds set within a square, and are then interspersed with plain blocks. A wide border and a narrow edge

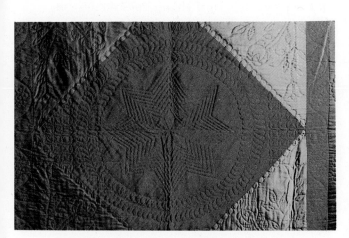

PLATE 23: *Amish Diamond Quilt* detail.

PLATE 25: *Amish Bars Quilt,* collection of Phyllis Haders.

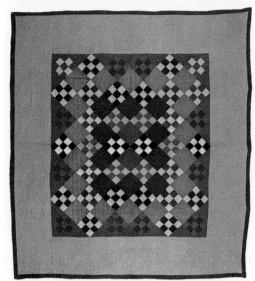

PLATE 26: *Amish Nine-Patch Quilt,* collection of Phyllis Haders.

PLATE 24: *Amish Diamond Quilt* detail.

PLATE 27: *Amish Sunshine and Shadow Quilt*, collection of Phyllis Haders.

PLATE 28: *Amish Sawtooth Quilt*, collection of Phyllis Haders.

frame the center motif. This quilt illustrates well the kinetic vibrancy that can result from skillfully placed colors. In spite of its subdued range, the effect is graceful and sophisticated.

Sunshine and Shadow (Plate 27) is a favorite Amish pattern. Known elsewhere as Trip around the World, it is composed of many squares set together in concentric diamonds, each row of which is a different hue. There is continuity and marvelous effect in this quilt, so evocative of walled fields fringed with trees, casting shadows over sunlit rows of many-flowered plants.

Sawtooth (Plate 28) is an elaboration of the Amish Diamond. It is an extremely difficult quilt to do if the corners are to meet perfectly. While we admire the technique of piecing this quilt, we feel that it has less impact than the startling simplicity of the Diamond. The zigzags clutter, and the hard-edge statement is diminished.

Basket (Plate 29), though not definitely Amish in origin, is handled by them with special excitement. The shapes are simplified and elegantly refined, and, of course, the stark, dark colors add sophistication. Triple Irish Chain (Plate 30) is made effectively vibrant by the use of two dissonant colors contained within a wide border.

Plate 31 illustrates a quilt that is Amish but from Tuscarawas County, Ohio. We do not know the name of the pattern, but the sharp grid, punctuated by yellow stars at its intersections, is as proclamatory as a flag.

Characteristics of Amish quilts are wide borders, beautiful quilting, and large corner blocks. The fabrics are always unpatterned, and although the late ones may be made of synthetics, most of them are made of wool or cotton. The

PLATE 29: *Amish Basket Quilt*, collection of Phyllis Haders.

PLATE 30: *Amish Triple Irish Chain Quilt*, collection of Phyllis Haders.

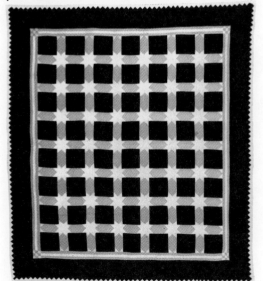

PLATE 31: *Ohio Amish Quilt*, collection of Audrey Heard.

colors are always those previously mentioned. These colors, incidentally, are also seen in the clothing of the Amish, but it is when they are juxtapositioned in the quilts that they achieve that special vibrancy characteristic of Amish quilts.

As early as 1870, all the quilts were pieced by machine and then quilted by hand. The quilting is superbly done, very bold and graphic, and we have traced many of the patterns from the quilts. They are shown to scale in Diagrams 3-92 through 3-101. The drawing of these quilting patterns has a special authority. It is sure, graphic, and beautifully proportioned. Many of the motifs are well known to quilters other than the Amish, but the Amish version seems to have reached a pinnacle of positive style.

With the exception of Diagram 3-99, which is from Tuscarawas County, Ohio, all these patterns have been taken from quilts made either in Lancaster or Mifflin counties, Pennsylvania. In order to give our readers a feeling for the placement of the patterns on a quilt, we have traced them in their proper relationship to each other. In this way, borders, corner blocks, grid fillers, center motifs, and so on, are illustrated in the position they will occupy on actual quilts. For example, Plate 22 is the quilt from which we have taken Diagram 3-94. Diagram 3-99 is the quilt pictured in Plate 31.

These designs recur in most of the quilts in this group, with slight variations on the theme. In Diagram 3-101, the feather wreath is used in the corner block and the Quaker feather repeats itself all around the outermost border. The next border, narrow and precise, is done in a sophisticated diaper pattern, reminiscent of the

Diagram 3-92/Amish Rose

Diagram 3-93/Amish Tulip

←2″→

Diagram 3-94/Amish Star

← 2" →

115

Diagram 3-95/Quaker Feathers

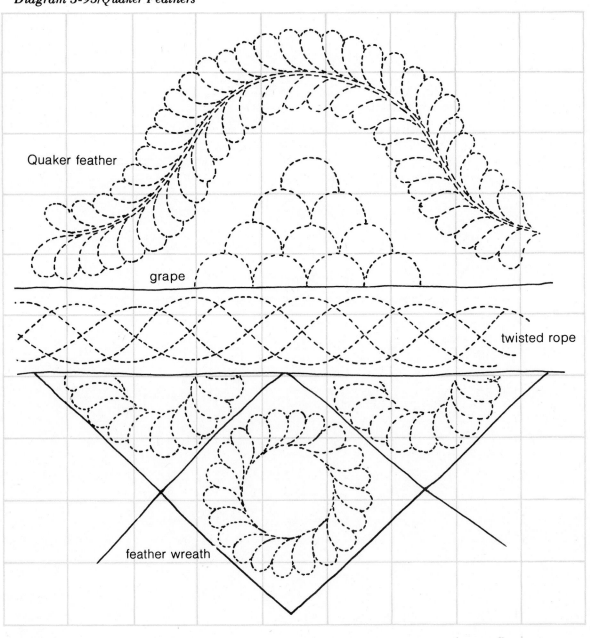

Quaker feather

grape

twisted rope

feather wreath

2"

116

Diagram 3-96/Grape

grape

Quaker feather

2"

Diagram 3-97/Amish Tulip

Diagram 3-98/Amish Primrose

← 2" →

119

Diagram 3-99/Quaker Feather and Wreath with Diagonal Grid Fillers

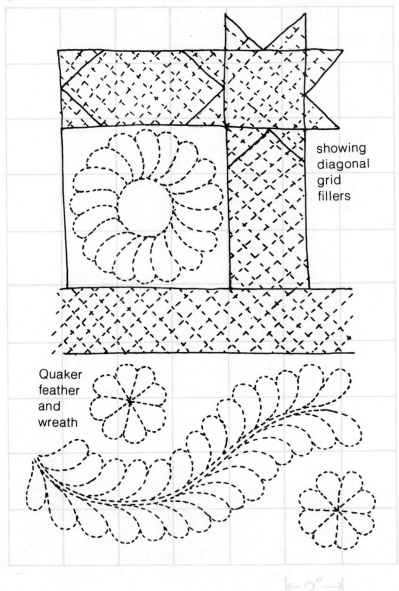

showing
diagonal
grid
fillers

Quaker
feather
and
wreath

2"

Diagram 3-100/Twisted Rope

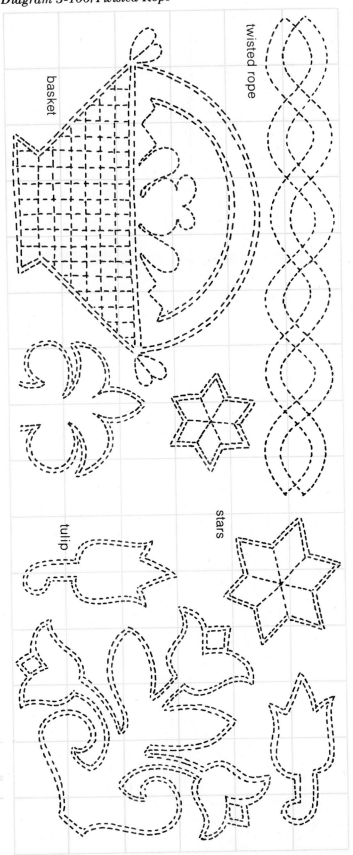

twisted rope

basket

stars

tulip

2"

Diagram 3-101/Amish Feather and Wreath

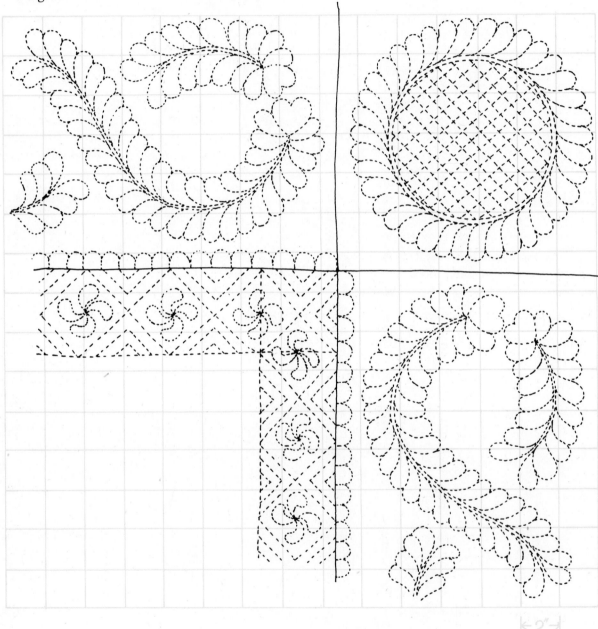

2"

Romanesque architecture of seventeenth-century Europe.

The twisted rope, as shown in Diagram 3-95, is a favorite pattern. Sometimes, double and triple strands are used.

These patterns have an elegance and grace that is not exactly analogous to the geometric simplicity of the quilts; stylistically, they are classical while the quilts are eclectic. But the blending of styles works and is exciting.

We have been using these patterns in making quilts for this book, and the results have been gratifying. The *jupon* skirt (see Plate 86A on page 238) is a medley of Amish quilting patterns, skillfully worked. The Modern Patchwork (Plate 64 on page 189) is another example. We asked a friend who is an innovative designer to make a quilt in the Amish manner. It is shown in Plate 85 on page 231. Interestingly, she was quite literal in her translation. The palette is her own, but the design is authentic. The same designer has done pillowcases (see Plate 102 on page 275) in the same patterns. They also utilize the unique quilting.

It was our original intention to illustrate Amish quilting done by machine rather than by hand. We traced one of the patterns accurately and tried it. It was complete disaster, for Amish quilting, to be effective, must be done by hand. The small inaccuracies, the slight puffiness of hand-stitching, the coarseness of the thread, the lack of absolute uniformity of the stitches—all combine to give the hand-quilted piece its fulfillment. We state, unequivocally, that Amish quilting—even the grid fillers, straight and diagonal—must be done by hand.

Adapt these quilt patterns to your own uses. They are not difficult to do, if you hone your sights to clean simplicity and use color in a way you never thought possible. The atonality and the starkness, the mysterious vibrancy of the odd colors, are marvelous decorative accents for modern homes. Make a quilt in the Amish style and hang it on your wall. You'll be amazed and delighted with the contemporary graphic you have created. These quilts are the most exciting when hung, for it is then that the design elements show to best advantage.

Copy the first quilt you make if you wish. This will set guidelines for you, and train your eye in selecting color and proportion. But, then, for the next one, do it your way, using the new thoughts, and you will find you have gained tremendous freedom and insight.

Indian Quilts

We were fascinated to discover a group of quilts made in India from handwoven fabrics in traditional Indian colors. The patterns, shown in Plates 32 through 35, are familiar and not familiar, leaving one with a feeling of déjà vu. They represent the transcendental quality of art, showing at the same time both the vertical and horizontal structure of cultural forms.

These quilts are reminiscent of American pieced patchwork, and yet their shapes and forms are closely related to those of the Caucasian areas of the Near East. Some will see Navajo forms in them.

So many derivative art forms seem to have sprung from a single well that we often wonder where it was that all of this really began.

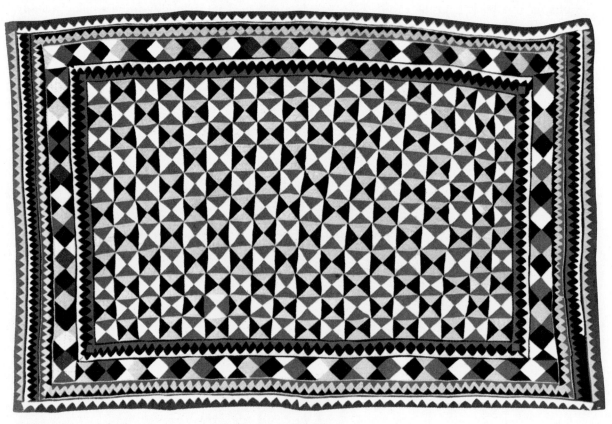

PLATE 32: *Patchwork Quilt from India,* collection of Joan Allen Walker.

124

PLATE 33: *Patchwork Quilt from India,* collection of Joan Allen Walker.

PLATE 34: *Patchwork Quilt from India,* collection of Joan Allen Walker.

PLATE 35: *Patchwork Quilt from India,* collection of Joan Allen Walker.

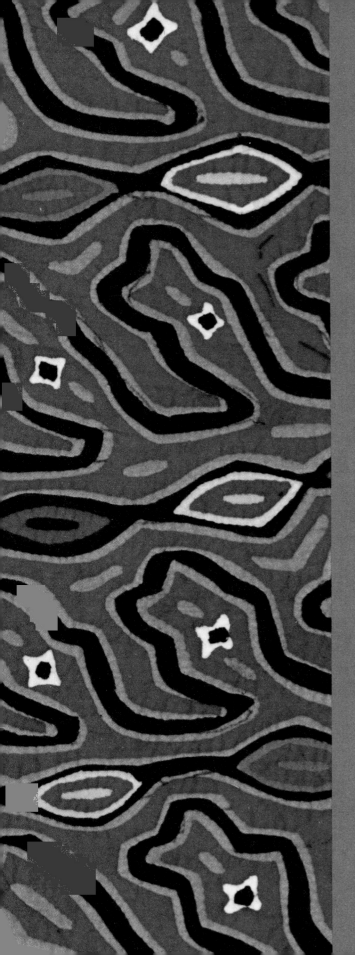

4
Appliqué
Quilts

Mola, collection of Audrey Heard.

Appliqué is simply the laying of one piece of fabric on top of another and securing it by means of stitches. This form of patchcraft has been used for centuries by civilizations throughout the world. Indians, Egyptians, the Chinese, and Europeans, too, have used appliqué work in their own individualistic and stylized versions. Needless to say, however, the ornate appliqué of renaissance Europe is very different from that of the Central American Indians. The latter's lively colors and primitive designs derived from nature reflect a totally different outlook from the highly civilized European work.

In America, the earliest form of appliqué can be traced to the early 1700s. Then, contraband calico and chintz were so scarce and so expensive that rarely could a household acquire enough of the precious stuff to cover an entire bed. Yet these fabrics were so soft and their prints so beautiful that the prints were often carefully cut from the bolts available and then applied to plain-background fabrics, either cotton or linen, which was woven domestically and was therefore in better supply. These were then made into bedcoverings and often embellished with elaborate embroidery, or *broderie Perse*, as will be discussed in Chapter 5.

Appliqué in America has come a long way since the days of the colonists. *Broderie Perse* has been replaced by iron-on appliqué, three-dimensional appliqué, reverse appliqué, stuffed appliqué, Hawaiian appliqué, felt appliqué, and plain, old, standard appliqué, done either by hand or by machine.

All these forms offer a freedom in design not afforded by the rigid structuring of geometric pieced patchwork. Traditional American appliqué is expressive, in the way that a picture is representative of its subject matter. It is pic-torial rather than graphic, and it lends itself to realistic interpretation. Animals, flowers, trees, birds, houses, and people are favorite subjects. Over the years, some remarkable examples of great folk art have been developed by the use of this technique.

It is not necessary, however, to be a trained artist to work with appliqué, for its charm often lies in the imagination and the craft skills of the maker. The simple, stylistic impressions of an innocent consciousness have a direct honesty and an integrity of *oneness*; they have purity and they are personal. In appliqué, it is possible to make a personal statement that has relevance and merit. It is a medium well-suited to an untaught craftsman, who can use the fabrics available in a plastic way, molding them to the vision of his inner eye for tremendous impact. The imperfections are a relief from the works of the slick professionals.

Primitive art is analogous to homely faces etched with lines and bent features, glowing with reality and with life. Primitive art, like a homely face, tells it like it is; the spirit and the mind and the dreams and the heartbreak, too, shine out. Communication happens, a reaching out, a giving of something personal, touching, and very beautiful.

MAKING AN APPLIQUED QUILT TOP

Fabrics selected for appliqué should be closely woven and should not fray easily. Calico, cotton broadcloth, and muslin are excellent. It's helpful, too, if the fabrics are preshrunk and colorfast. Unbleached muslin or off-white broadcloth are suitable for the foundation block. Combine plain and printed fabrics to complement your design. Consider the strength of their colors in

PLATE 36: *Album Quilt*, designed and made by Diane Wilson.

relation to each other, as well as the scale of the designs in them. Try to achieve a happy balance, and know that as you work with fabrics, your eye will improve with the experience.

Designs to be appliquéd are always traced on the right side of the fabric because it is necessary to see the seam line as you turn it under for hemming. Appliqués are always sewn, as well as quilted, with thread that matches them in

color. An appliqué design can be worked on a small block of fabric, or it can be enlarged to the full dimensions of a bed. Choosing the pattern, designing the layout, and picking the colors are the preparation for making the quilt.

For your first project, select a simple pattern and do it on a small 12- or 14-inch block. We recommend using one of the patterns that follow. (These patterns are arranged in order of diffi-

131

Diagram 4-1 / Tiger Lily

→|1"|←

culty, with the easiest being first.) Later, you will be able to work with any kind of picture or photograph, for you will know how to enlarge it to the exact dimensions you want. (Instructions for enlarging and reducing a design are in Chapter 6.) For now, this should be an exercise in developing skills, as from it, you will learn to draft the pattern, cut it out, and sew it to the background. Save your first block; you may want to use it in your first appliqué quilt. Your abilities will improve in very little time, and it will be fun to look back to the very first effort.

Plate 36 shows the first quilt a friend of ours made. She didn't know the first thing about quilts or quilting, but she wanted to try one. As we have seen from some of her recent quilts, she's come a long way, in technique and concept, as will happen to you, too.

Diagram 4-2 / Tulip #1

→|1"|←

The Reel, Plate 37 on page 146, is a difficult appliqué pattern to do. This beautiful old quilt was undoubtedly the work of a superb sewer. The symmetry of the arcs and the precision of the joining are extraordinary.

The Lobster appliqué, Plate 38 on page 147, is almost like a paper cutout. These are fun to do, and are most like the Hawaiian appliqués discussed later in the chapter.

APPLIQUE PATTERNS

To copy a pattern from a book, you must first transfer it from the book to a template in the manner described in Chapter 2 in "Making and Using a Template." Then cut out the pieces carefully. When all the pieces have been cut out, place them on the foundation block exactly as they will appear. Where pieces overlap, pin

133

Diagram 4-3 / Tulip #2

→|1"|←

Diagram 4-4 / Charter Oak

→|1"|←

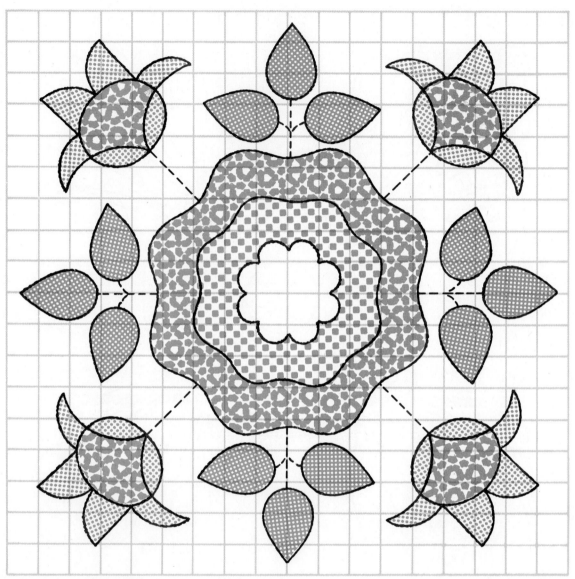

Diagram 4-5 / Whig Rose

Diagram 4-6 / Wreath of Paradise

→|1"|←

Diagram 4-7 / Prairie Flower

→|1"|←

Diagram 4-8 / Rose of Sharon

→|1"|←

139

Diagram 4-9 / Harrison Rose

→|1"|←

Diagram 4-10 | Ohio Rose

Diagram 4-11 / Poinsettia

→|1"|←

142

Diagram 4-12 / Original Pennsylvania Dutch

→|1"|←

143

Diagram 4-13 / Original Dove

Diagram 4-14 / Original George Washington

→|1"|←

145

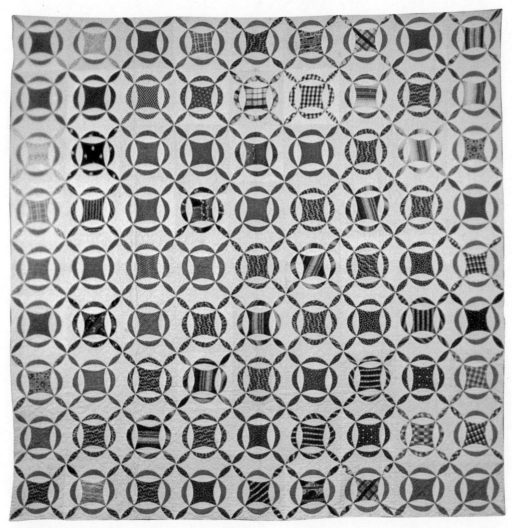

PLATE 37: *The Reel Quilt*, collection of Alice Potter.

PLATE 38: *Lobster Appliqué Quilt*, collection of Audrey Heard.

the bottom one to the block, remove the others, and sew this one first. Then, place the second piece on top of the first one, and sew again. Continue until all the pieces are sewn.

Although some quilters prefer to baste the pieces in place, it is not necessary if they are securely pinned. Turn the hem under to the seam line as you sew, and clip concave curves as shown in Diagram 4-15, to allow the fabric to follow the line of the curve properly. The tighter the curve is, the more clipping will be needed.

Sewing sharp corners can be a problem unless they are adequately fastened first. Following Diagram 4-16, fold the corner and tuck under the edges. Take three small stitches right at the corner to prevent the raw edges from slipping out.

Appliqué stitches are shown in Diagrams 4-17 and 4-18. A small, neat, running stitch (Diagram 4-17) can be used on top of the fabric, or a slip stitch (Diagram 4-18), nearly invisible, can be used along the seam line; an embroidery stitch is also sometimes used. For either a running stitch or a slip stitch, use thread the same color as the pattern piece. The stitches should be evenly spaced, about ⅛ inch apart, and they should be of uniform size. If you are obsessively neat and precise while learning, the methods

Diagram 4-15

147

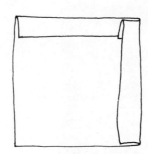

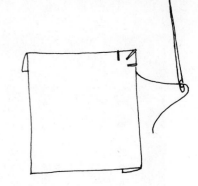

Diagram 4-16

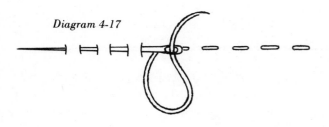

Diagram 4-17

Diagram 4-18

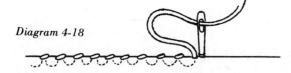

will become automatic, and, very soon, your hands will know just what to do.

Even though we prefer to sew appliqués by hand, the sewing machine is a wonderful tool. Not only does it save time, but usually the stitches are stronger and will withstand the rigors of laundry and bed more successfully. This is an especially important consideration when making quilts for children.

Appliqués can be sewn by machine in several ways. One way is to topstitch them (Diagram 4-19); by this method, the ¼-inch seam allowance is turned under, clipped where necessary, and pressed. The appliqué is then pinned to the foundation and topstitched ⅛ of an inch from the edge. The zigzag stitch is shown in Diagram 4-20. For this method, do not turn the edges under; they will be covered by the zigzags. Loosen the tension of the machine; sew once with a wide zigzag and, again, with a narrower zigzag stitch. (Fancier stitches can be used if you enlarge the seam allowance by at least an inch to allow for the space they will take.) Then sew on the seam line, and cut away the excess, as shown in Diagram 4-21. (Hint: If the fabric bunches and does not lie flat while being appliquéd by machine, the tension of your machine needs adjusting. Usually, it needs to be loosened.)

When all the blocks are finished, lay them out in the way they are to be assembled. They will be either joined to each other, separated by lattice strips, or alternated with plain blocks. The directions for doing this are in Chapters 1 and 2, along with those for making the borders, the interlining, and the backing and for doing the quilting.

Choose any quilting pattern you like, remem-

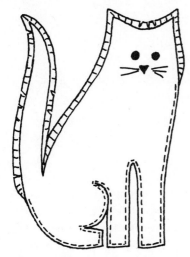

Diagram 4-19

Diagram 4-20

Diagram 4-21

bering that outline, diagonal, and curved quilting are the easiest. If you prefer, you can tie your quilt, eliminating the hours of stitching required to quilt it (see "Tying the Quilt" in Chapter 2).

Stuffed Appliqué: Added dimension can be given to appliqué by stuffing it first. Animals and flowers thrive when stuffed, and it's fun to do. The Jungle Quilt (see Plate 63 on page 188) illustrates this; the giraffe's spots and the alligator's scales are padded. It makes them really stand out!

In order to stuff an appliqué, leave a small opening when sewing around the edge; through this, gently insert Dacron or cotton. Distribute it evenly and lightly, using either the point of your scissors or a seam ripper. Remember, enough is a puff, too much is a bulge. Sew the opening closed.

Three-dimensional Appliqué: Three-dimensional appliqué is an appliqué that is partially sewn to the foundation block but yet has pieces which are backed and hang free. Fortunately, we have a photograph of this; a verbal explanation of the process without illustration would boggle the mind. Plate 39 is the photograph that is worth its weight in words; it shows a flower whose petals are attached only at their bases. This is done by sewing the petal pieces, right sides together, around their outside edges, leaving the base open. The petal is then turned right side out, the raw edges are turned in, and it is appliquéd at its base only. This technique gives a wonderful, full look as in high relief carving. Space underneath the appliqué becomes important, and the shape is revealed in its roundness.

This technique can be used effectively in children's quilts, especially. A rabbit's ear could curve and flop, or a basket of strawberries

PLATE 39: *Basket Ribbon Quilt,* designed by Audrey Heard, made by Rosemary Buckley.

could spill its leaves in everlasting summer.

Felt Appliqué: Felt is easy to work with because it does not fray so that the edges do not need to be turned under. It has great texture, is available in widths up to 72 inches, and comes in divine colors. There are various qualities to choose from, which are categorized according to the wool content. Use a 12-ounce felt if you can find it; the cheaper grades are sleazy and stretchy. Unfortunately, the main drawback of felt is its tendency to shrink. It also must be dry-cleaned, and you must use care when pressing it, for unless it is firmly held to size, steam can shrink it.

We like to use felt appliqué on a felt background, as it is possible to do a very handsome quilt in this material. First, the ground color is cut exactly to size. If the desired width is greater than 72 inches, strips of felt the full length of the quilt by the width needed are added to either side of the 72-inch strip. The seam can be overlapped and stitched or joined in the usual manner and pressed open. The edges can be scalloped, left straight, or zigzagged. Then mount the felt top to a firmly woven fabric, such as denim or broadcloth, to give it body and prevent its stretching or shrinking out of shape. These two, joined, then become the "foundation." Machine-stitch all around the perimeter, joining both layers. Baste the center lines and the diagonals; also baste a grid of lines spaced about 8 inches apart over the surface.

The appliqués are cut exactly to size, with no seam allowance; they are then placed on the *foundation,* pinned, and sewn. We prefer to sew the appliqués by machine, using a straight stitch, 1/8 inch in from the edge. However, they can also be machine-zigzagged or attached by numerous fancy hand-sewn stitches.

The quilt top is effective also when covered with decorative stitchery, such as crewel or other embroidery. When it is finished, it is interlined, backed, and quilted, as has been previously discussed in Chapters 1 and 2. The backing should be of a strong, nonstretchy fabric, heavier than you would normally use.

Reverse Appliqué: Reverse appliqué is an old form with beautiful dimensions that has been primarily identified with the Indians of Panama and northern South America. The examples we have shown here in Plates 40 through 44 come from Colombia, where they were made by women in a federally run co-op. They are called *molas* by the natives and were originally used in making native blouses. Recently, dress designers have incorporated these *molas* into high-style fashion, using them as the back or front of a dinner dress or as a yoke in a jacket. The outfits are very handsome—expensive, too.

The technique calls for sandwiching together three to five layers of fabrics in different colors; the design is created by cutting through the layers to expose the underlying colors. The top layer is cut first and the opening turned under and hemmed; the second, third, and so on are done in the same way so that narrow edges of new color are left each time a cut is made. This technique is the opposite of appliqué, in which layers are stacked one on top of the other.

The *molas* of the Indian women are inspired by nature, from which they adapt the forms of animals, flowers, and sea creatures into stylized, often geometric, statements. Usually, for unknown reasons, red is the top color, and

PLATE 40: *Mola*, collection of Audrey Heard.

PLATE 41: *Mola*, collection of Audrey Heard.

black the bottom. Electric blue, orange, pink, yellow, and green are the filler colors. The women cut their designs freehand, and the sewing is done with tiny, invisible stitches.

We are fascinated by the *mola* in Plate 44 because its maker was most inventive. She used red for the top and gold for the bottom, but, in between, she placed a piece of fabric made of patchwork squares in varied hues. When she cut

through for the design, the colors that emerged were fantastic; it looks as though she had done twenty layers.

A wall hanging of a turtle that shows the technique of reverse appliqué is shown in Plate 45. The designer has followed tradition in making it, but the boldness and scale of her *mola* is her own. Beverly Pryor's *mola* (Plate 46) was adapted from a design we found in a local artist's collection. It represents another approach.

Reverse appliqué is fun; puzzlelike in its enchantment, it consumes hours of painstaking work, not only in cutting but in sewing thousands of tiny stitches. It makes a stunning quilt, had one "but world enough, and time." Blocks can be made in squares, or they can be irregularly shaped and fitted together. A center medallion could be made in reverse appliqué and set into a plain or pieced quilt top.

It is an intriguing technique, and it is possible to think small; a baby quilt using it would be lovely, or a wall hanging, or a chair seat.

Making a Reverse Appliqué:
1. Plan the design, keeping in mind the sequence in which colors will be exposed. Do something relatively simple, without complex curves and intricate squiggles.
2. Choose the fabrics. We recommend percale

PLATE 42: *Mola*, collection of Audrey Heard.

PLATE 44: *Mola*, collection of Audrey Heard.

PLATE 45: *Turtle Wall Hanging*, designed and made by Diane Wilson.

PLATE 46: *Elephant Wall Hanging*, concept by Kathryn Forest, designed and made by Beverly Pryor.

or 100-percent cotton broadcloth. Don't use synthetic mixtures, as they are slippery and won't cling to each other. Heavier fabrics won't work, either, nor will those that are stretchy or loosely woven. You will need a layer of fabric for each major color in your design.

3. Cut all the layers exactly the same size, and arrange them from top to bottom in planned sequence, as you wish them to appear when the *mola* is finished. Baste the layers together around the edges and on both diagonals, from corner to corner.

4. Using a pencil, trace the design onto the top layer. Very carefully, cut through to the second layer, leaving a ¼-inch seam allowance that is to be turned under and sewn down.

5. Clip all curves and corners to the seam line, turn the seam allowance under, and sew with small slip stitches, closely spaced, through all the layers. The thread should match the color of the fabric being sewed.

6. Cut through to the third layer, following your design, and remember to leave the ¼-inch seam allowance. Continue in this way until only the bottom layer is left. Do not cut this.

7. If you wish to add a dash of different color, it is possible to do this by inserting a small piece of fabric in selected spots between layers. The piece to be inserted is cut larger than the opening in which it is to go. This piece is slipped in, and the layer above it is sewn through it and the layers underneath.

8. Appliqué can also be used on a *mola*, as can be seen in Plates 41 and 42. Here, the appliqués are sewn to the top of the complete *mola*.

9. When the blocks are finished, they are set together in the same ways as previously described. The top, interlining, and backing are joined, and the quilt is quilted in whatever design you wish.

PLATE 47: *Kukui Nut Hawaiian Quilt*, designed and made by Barbara McKie.

PLATE 48: *Kukui Nut Hawaiian Quilt* detail.

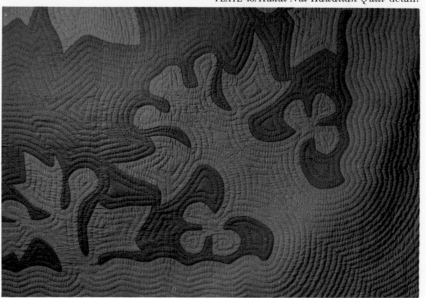

HAWAIIAN QUILTS

Quilting was introduced to the Hawaiian Islanders in 1820 by American missionaries. They brought with them their patterns, their scrap bags, and their memories, and they taught quilt making, as they knew it, to the Islanders, who soon evolved their own gorgeous techniques.

Hawaiian quilts are unique in that they are made from two whole pieces of material, one of which is a giant free-form cutout that is appliquéd to the other. The designs are cut freehand, in lush, rhythmic forms reminiscent of the scenery and vegetation of the Islands. Usually, only two colors are used, one for the background, one for the appliqué, and these are almost always solid colors. Prints are rarely used. The quilting is done by following the lines of the appliquéd design.

The lore and the language surrounding Hawaiian quilts is fascinating; the words are lovely melodic sounds, and the folklore, fact, and superstition surrounding Hawaiian quilt making combine to make the quilts an important facet of Hawaiian culture. The craft of making a Hawaiian quilt, or *kapa*, is taught by a *tutu*, or grandmother teacher, and the patterns are carefully guarded family treasures. Traditionally, untold wraths and furies descend on one who steals another's precious pattern, the inspiration for which might have been taken from a dream, a national or family event, or a dearly loved scene. Occasionally, permission is granted to copy a pattern, but the copier is honor-bound to alter the pattern in some way. Usually, it is altered by adding little openings, or *pukas*, to the original.

Men, as well as women, make quilts, and the degree of skill they show is unbelievable. The quilt makers have a reverence for their work, considering it personal and private. In fact, when the Honolulu Academy of Art recently had a show of quilts, the organizers had a difficult time getting the owners of the quilts to exhibit them, for an unwritten ethic walks always with the quilts.

Once a year, in May, the Waianae Library has a quilt festival. Then, from thirty to forty patterns are made available to the public to be copied. Hundreds of people, *Kamaaina* (natives) and *Malihini* (newcomers), flock to the library and patiently await their turn. During the hours that the exhibition is open—from 10 AM to 4 PM—only a few people are admitted at a time. Each is given five sheets of paper and a pencil, and each may copy only five patterns. Some merely sketch, but others use rulers and other devices to meticulously copy the treasured patterns.

Most Hawaiian quilts take their forms and colors from nature—flowers and birds, animals and fish, mountains and sea. All, however, are stylistically represented. Rarely, the subject matter is an event of historical importance, with the appliqués of human figures realistically portrayed. Red and yellow (the royal colors) are favorites; they represent the plumage of a macaw-like bird native to the Islands. Other colors used are, for the most part, also Island colors—blue, orange, purple, and green. Sometimes, one color is combined with white, as red on white, but often, tints of the same color are used.

MAKING A PATTERN

Hawaiian quilting is considered a "scissors' art"; designs are cut from fabric folded to precise specifications so that a perfectly symmetrical pattern is formed. Patterns are always either

157

eight-point or four-point. To learn how to work with them, we suggest you practice with paper first. It won't take long to get the hang of it.

The eight-point pattern:

1. Place a sheet of 8½- by 11-inch paper in front of you. Fold the bottom to the top and crease the fold, as shown in Diagram 4-22A..

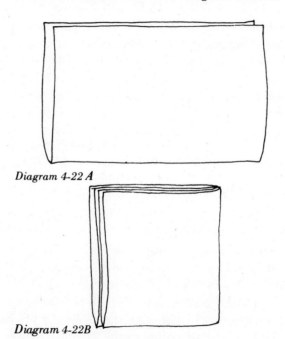

Diagram 4-22 A

Diagram 4-22B

2. Following Diagram 4-22B, fold from right to left and crease the fold. There is now one fold on the right, two on the bottom, and open edges on the top and on the left.

3. Make a triangle by folding the lower left corners to the right folded edge, as shown in Diagram 4-22C. Crease the fold.

4. The point at the lower right is the *pico*, or middle. Mark it with a pencil. The rectangle of fabric extending above the triangle now formed may be used later if you wish to make a border.

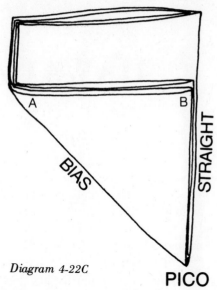

Diagram 4-22C

5. Make the two folds to your right the "straight"; the hypotenuse on your left is the "bias." Draw your design in any way you like, keeping within the area shown in Diagram 4-22C. Draw a continuous line from point A toward the pico and end at point B. *Do not let this line touch either the folds or the* pico, *or the design will fall apart when it is cut and unfolded.* *Pukas* are made by cutting openings inward from the folds, or the *pico*. These are small and leave most of the folds intact so that the design holds together when unfolded.

6. Cut along the drawn lines through all eight thicknesses, keeping the paper folded.

7. Save the paper cut from the center between the folds and also the rectangular strip at the end; you may want to use the latter for borders. To do this, cut a design into the rectangular piece, through eight thicknesses.

8. Unfold the triangle; you will have a snowflakelike pattern with eight points, which have four each of two alternating designs.

The four-point pattern: This pattern is preferred for making pillows.

1. Fold the paper for the pattern as described in steps 1 and 2 above. Omit step 3.

2. Mark the *pico*, the point at the lower right.

3. Draw the design as described in step 5 above. You are now working with a square instead of a triangle so that you will have two

straights and no bias. The design is cut between the folds. When it is unfolded, you will have a four-point pattern, with two alternating designs.

4. When you have completed a paper pattern that you like, set it aside.

MAKING THE QUILT TOP

You must now assemble the fabrics you are going to use and preshrink them by washing them. Then, by joining lengths of fabric as shown in Diagram 4-23, form them into three large units, the quilt top, the appliqué overlay, and the backing. Each unit should be pieced to reach its full size in exactly the same way as the other two. This ensures that all the seams come out at the same place and guarantees uniformity. For example, if you plan to make a quilt that measures 84 by 84 inches, you first make the quilt top to be this size. Then you make the backing and, finally, the piece from which the appliqué is to be cut. All should be exactly the same in size, and all their seams should be in the same places.

The following chart is intended to serve only as a guide to how much fabric you will need to make your quilt. Because of their design, native Hawaiian quilts are always square. We recom-

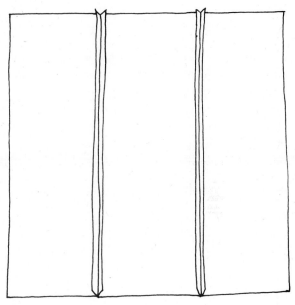

Diagram 4-23

mend using 36-inch fabric for two reasons: Usually, the most interesting fabrics come in this width and it is more economical because 45-inch fabrics entail a lot of waste. If you wish to make an oblong quilt, however, you can do it in either of two ways: (1) Use the center design in the middle, and cut other designs to use in the corners; (2) Elongate sections of the pattern for the lengthwise direction. Be inventive! Diagram 8-3 on page 246 shows how this can be done.

Type of Bed	Size (in inches)	Width of Fabric (in inches)	Required Yardage			Finished Quilt Size (in inches)
			Appliqué (in yards)	Background (in yards)	Lining (in yards)	
Crib	27 × 52 ..	36 ..	2 ..	2 ..	2	.. 40 × 40
Twin	39 × 75 ..	36 ..	7 ..	7 ..	7	.. 84 × 84
Double	54 × 75 ..	36 ..	9 ..	9 ..	9	.. 96 × 96
Queen	60 × 80 ..	36 ..	9¾ ..	9¾ ..	9¾	..108 × 108
King	80 × 80 ..	36 ..	9¾ ..	9¾ ..	9¾	..115 × 115

After you have bought and ironed all the fabrics you need, fold the fabric that is to be the appliqué (Diagrams 4-24 A and 4-24 B) in exactly the same way as your paper pattern (steps 1 through 4 in the case of the eight-pointed pattern; steps 1, 2, and 4 for the four-pointed).

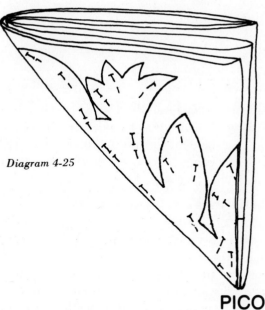

Diagram 4-25

PICO

You now have the size of one section of the pattern that is one-eighth the overall size for an eight-point pattern and one-quarter for a four-point.

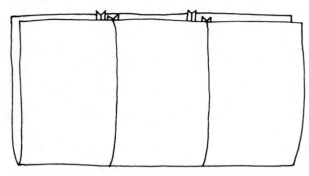

Diagram 4-24A

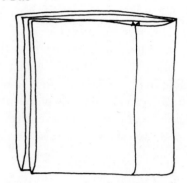

Diagram 4-24B

Lay the folded fabric over a piece of paper that is large enough to accommodate it. Newspaper or shelf paper can be used; if it is not long enough or wide enough, tape on additional paper. Lay the folded fabric on top of the prepared paper, and cut the paper to the same size.

You must now enlarge your small paper pattern to the size of the paper you have just cut. Remember that this is just one segment of the design and that the paper is only one thickness. Mark your pico, the straight, and the bias. You have already done this on the folded fabric. Transfer the design to the new paper, being accurate but drawing in as free a manner as you can.

When the drawing is completed, lay the pattern on top of the folded fabric. Pin it securely through all the layers, as shown in Diagram 4-25, and cut through all the layers. Unfold the fabric, line the seams up so they match the top, and lay it down so that the back of the appliqué is to the front ot the top. Do not pull or stretch the appliqué because so much of it is on the bias. Pat it out gently, and it will fall in place. Be sure it's centered, and then stand back and look at it for a while to be sure it's right. Pin it in place, by starting at the center and working out toward the edges (Diagram 4-26). Baste across the middle,

up and down the center, and through each section of the appliqué, always starting in the center and going to the edges, as shown in Diagram 4-27. (You first make a cross, and then an X.) This is the time to do a final check on the spacing of the appliqué on the quilt top; because of its absolute symmetry, it must be exactly placed, with equal space all around. If it is not perfect, do it again.

When all is satisfactory, baste around the outside edges of the appliqué, about ½ inch in if possible.

The technique of sewing a Hawaiian appliqué is an interesting one. The edges of the fabric are first turned under with a needle, as shown in the photo. To do this, place the point of the needle under the edge of the fabric and then draw it in the direction in which you are sewing. Do this for an inch or two, and then overcast it with tiny stitches in thread color to match. The fabric rolls over the needle, and from $\frac{1}{16}$ to $\frac{1}{8}$ of an inch is

Diagram 4-27

folded under. This works on both convex and concave curves as well as on straight areas. It eliminates the need for clipping and takes advantage of the natural tendency of biases to stretch. It is imperative, however, that the stitches be small and close together so that raw edges will not pull out and ruin the effect. To turn a sharp corner, as at the point of a leaf, use the needle to turn the fabric under to the very point, overcast to the point, and then take several tiny stitches, almost on top of each other, to secure the point. Push the following edge under with your needle, sewing closely, and continue until all edges are sewn. Then remove the basting stitches.

If you wish to make a border, cut it out in the same way as the center, using the folded rectangle you saved earlier. Do not unfold this section before pinning and cutting the pattern. This pattern is cut to fit one-eighth or one-quarter of the total size, depending on the design used; it is pinned to the fabric and cut through all the layers.

The quilt top, interlining, and backing are then joined in the usual way, as shown in Diagram 4-28. Because the precision of the quilting is so vitally important in this type of quilt, we recommend using a quilting frame or hoop.

Diagram 4-26

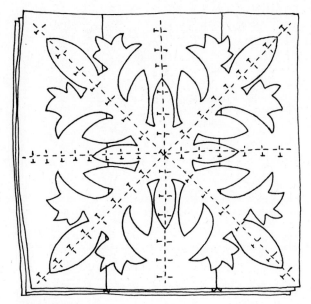

Diagram 4-28

Diagram 4-29

QUILTING THE QUILT

Hawaiian quilting *(humu lau)* follows the line of the design. Look closely at the quilts and their details pictured in Plates 47 through 50. The technique used is outline quilting. Waves of stitching go outward from the outline of the appliqué at intervals of from ½ to ⅝ of an inch, as shown in Diagram 4-29. The first row of quilting is done exactly at the outside edge of the appliqué and follows it completely around. Study again the details of both quilts, and notice how the rows of quilting are handled when they meet.

It takes time and thought to do a Hawaiian quilt well, but the results are spectacular. The appliquéd skirt shown in Plate 86C on page 239 uses the Kukui Nut pattern, which is the same pattern that was used to make the quilt pictured in Plates 47 and 48. It's interesting to see different approaches to the same pattern.

Plate 49 shows an intricate Hawaiian quilt that was done under the aegis of a *tutu* when the quilt maker was living in Hawaii. The name of the pattern is Orchid, and if you look at the detail (Plate 50), you will understand how much work goes into a well-done quilt of this type. The fastest quilter we have ever known made this quilt, but she estimates that it took her more than three months to do, sewing four to five hours a day.

A *kapa pohopoho* is a Hawaiian quilt form that follows the traditional New England missionary placement of blocks—side by side. However, the Hawaiian interpretation bears little resemblance to its predecessors. A wall hanging using this form is shown in Plate 80 on page 206.

Once you have learned the technique of outline quilting in the Hawaiian style, you will find many uses for it. The Vermont Quilt shown on

PLATE 49: *Orchid Hawaiian Quilt*, designed and made by Diane Wilson.

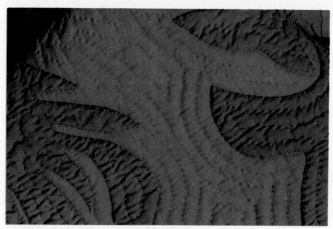

PLATE 50: *Orchid Hawaiian Quilt* detail.

163

the cover and on page 187, so far away in design from the Hawaiian quilts, uses this quilting technique. It gives marvelous depth and motion, as you will be able to see when you examine the details.

FINISHING THE QUILT

After the quilt has been quilted, it is bound with a strip of binding. This can match the background color, or if a border has been used, then match the binding to it. Cut four 2-inch-wide strips, on the straight grain, two as long as the width of the quilt and two as long as the length. Then sew the binding strips to the back of the quilt, either lapping or mitering the corners, turn it to the desired width, and blindstitch it to the front.

We include here several Hawaiian quilting patterns, which can easily be enlarged to the dimensions you wish (see instructions for enlarging designs in Chapter 6). Diagrams 4-30, 4-31, and 4-32 are all eight-point quilt patterns. Diagrams 4-33, 4-34, 4-35, and 4-36 are four-point patterns suitable for pillows. These patterns can easily be adapted to make the skirt and tablecloth shown in Chapter 8, once you have learned the basic methods of folding and cutting.

We have given a great deal of space to this most fascinating of quilting techniques because we enjoy its freedom and vitality and know that you will, too. *Aloha* and *maholo nui*.

Hawaiian Quilting Patterns

Diagram 4-30 | *Plumeria (eight-point)*

|2½|

Diagram 4-31   Baby Rose (eight-point)

$2\frac{1}{2}$

Diagram 4-32   Bread Fruit (eight-point)

2"

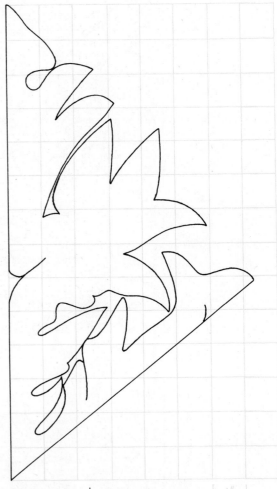

Diagram 4-34 | *Mi Pia (four-point)* ⊢1″⊣

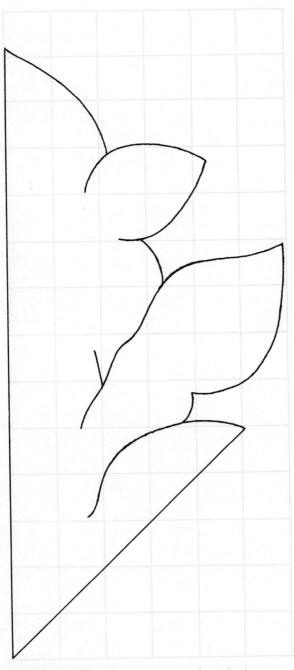

Diagram 4-33
  Calla Lily (four-point)   ⊢1″⊣

168

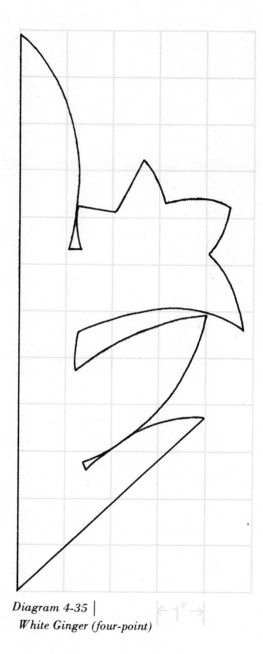

Diagram 4-35 |
  White Ginger (four-point)

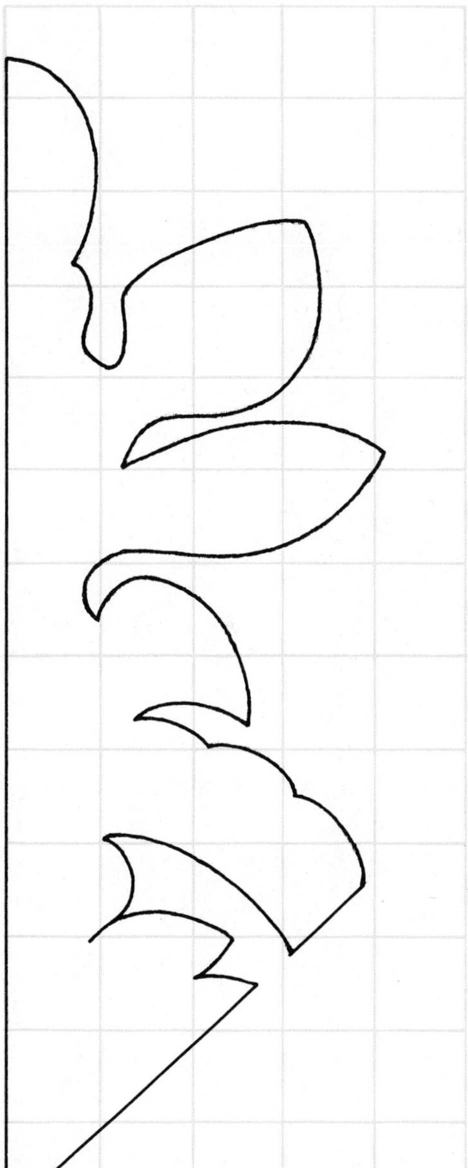

← 1″ →

Diagram 4-36 |
  Light House Lily (four-point)

← 1″ →

5
Needlework Quilts

Bates Family Quilt, broderie Perse detail.

PLATE 52: *Bates Family Quilt, broderie Perse,* designed and made by Kathryn Forest, collection of Mrs. Kenneth Bates.

PLATE 53: For *Bates Family Quilt* detail, see pages 170-71

NEEDLEWORK QUILTS

Needlework quilts, whose primary decorative qualities stem from the intricacies of stitchery, were popular in the late eighteenth and early nineteenth centuries, before the invention of the Jacquard loom. This loom made bedcoverings similar to those being made by hand, supplanting them because "a machine is quicker and cheaper." The handworked quilts of long ago are treasured today, and many of them are preserved in museums throughout the world.

The modern quilt maker who approaches her craft with deliberate creativity and imagination will, perhaps, bring about a renaissance of fine needlework quilting, perhaps as her response to everything she uses and wears being mass-produced. The quilt maker of the eighteenth century considered needlework a pastime, an entertainment. If she were limited for time, she did pieced patchwork or appliqué; if she were more ambitious, she applied her skills to fine needlework. There are several kinds of quilts that fall into this needlework category.

"WORKT," OR CREWEL, QUILTS

During the past fifteen years, there has been a revival of interest in crewel embroidery. Most embroidered articles being made now are small—pillows, eyeglass cases, wall hangings, etc. Two hundred years ago, whole quilts, with valances and curtains, were "workt." Some of them took years to make.

In the old days, the crewel embroidery was done on a background fabric of lightweight wool or English harrateen, on cotton, or on linen. The yarn was made of wool and imported from France. At this time, the China Trade clippers were bringing home Chinese bedcoverings made of silk and embroidered in silk threads. The

PLATE 51: *Fruits and Berries, Gloucester Quilt* crewel detail, designed and made by Peggy Norton, Women's Auxiliary to the Addison Gilbert Hospital, Gloucester, Massachusetts.

women of the colonies could not match the delicacy and minute skills of the Chinese, and their work was considerably coarser both in technique and in design. Nonetheless, they were influenced by the art of China, as well as of India and Persia.

Plate 51, a detail from the Gloucester quilt shown in Chapter 6 on page 192, illustrates a modern-day example of crewel used on a quilt.

BRODERIE PERSE QUILTS

Broderie Perse, or Persian embroidery, is the name given to the quilts made in the colonies and in England of cutouts from pictorial chintzes. Usually, these were designed with a center medallion and surrounded by rambling flowery borders. Individual flowers were then cut out of the chintz and appliquéd to the foundation fabric wherever the fancy of the maker dictated. The effect was that of lavish embroidery work.

Plate 52 shows a contemporary approach to *broderie Perse*. Plate 53 opening this chapter is a detail of one of the blocks. The artist who designed the quilt some thirty years ago used printed fabric pictures to give the illusion of intricate appliqué and then embroidered it elaborately to add to the effect. This work differs from the old work because appropriate fabrics were used to make more realistic the shapes of the objects and people she designed. The modern quilt maker uses the same techniques when she uses green-flowered calico for a grassy slope or a black-and-white striped fabric for a zebra. Prints add a realistic note; when embellished with embroidery, they look like the "real thing."

173

PLATE 55: *Whitework Quilt* detail.

WHITEWORK QUILTS

The whitework quilt is not to be confused with trapunto, or Italian, quilting (discussed later in this chapter), though, at first glance, it may resemble it. It is not stuffed as trapunto is nor does it have the contrast of high relief. Instead, a whitework quilt is flat, and its design is done in tiny stitches that match the background, usually white. The designs stitched into the quilt are always pictorial. The technique is literally that of drawing with a needle and thread (Plates 54 and 55).

To make this kind of quilt, the top, the flat interlining, and the backing are basted together. The design is then drawn on the back. The quilting stitches start in the center and work toward the edges. They must be tiny, uniform, and close together. It takes hours and days and months to do, for the designs must be ornate. These quilts are remarkable for their delicate workmanship.

PATCHED NEEDLEWORK QUILTS

The patched needlework quilt differs from other needlework quilts because the stitching is worked on small individual blocks that are later joined to make the quilt top. Sometimes, the blocks are the same colors; at other times, two colors are alternated in checkerboard fashion. The blocks are embroidered or decorated with fancy stitching, depending on the choice of the maker.

During the 1890s and early 1900s, "Turkey red" quilting was a popular pastime. Small patterns were bought at local stores, transferred to squares of white fabric, and then embroidered in Turkey red thread. When a sufficient number of blocks had been completed, they were joined together, a border was added, and a quilt was made of them.

PLATE 54: *Whitework Quilt*, collection of Phyllis Haders.

174

PLATE 56: *Turkey Red Quilt*, collection of Beverly Pryor.

Most of the patterns were trite—birds, hearts, flowers, and all manner of sentimental trivia were used. Every now and then, however, one can find a quilt made in this manner that is personal and wonderful. The one we have chosen as an illustration, shown in Plate 56, is of this ilk. The woman who made it was a real character; in it, she has commemorated both of her marriages and the demise of both spouses, as well as numerous other events in her life.

TRAPUNTO QUILTS

Trapunto, sometimes called Italian quilting or cord quilting, is a technique in which the designs are raised by being stuffed between the stitched lines of the design (Plate 57). The stuffed areas are thrown into high relief by this method, giving tremendous depth and dimension to the quilt. This form of needlework was popular in Europe during the seventeenth and eighteenth centuries, and, in America, it was a

PLATE 57: *Strawberry Quilt*, trapunto, collection of Phyllis Haders.

Diagram 5-1

favorite in the South, where many able hands could be enlisted to perform this most arduous of tasks.

Traditionally, feathers, fruit, flowers, vines, birds, and other rococo motifs were used. They were classically placed and very rigid. The background areas were stitched in a diaper effect. The diagonals formed diamonds, which were also stuffed.

A trapunto quilt is made by joining a top of fine white cotton to a backing of a more loosely woven white fabric. Since the effect of the quilt depends on stuffing the channels and areas that have been formed by stitching the top and the backing together in a decorative design, the need for an interlining is eliminated.

After the top and the backing have been joined together and the design marked, the design is worked in fine stitches through both layers. Then, with a sharp instrument, a hole is poked into the loosely woven backing material, pushing the threads apart to form an entry for the stuffing. Through it, bits of batt, cotton, or Dacron are gently pushed with the sharp instrument to stuff the area. After the area has been stuffed, the threads are pushed together again. If the fabric is too closely woven to allow for this, a small opening is cut into the backing fabric to allow for stuffing and is then sewn closed, as shown in Diagram 5-1. A proper balance must be achieved in order to stuff enough and not too much.

Often, two lines of stitching will outline a stem or other narrow design element. These are stuffed by inserting a needle threaded with yarn or cord through the back into the channel. The yarn or cord is drawn the full length of the design until a curve or angle is reached. The needle is

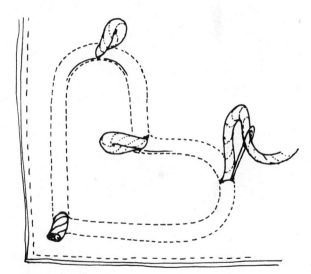

Diagram 5-2

then withdrawn on the back side—never on the top—and a loop is left before reinserting it to continue the design (Diagram 5-2). The loop is insurance that should the cord shrink, the design would not be drawn up.

Making a trapunto quilt requires patience and skilled craftsmanship. It represents thousands of tiny stitches and hours of painstaking stuffing. The effect is sumptuous, but the technique is just not geared to modern-day thinking. The subtleties are foreign to today's temperament. We are a design- and color-oriented group, lacking the patience for the skill required.

177

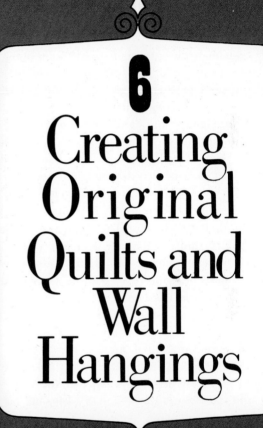

6
Creating Original Quilts and Wall Hangings

Happy Day Wall Hanging, detail designed and made by Rieta Park.

Throughout Chapters 1 through 5, we have told you what we know about the techniques of quilt making. A constant theme runs through the pages: learn the techniques, master the craftsmanship, and then create something that is entirely your own. Dream up the design, transfer it to fabric; see it your way, in colors that please you. Trust your own standards of taste and judgment and dare to be wrong, dare to be different. It's important to make a statement, to say something that no one else has ever said. Listen to your private thoughts; see with the clarity you had when you were very young.

A wonderful legacy of original thought has been left to us by the talented women who made the first quilts in the now well-known patterns. The first quilt maker started with nothing but the vision of her inner eye, and the second added hers, and the third hers. It has been a spiraling involvement, and the end is nowhere in sight.

It is fascinating to study the old quilts, especially the appliquéd ones, and to realize how personal an expression they really are. Pictures and symbols depict the objects, the interests, and the feelings of the maker's life, her hopes, her achievements, her sorrows. Translating these into the medium of cloth emphasizes the importance of these things to the quilt maker.

Many of the old quilts belong in the folk art category, for they are primitive and naïve in their concept, although the workmanship is often superb. They are the expression of untaught women, recording a way of life that is no more. They are charming, and often very capable in craftsmanship and in inherent artistic sensibility.

These wonderful old quilts are for looking at, for admiring, and for appreciating, but not for copying. Our world has come too far, and we are too sophisticated; our modes and mores are of a different idiom, and we must say what is our generation's. The old quilts are delightful nostalgia, and we all succumb to the enchantment of a simpler era. If we are recreating or reproducing an earlier interior and if we wish analogous decoration, then we copy. But if we wish to represent the present, then we must express what is ours.

Of the old quilts, a large group represented, in rituallike way, the commemoration of occasions. There were Friendship, Marriage, Album, and Memory quilts; some were tokens of esteem, made to be presented to special people, while others are recordings of history or of daily life.

A large body of the old quilts, especially those in the pieced patchwork and repeat decorated-block appliqué, are simply triumphs of design, expressing only the joy of creativity.

This chapter is broken down into three sections. In the first, we shall explore for you the mechanics of creating an original quilt, from the seed of an idea to the final stitch. Section II is all about creating quilts for children. The third section deals with creating your own wall hanging and includes instructions on how to mount it.

I. CREATING AN ORIGINAL QUILT

Basically, there are five elements (each of which is elaborated upon in other sections of the book) to take into consideration in creating a quilt. They are, in order:

1. The concept
2. The plan: design, structure, and color
3. The mechanics: drafting the pattern to scale
4. The fabrics
5. The quilting

1. THE CONCEPT

Once you have decided to make an original quilt, give thought to what you want to say. Let your ideas float in and out of consciousness, like butterflies waiting to be captured. Keep paper and pen handy, and make rough sketches. Soon the image will jell, and, usually, the total picture is there, waiting to be developed and refined.

2. THE PLAN

Design: Formulating the design takes work, for it is an exact thing. First, you must decide on the size you wish your completed quilt to be. To draft it, mark it off on either premeasured graph paper or on a grid that you have drawn. The measured squares will provide a visual accounting of the units in relationship to each other.

Sketch your rough design into the overall dimensions marked on the graph paper to see whether it works and whether it says what you want it to. Study it closely. Often, a small sketch enlarged to the size of a quilt will leave enormous empty spaces, or sometimes the design elements will have become too large or too small to be effective.

When planning your design, then, it is important to consider the size of the subject matter contained in each block in relationship to that in each of the other blocks and in relationship to the entire quilt. There must be balance and harmony. If one area is heavy with detail without a counterpoint elsewhere, the composition will be out of scale.

Now, you must refine the design elements. They have to be drawn in exactly the way they will appear in the finished quilt. Many of us are not artists, but this is not a deterrent. Photo-graphs, drawings, and other delineated forms all suggest ideas for design. Sometimes, we ask an artistic friend to help us. We have all learned to be somewhat dexterous with a ruler and a compass to work out the basic geometry involved in pieced patchwork. Designing is one part inspiration, one part patience, and one part technique.

Structure: This is the time to decide how the quilt will be made—whether it is to be in blocks, pieced, or appliquéd; whether or not lattices and borders are to be used. Will you do it by hand, by machine, or with a combination of both? You must decide, at this point, exactly how you are going to make the quilt.

The design often determines the technique to be used. For example, the drawing of an elephant sitting on a globe should not be interpreted in pieced patchwork because the curved lines would be too difficult to match. Also, the design would lack the dimension that could be achieved through either reverse appliqué or appliqué. The Indian elephants in Plate 45 on page 155, for instance, are a combination of appliqué and reverse appliqué; parts of the design are five layers thick.

One large, overall picture can be used, as is shown in the Jungle Quilt on page 188 (Plate 63), or different designs can be used in blocks separated by lattices, as in the Man and Wife Quilt on page 192 (Plate 67). Various-sized blocks, each with its own picture, can be sewn together flush (see Kent Family Quilt, Plate 59 on page 186), or one design can be repeated over and over in different colors (see Owl Quilt, Plate 72 on page 196). In the Modern Patchwork Quilt on page 189 (Plate 64), two interreacting designs have been combined to form one motif.

The combinations for possible layouts are limitless. Look at Diagrams 1-1 thru 1-5 in Chapter 1, and examine the various methods of arranging blocks into an overall "set."

The border designs, if borders are to be used, must be planned now. They must complement and finish the central design, as well as be a part of the composition. They should decoratively enhance the quilt, for they are, literally, the frame. Border designs can be pieced, appliquéd, or plain, and, of course, when the entire quilt is sewn, the borders should be in proper relationship to the rest.

Color: Choice of color is vitally important to the quilt. Once you learn the basic rules of color harmony, you should have no trouble. Most beginners are carried away by the wide spectrum available to them and tend to use too much color, which overwhelms the design.

It helps to have some knowledge of the techniques of color harmony. There are many good books available on the subject; you can also learn a lot by looking at printed fabrics, especially those done for the home furnishings market that use many screens. From studying them, you can get a feeling for basic color relationships.

Red, blue, and yellow are primary colors; all others—secondary and tertiary—stem from these (Diagram 6-1).

Red and blue combine to form purple; blue and yellow, green; yellow and red, orange. These are the secondary colors, and they complement their opposing primary color. For example, purple is the complement of yellow, orange of blue, and green of red.

Tertiary colors extend the spectrum in the

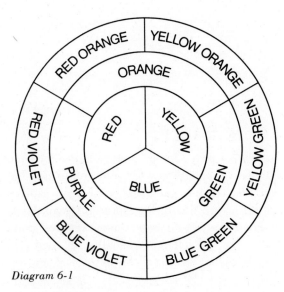

Diagram 6-1

same relationships. Depending on the amount of secondaries you use, varying hues are arrived at, which finally evolve into gray when equal amounts of each are used.

The cool colors are the run of mixes from red to blue, warming as yellow approaches and getting hottest at red.

If you use colors that are opposite on the wheel, your schemes will be complementary; if you use those that are adjacent to each other, your scheme will be monochromatic. Tints and hues of each color are made by adding white.

This is only a capsule lesson in color; it can be very useful to pursue this further.

As far as the quilt maker is concerned, colors must be used in proper relationship. It takes a lot of skill to flaunt the basic rules, although the results can be exciting.

Old Maid's Puzzle, made by Beverly Pryor in tie and shirt prints (see Plate 8 on page 55), is an example of a well-planned, multicolor design. In spite of the number of complementary colors used in the prints, it works because each print is set next to a white background print. On the other hand, the quilt pictured in Plate 58 is not as good. This is one of Bev's first quilts, and we show it to let you see what happens when too many colors are used.

Color is a powerful tool, and you must make it

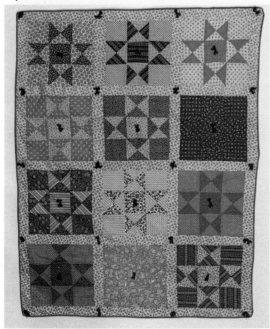

PLATE 58: *Jackknife Quilt*, designed and made by Beverly Pryor.

work for you. You will learn to handle colors by trial and error. Time spent in planning your scheme is never wasted, for through the process of selection and elimination, you will arrive at just the right combination.

Printed fabrics add a new dimension to color choice. It is here that most beginners have problems. Regardless of design and color in the printed fabrics you choose, the factor that makes them work together is scale. The drawings of the patterns must relate in size and scale and in their reaction on each other. Usually, the smaller prints are the most suitable, although a large print can be used effectively in a picture design, as in *broderie Perse*. There is no way we can tell you exactly how to choose color; it is a matter of experimentation, of rejection and acceptance. You train your eye to the degree that it picks suitable combinations. And, of course, the final choice is always a personal thing.

3. THE MECHANICS: DRAFTING THE PATTERN TO SCALE BY ENLARGING OR REDUCING THE DESIGNS

Almost everyone has access to excellent artwork of all kinds. If you cannot draw, books, sketches, photographs, paintings, wallpaper, printed fabrics, and magazines are all good sources for finished artwork to use in your quilt.

The picture you wish to use can be quickly enlarged or reduced to fit your concept. Its shape can also be altered to make it more suitable for your purposes. There are three devices used to scale a design: a grid, a pantograph, and a projector. Following is a description of how to use each method.

1. Grid: Trace the picture on tracing paper, and divide it into equally sized squares, as shown in Diagram 6-2. Cut another piece of paper to the exact size you wish to make the picture you have traced. Following Diagram 6-3, mark it with a grid having exactly the same number of evenly spaced squares as your first drawing. Number the squares, vertically and horizontally, for quick reference. Then copy the placement of each line from the small drawing on the corresponding square of the full-size grid. This will give you an exact reproduction, only on a larger scale.

To reduce the drawing, reverse the procedure, starting large and ending small.

2. Pantograph: A pantograph is an instrument made of four measured strips that are joined together to form a kind of movable parallelogram (Diagram 6-4). The measurements on these strips are scaled so that the instrument can be adjusted to enlarge to any required dimension.

Notice in the diagram that the pantograph has

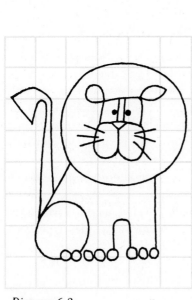

Diagram 6-2

⊢1"⊣

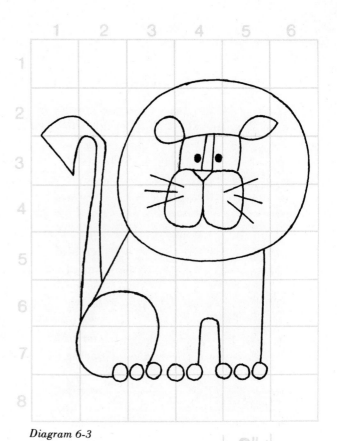

Diagram 6-3

⊢2"⊣

Diagram 6-4

Point A

Point B

184

two points: Point A for tracing and Point B for drawing. Point A, a needle, is moved over the outline of the design being traced, and Point B, a pencil, makes the enlarged copy.

Pantographs are inexpensive and are available at most drafting supplies stores.

3. Projector: A projector, whether slide or opaque, is also useful in making an accurate enlargement of a design. The slide projector throws the image of a transparent design on the wall. The size of the image can be altered by changing the distance of the projector from the wall. The design is then traced on tracing paper placed over the image on the wall.

An opaque projector works in the same way except that it has the capacity to transmit printed pictures or photographs instead of only transparencies. With it, any photograph can be mounted in the projector and enlarged or reduced to any size you wish when it is projected on the wall.

4. THE FABRICS
Fabrics are the medium through which the quilt maker expresses her art. Reread the section in Chapter 1 on fabrics. The world is full of marvelous materials, and your personal choice is what will make your quilt. The rules of color harmony, of design scale, of suitability—all must be considered.

Many times, while making the quilts for this book, we could not find at the local stores the fabrics we wanted. Those we could find had a sameness and a dullness; we made several trips to New York, the world's great marketplace. There, we were able to find madras in glowing crossweaves and wax-resist batiks in subtle small designs, one color on white. The Japanese cotton prints offered lots of interest. We also bought marvelous French cottons, in clear, bright colors, and gorgeously colored felts directly from the manufacturer. Finding just the right fabric is a challenge; it's very important, though, for it makes a quilt special.

5. THE QUILTING
The method used to join the three layers of the quilt is crucial, for the quilting becomes a design component that adds interest to it. The design for the quilting should be as carefully worked out as the piecing or appliquéing. The quilting brings the quilt, quilted object, or hanging to life, by adding a dimension in which light and shadow can interplay. In the case of a quilt to be used on a bed or in clothing, it also adds warmth and comfort.

The finest quilting is done by hand, but by using one of the large stitch settings on your machine, you can do a creditable job, especially in simple outline, square, or diagonal quilting. The wonderful Amish patterns represent a pinnacle in quilting design. Use them as we showed them in Chapter 3, or simplify them. Contour or wave quilting done in the Hawaiian manner, as shown in Chapter 4, is also a fascinating quilting technique.

We have shown many quilting methods and patterns in these chapters. Adapt them to your own inclination. Make them work for you, to enhance the total effect. Devise your own patterns or use designs from your quilt top. The repetition of design motifs in varied situations is an effective technique.

Originality is an intangible; usually, it is a subconscious adaptation of the sum of experience, plus a divine inspiration. The implication is freedom, a willingness to experiment, and the

PLATE 59

capability to think things through. It means seeing the structure and bones of forms; it means curiosity, the whys and how-tos. If you try for it, it's yours.

We have made a number of original quilts for this book. Many of them are interspersed in other chapters. We have reserved several to give meaning to this chapter.

Family, Album, and Marriage quilts are the most personal expression of all. By their nature, they are usually appliquéd in a more or less realistic interpretation of known objects, places, and people.

The Kent Family Quilt shown in Plate 59 illustrates how a quilt can portray the many strong interests natural to a big, involved family. Among those interests depicted are teaching, choral singing, and lobstering. The quilt maker, who is a member of the family, evolved the basic design by making rough sketches of the portrayals she decided would most commemorate their lives. The format she chose for these portrayals

was that of varied blocks, the sizes of which were determined by the subject matter. These blocks were then to be sewn together flush.

Based on this format, an artist friend refined the sketches and made a small, complete line drawing of the entire quilt. Following this drawing, the quilt maker made the quilt in sections, which enabled her to work on the quilt wherever her busy day took her.

The artist for this book designed the Hines Marriage Quilt shown in Plate 60. Very cleverly, she used the letter H as a design motif. Bands of fabric were pieced to form the H's, while the areas between the verticals and the cross members are oblong blocks. The blocks are done in a combination of pieced patchwork, appliqué, and reverse appliqué. The designs depict the quilt maker's home, her career, her astrological sign of Aquarius, her small daughter, and her life with her husband. The quilt was then given to another quilt maker to be made.

Ed Pryor's Birthday Quilt (Plate 61) is an

PLATE 60

interesting one. For it, Beverly cut from black fabric silhouettes of their children. She mounted these on squares of off-white cotton, embroidering the name of each child under the neck. Then, she enlarged one repeat of the old pattern Storm at Sea (Diagram 3-29 in Chapter 3) to the dimensions of the whole quilt. The blocks containing the children are set in the pattern as a block segment. The small off-white squares are embellished with other interests in her husband's life—his guitar, their house, their summer camp, his school, etc. The fabrics are

PLATE 62: *Vermont Farm Quilt* detail, designed and made by Diane Wilson, collection of Mr. and Mrs. Steven W. Parker.

187

PLATE 63: *Jungle Quilt*, concept by Audrey Heard, designed by Carol Hines, made by Joyce Payer.

Victorian in their concept, rich and strong and masculine.

Bev and her husband lived in Noank, Connecticut, for a while when they were first married, and they are very fond of the little waterfront village. The same Connecticut artist who made the *broderie Perse* quilt in Chapter 5 did, many years ago, a small wood-block print of the village, depicting the hilly terrain, the church, the shipyard with the tall-masted boats, the winding streets, the docks and boats, and the lighthouse. It showed the old trolley that ran to Mystic and the beach and the sea. It had all the

flavor of a favorite place. Bev enlarged the print to quilt size, and, of course, since the print was black and white, interpreted the forms in the colors of her choice. The result is found in the Noank Wall Hanging shown on the dedication page of this book. To make the quilt, she used a combination of techniques—mostly appliqué, some reverse, and a little embroidery. It is truly a commemorative quilt.

The quilt shown in Plate 62 was commissioned by a Vermont family who wished to show their farm, with the animals and scenes that they love. The quilt, shown on the cover of this book, was done in appliqué, utilizing the border to continue the story. Plate 62 here shows the quilting detail. It was quilted in the Hawaiian manner, thereby adding great depth and motion.

The idea of doing a jungle quilt happened one day when we were driving along a country road. Stopping quickly, we made a rough sketch, and our book artist worked it into the marvelous composition that is shown here in Plate 63. It's a story quilt, with its friendly animals padded into low relief. After the color scheme was set, the choice of fabrics became crucial. They had to be just right so that the subtle, imaginative quality would not be lost. We spent many hours finding the fabrics before giving them to another quilt maker to begin the work. With meticulous attention to detail and elegant flair, she appliquéd the large center square, embroidering the animals for best effect. She then added her own very special touches.

The artist for this book, like all the rest of us, is intrigued with the design possibilities of pieced patchwork. To satisfy her desire to work with it, she designed a cohesive, original patchwork pattern that involves two separate designs joined to create an exciting overall effect (Plate 64). It's a precise, detailed pattern, requiring patience and skill to execute. The quilt maker did this quilt twice, as a matter of fact, because the first time the corner joinings were not perfect enough to please her. We call this Modern Patchwork, even though we know it deserves its own special name.

It was hard to find the right materials for this quilt. The artist had planned grayed solid colors, but they lacked interest when translated into fabric. Instead, we used subtle prints, which brought the design to life.

PLATE 64: *Modern Patchwork Quilt*, concept by Beverly Pryor, designed by Carol Hines, made by Lynn Kent.

The Black and White Tulip Quilt shown in Plate 65 is an unusual concept in quilt making. For it, the designer used two lengths of fabric, one white, the other black. After cutting pre-planned holes in the black fabric, she appliquéd it to the white ground. Then, she appliquéd red tulips in some of the spaces, carrying the stems from one hole to another. It's a fascinating viewpoint, and one that is very striking. She quilted it in the Hawaiian manner, which added vitality to the plain surfaces.

The black and white Interacting Pyramids Quilt, done by the same quilt maker, provides a wonderful optical illusion (Plate 66). For it, she varied the Thousand Pyramids pattern by using a technique seen in the Robbing Peter to Pay Paul pattern (Diagram 3-48 in Chapter 3).

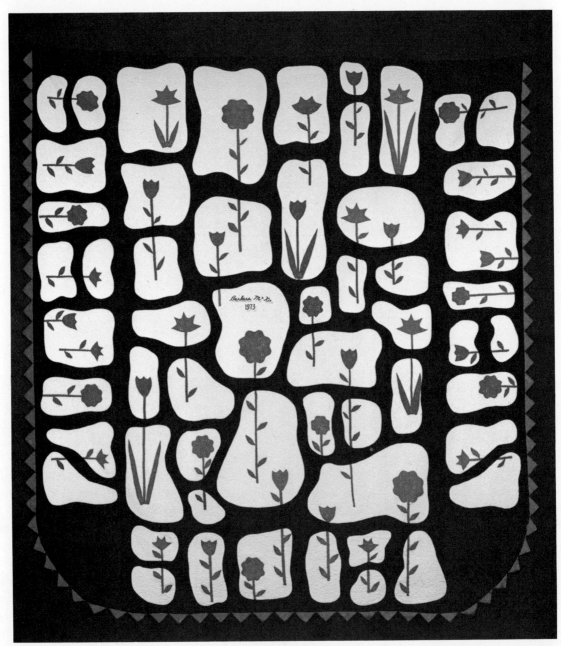

PLATE 65: *Tulip Quilt*, designed and made by Barbara McKie.

PLATE 66: *Interacting Pyramids Quilt*, designed and made by Barbara McKie.

In the Man and Wife Quilt, Beverly used one design set between lattices (Plate 67). Because each appliqué block is colored differently, great interest is added to the overall scheme. It's a very busy quilt, but it works. All the fabrics used have tiny patterns; the greens and blues cool the dominant cranberry, contrast with the burgundy, and are accented by the burnt orange. Bev quilted it in outline, using an old blanket as the interlining. She wanted it to be flat so that it resembled a series of portraits.

1976 is the bicentennial year for our country. It has been our thought that either individuals or groups could celebrate this event by depicting in quilt form the history of either their communities or states. We were thrilled the other day to find out from a friend that a group of ladies in Gloucester, Massachusetts, had done just this. Our friend's mother had persuaded the Women's Auxiliary to the Addison Gilbert Hospital in

PLATE 68: *Gloucester Quilt*, concept by Beatrice Dyer, designed and made by the Women's Auxiliary to the Addison Gilbert Hospital, Gloucester, Massachusetts.

PLATE 67: *Man and Wife Quilt*, designed and made by Beverly Pryor.

Gloucester to make a quilt celebrating the town's 350th anniversary (Plate 68).

The quilt they made is composed of thirty-five squares, each commemorating a different event in Gloucester's long history, many of them relating to the sea. Each square was made by a different person and later joined to the others. Gloucester is so proud of the quilt that when the new wing of the public library is completed, it will hang there permanently.

We have tried to describe to you how some of these quilts evolved. It's not difficult to be original; you don't even have to be completely original. You simply have to say things in your way, with special inflection and with perception.

II. CREATING A CHILDREN'S QUILT

We see what we think we see,
We see what we want to see.
To see what is really there
Is to look with brand new eyes.

Children's quilts are a different breed of cat. They have to be seen with brand new eyes. Study the drawings of children, the uninhibited ones who make show-and-tell such a delight—and such a nightmare. The colors, even when done with Crayola, are in nonhackneyed combinations and are all the more compelling because of their dissonance. Note the marvelous shapes, more real than real, done in the way that George Bracque's painting of a banana makes a banana look ordinary. Scale and perspective are secondary to story. A twelve-foot-tall mouse is astride a three-inch giraffe—that is, he's twelve feet tall if he's the star of the show. Kids have a way of seeing what's really important. They see the microcosm, and they know it for the world.

It's learning this trick that makes a successful quilt for a child. Capturing the magic of a child's wonder and joy in the medium of material and thread is fun. It's easy, requiring only basic skills in craftsmanship and design. The beginner can produce a spectacular quilt that will not only be useful and decorative but can become a proud and stalwart heirloom to be treasured by generations to come. A hundred years from now, your descendents will be talking about how talented and clever great-granny was.

Philosophers talk about leaving footprints in the sands of time. It is important to leave a part of yourself in a personal, tangible way, and a quilt is a lovely way to record the present for the future. We value the quilts handed down to us, not only for sentimental reasons but also for their intrinsic artistry and for their way of showing a life that will never again be.

Before you start a quilt for a child, spend a lot of time just looking, seeing, thinking. Leave your mind open and observe the world around you. The sources for subject material are endless, even within the confines of your own home. Look at the framed pictures on the wall, the pictures in the coloring books, the illustrations in the birthday-present-from-relatives books. Even the cereal box on the breakfast table holds inspiration.

Carefully savor the pictures that are handed to you after a long hard day at school. One freewheeling masterpiece might just be the perfect design to interpret as a quilt. Watch the birds at the feeder, the crazy squirrels trying to steal the seed, the striped yellow cat stalking through the autumn leaves, the silly puppy, bright eyes and red tongue, legs all akimbo in the way that puppies sit. See the precise geometry of canned soups and vegetables soldiering on the shelves, the concentric patterns of pots hanging over the stove, the fragmenting of sunlight shining through the drops of the chandelier, snowflakes on the window, daffodils lying on a black-and-white striped towel, one pink tulip. There are a million things to see if you look with brand new eyes.

Crib quilts: You have decided to make a crib quilt. Make a rough sketch on paper of the image you have in mind. If you can't draw a line, find illustrations that appeal to you.

More often than not, the illustration of your choice will be either too big or too small for the place it is to occupy in your quilt. Enlarging or reducing its size is a necessary step. This pro-

193

cess is discussed earlier in this chapter. Sometimes, the picture you choose will be too staid or too realistic for a child's taste. If that is the case, alter it for whimsical effect or for humor. Put a smile on a cow, eyelashes on a bee. Lengthen the tail of a dog, or accentuate the roundness of an elephant.

In choosing a design or illustration for an appliqué crib quilt, consider that pictures with clear, easy lines are simpler to execute than pictures with jagged, complicated structures. For instance, the long smooth lines of an elephant sitting on an egg present no problem. But a porcupine with every quill erect in fighting trim—very difficult!

After you have chosen your design and have scaled it to the size you want, you must now work out your color scheme. Block in your rough sketch with watercolors or colored pencils. Round up all the fabrics you think you'll need, and test them, one against the others, until you find just the right combination. As discussed earlier, there are basic rules for color harmony, but it isn't always necessary to follow these in making a quilt. Sometimes it is the off-beat, unplanned color that gives zing to a quilt. If you've looked at enough of the old ones made from available scraps, you'll agree.

Probably, the easiest way to achieve a good color scheme is to find a picture that you really like and use those colors. Be sure to keep the mass relationships. For example, one-third is olive green, one-sixth brown yellow, one-sixth golden yellow, one-sixth rich cream, one-sixth claret wine, and just a dollop of bright teal blue.

We particularly like illustrative quilts for babies. We like their imaginativeness and the fact that they are pictorial.

PLATE 69: *Beatrix Potter Crib Quilt*, designed and made by Barbara McKie.

Here, Plate 69 shows a charming crib quilt depicting a group of Beatrix Potter figures. The little creatures are appliquéd onto a plain ground.

Patchwork is also good for crib quilts, and any of the standard patterns can be scaled down to requisite size. The color range is diverse. Our ancestors didn't limit their palette to blue for boys and pink for girls, or maybe yellow and white for a nursery. We don't have to either. Plate 70 shows how attractive a patchwork crib quilt looks when done in nontraditional colors.

TWIN-SIZE QUILTS

Quilts to fit twin beds afford room for expanded styles and designs. The following illustrations and descriptions explain how to make children's quilts by using either the diversified or the repeat pattern method.

194

PLATE 70: *Bits and Pieces Crib Quilt,* designed and made by Diane Wilson.

PLATE 71: *Animal Quilt*, designed and made by Beverly Pryor.

Diversified quilts: When the blocks of the quilt vary from square to square, either in size or in design content, the quilt belongs in the diversified category. Appliqués can be presented either in blocks, as shown in Plate 71, or as a total picture, as shown in the Jungle Quilt on page 188 (Plate 63). The sections of the quilt can be of any size, as long as the finished spread adds up to the twin-size measurements. Remember to allow for borders, if you plan to use them, in figuring overall size (see Chapter 2).

The sources of subject matter for these quilts are unlimited. For a special child, you could make a quilt depicting important events and people in his life. Show his house, his brothers and sisters, his favorite pets, the airplane trip he took to Florida when he was four, the Halloween costume he wore for his first trick-or-treat night.

A quilt for a little girl can be wonderfully symbolic if you use materials from dresses she has outgrown. Each patch will have a special meaning, and memories will stay alive.

Again, favorite storybooks can provide inspiration for a diversified quilt in such stories

as *Babar, Jamima Puddle Duck, Peter Rabbit,* and *Green Eggs and Ham.*

Repeat pattern quilts: If you want to make a birthday present and time is short, the repeat pattern quilt can be a quick, easy solution. Choose a design that appeals to you and repeat it over and over again, changing it only by alternating the colors from square to square. The Owl Quilt shown in Plate 72 illustrates this technique well. Since you will be using the same design repeatedly, we suggest that you cut a cardboard master pattern. Cardboard is much stronger than paper and it is much easier to trace around.

PLATE 72: *Owl Quilt*, designed and made by Beverly Pryor.

The pieced patchwork crib quilt shown in Plate 70 on page 195 is also a good example of a repeat pattern quilt. The colors and fabrics have been varied in each square, giving each one a different effect from the next.

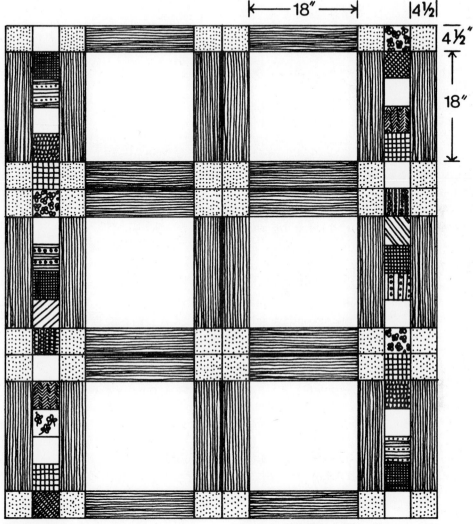

Diagram 6-5

ASSEMBLING A CHILD'S QUILT

Assembling or setting a quilt for a child can be done by various methods (see Chapter 1), but the following illustrations show you two techniques frequently used in making children's quilts. The first shows how to use small borders to frame the squares of your quilt, and the second shows how to use larger borders to surround those framed squares so that the quilt is brought to its required measurements.

Bordered quilt tops: Before buying material for your quilt, carefully calculate on paper what the measurements of your border pieces should be (see Chapters 1 and 2). Once again, keep in mind that when each piece is sewn, it will lose ¼ inch on all sides for the seam allowance. The following example of a 72- by 80-inch twin-size quilt illustrates step-by-step measuring and piecing together of six 18-inch squares that are

197

framed by borders of equal width (Diagram 6-5).

By examining the diagram, you can see that we've chosen a base width of 5 inches for all border pieces which allows for a seam of ¼ inch on all sides. The width of each piece will be 4½ inches after sewing. The length of each piece should also allow for a ¼-inch seam on each end. It should be 18 inches plus ¼ inch plus ¼ inch, or a total of 18½ inches. The 5-inch squares will lose ¼ inch on all sides, becoming 4½-inch squares after sewing.

Pieced quilt tops (unbordered):

1. Cut four strips, each measuring 5 by 18½ inches, from the primary color you are using and four 5-inch squares from the secondary color. Machine-sew two strips to the 18-inch square, right sides together and flat (Diagram 6-6).
2. Now machine-sew one 5-inch square to each of the remaining strips (Diagram 6-7).
3. Place one of the strips next to the square. Accurately mark with a pencil the exact point at which the second square is to be sewn, making sure to line up the corners of the blocks. Attach the second square and iron (Diagram 6-8).
4. Pin the strip to the square, right sides facing,

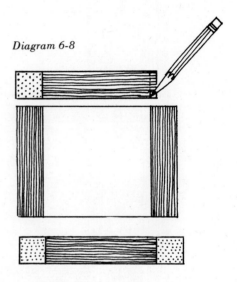

Diagram 6-8

and machine-sew (Diagram 6-9). Attach the fourth strip in the same manner as strip three (Diagram 6-10).
5. The remaining five squares for your quilt should be bordered in the same manner. When they are all sewn, put all six pieces together (Diagram 6-11).
6. The outer borders are made from patchwork strips. Sew together 5-inch squares that have been selected at random from your appliqué colors (Diagram 6-12). Iron the patchwork strips before pinning and sewing them onto your quilt.
7. The outermost borders are a repeat of the inner borders. They should be sewn in long strips, taking care that the measurements are precise and that the squares on this outside piece are exactly matched to those on the inside of the quilt (Diagram 6-13).
8. When the quilt top is finished, you are ready to pin together the top, the batting, and the back layers, and then quilt it as shown in Chapter 4.

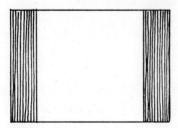

Diagram 6-6

Diagram 6-7

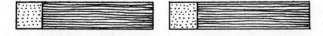

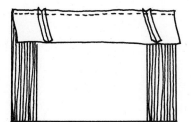

Diagram 6-9

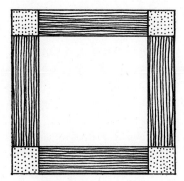

Diagram 6-10

Diagram 6-12

Diagram 6-11

Diagram 6-13

III. CREATING A WALL HANGING

It is exciting to open any one of the popular home-furnishings magazines and see a photograph of a quilt hanging on a wall, where it is serving as a focal point of decoration. The dazzling geometry of pieced patchwork and the meticulous arrangement of appliqué have finally come into their own, having been taken out of the bedroom and put into the living room to receive their rightful due as an important art form.

Soft is a definitive term used in retailing and in art circles to refer to objects made of fabric as opposed to those made of metal or wood. We are currently seeing a revival of the soft arts. This is not a new form, for fabrics have been used decoratively for centuries, usually as wall hangings. Old walls made of stone, wood, or plaster were cold, and so the first use of fabric wall hangings was for insulation purposes. Later, the cloths were embellished, either in the fabric itself as in weaving or by stitchery or appliqué.

The acme of soft art was reached probably between the fourteenth and sixteenth centuries in the famed medieval tapestries depicting the Hunt of the Unicorn. These were a sublime achievement, drawn by masters and executed by inspired artisans, whose skills and patience belong to the past. However, there has always been an interest in fabric-and-thread wall decoration. The samplers made by children in colonial days were pictorial. The letters of the alphabet and simple geometric shapes were embroidered, as were representations of scenes, people, houses, and objects.

In England and on the Continent, stitchery decorations were an important art form, some of them incredibly elaborate, done in threads of

200

precious metals combined with silk and cotton floss. Ivory pallets were shaved into thin layers and cut into shapes, to be used as faces and arms in the depiction of human figures. The hair, clothing, and scenery were embroidered. When areas were stuffed, the work was known as stump work.

To the best of our knowledge, it was not until the nineteenth century that appliqué became a medium for wall decoration. At this time, the representations were always pictorial. In Plate 73, we show a sample of the Egyptian marketplace appliqué, sold for the edification of tourists on the then-fashionable Grand Tour. It is a flat, nondimensional copy of an Egyptian fresco.

A neighbor of ours owns the appliquéd wall hanging of George Washington shown in Plate 74. We guess it to have been done for the Centennial Celebration of 1876, relying on our knowledge of the fabrics used and the fact that interest in Washington peaked at that time. In it, large simple forms are combined in overlapping appliques. It is interesting to note the realistic complexity of the figure in contrast to the stark abstraction of the trees, the somber violet of the sky, the luminous, larger-than-life stars, and the burning campfire. We do not know the origin of this work, but we are intrigued by the similarity of palette to that used by the Amish people. The image is unmistakably that of George Washington, praying alone in the snow on a frigid Christmas Eve. The Star of Bethlehem glows brighter than the rest, and the dedication of the general on the eve of battle shines through with a great intensity. It is a fine piece of folk art.

We have not seen many fabric wall decorations that interest us in the work done between 1700 and recent years. The samplers, of course, are fascinating in a historical sense and as an illustration of craft skills, folklore, and sociological comment on a way of life.

In the era of Mission Oak furniture at the beginning of this century, poorly made commercial tapestries hung in living rooms around the country or were earnestly draped over sideboards in the dining room. They were usually ecru and outlined in black with touches of old rose and muted spruce green. The designs show neoclassic scenes or stereotyped European landscapes. Later, in the twenties and thirties, there was renewed interest in tapestries, but this was the age of baronial reproduction and of Tudor-style houses. Those who could afford them bought the original tapestries while the rest bought reproductions.

PLATE 75: *Winter Wall Hanging*, designed and made by Barbara McKie.

PLATE 76: *Summer Wall Hanging*, designed and made by Barbara McKie.

We theorize that art movements are horizontal, cutting across the consciousnesses of peoples all over the world at the same point in time. A new idea does not seem to develop by itself, in total isolation, but rather seems to emerge spontaneously in different cultures, in different parts of the world at about the same time. All that has gone before is the atmosphere in which the form develops, and, as though by preplanned evolution, congruous ideas are all around us. The climate is right, the acceptance is widespread, and the new, or the new-old art form, has a total welcome all over the world.

This is what has happened with quilts, especially those fashioned of pieced patchwork. We don't know why; it is possible to trace the art movements of this century and to arrive at an explanation, but art history is not the province of this book. We simply know that the basic components of hard geometry, the excitement of color, and the eclecticism of shape are compatible to today's thinking. The quality of the needlework is not as important as is the impact of the design.

Quilts, of course, can be made for hanging on walls, but also the techniques of quilt making can be utilized for making unquilted panels specifically for wall hangings.

Modern wall hangings utilize many techniques and a wide range of materials. Since they will not be used as bedcoverings, it is not necessary to be practical about the selection of fabrics nor the washability or durability of the component parts. Wall hangings are simply decorative.

Usually, they are small in size and quickly sewn because the embellishment is all surface—they do not need the preparation, the

interlining and backing, and the quilting that goes into a quilt. String, ribbons, pieces of mirror, stitchery, and raffia are but a few of the materials that are used in wall hangings. Macramé can be used in conjunction with a hanging, as can strips of wood and bamboo, ceramic pieces, or small stones. The innovative quilt maker sees unlimited possibilities.

The Winter and Summer House hangings shown in Plates 75 and 76 are a lively, humorous involvement. They are unabashedly sentimental, and the awry perspectives and naïve subjects are charming.

Plate 77 shows a wall hanging of hands appliquéd on burlap. The hands have been padded, adding dimension and superrealism to the hanging.

The hanging shown in Plate 78 was created using broadcloth and machine appliqué. The maker of this quilt works quickly, with a happy spontaneity that is obvious in her design.

Geometric representations are particularly effective. Red and blue diminishing oblongs, shown in Plate 79, has the appeal of a modern painting. The artist's statement is strong in its simplicity. Plate 80 shows a Hawaiian quilt

PLATE 78: *Happy Day Wall Hanging*, designed and made by Rieta Park.

made in the American style. A complex composition involving hours of planning, cutting, and sewing, it says a lot about Hawaiian quilting, for it is the result of years of working with them. The compilation of patterns used is encyclopedic in its impact.

Plate 81 shows a quilt maker's interpretation of the old Kaleidoscope pattern. The strong colors are equally dominant and the optical illusion is fascinating.

Audrey Heard and the artist for this book used felt to interpret the famous Cluny tapestries in the wall hanging shown in Plate 82.

Some of the best wall hangings are done by children because they can be completely free in their expression, inventing their own designs and color combinations. They are uninhibited by precedent, by fashion, and by learned standards of taste, good or bad. They express things the way they see them and feel them. The results are most original.

This approach is refreshing, as great artistic expression is never imitative. Adults, unless reassured by past experience of confirmed talent, tend to be self-conscious about their work and ultimately resort to collecting ideas and designs from outside proven sources.

Wall hangings made *for* children can be modern or traditional, brightly colored or conservative. Much depends on the materials used. Again, these need not be chosen for their wearability and durability. This gives tremendous leeway in choice, and using oddball scraps of material adds ingenuity and charm. Since hangings need no laundering, the assortment of decorative items you may add is endless. Buttons, tassles, fringe, yarn, beads, netting, string, mirrors —all incorporate well into a child's wall hanging.

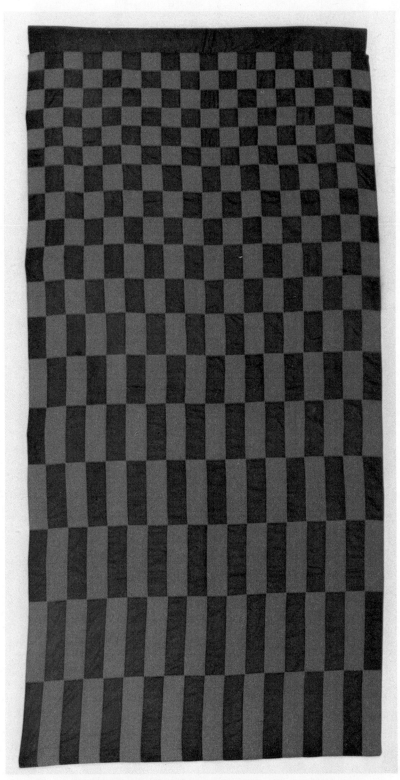

PLATE 79: *Diminishing Oblongs Wall Hanging*, designed
and made by Sharon McKain.

For making the backing, cotton, wool, felt, or burlap are best. Felt is exceptionally good because the edges do not ravel so that they need not be hemmed. It also comes in a great variety of colors. Both burlap and felt have enough body so that an interlining is not required. Most other materials do not, however, so that in order for them to hang well, they must be used with an interlining.

We asked our local art school teacher to have her children's class do an original wall hanging. We showed her some of the crib quilts we had done, briefed her on the techniques involved, and sat back. Beyond showing the children what a wall hanging is, how it is put together, and how it is used, no instructions were given. We wanted to give the children free rein to see what they would come up with in terms of design and materials.

The children were most enthusiastic, and the photograph below shows them at work, designing, executing, and finally—the opus (Plate 83). We think it is superb.

In Waterford, Connecticut, the group of children shown above (average age: nine) decided to make a quilt to raise money for their annual bazaar. Each child made his own square, and when all the squares were finished, their mothers set the quilt. A group of elderly ladies at a local nursing home quilted it. It was a fun project, and shows how very able children can be.

207

HANGING A WALL HANGING

When the wall hanging is completed, it must be secured to the wall in some fashion. There are a number of methods to use.

Hanging a quilted or tied quilt: A quilt has considerable bulk; consequently, it must be carefully hung to protect it and to allow it to be seen to its full advantage. The simplest way of hanging it (we do not recommend stapling or nailing it to the wall) is to cover with muslin a strip of wood that measures 2 by 1 inch and that is as long as the top of the quilt. The muslin is cut in a 7-inch strip and should be 4 inches longer than the wood. Lay the wood in the center of the muslin, and bring the ends up until they overlap. Staple them down. Carefully fold the ends over and staple them. The unstapled side is the front. Insert a screweye one-quarter of the total distance from either side. Attach picture wire to the screweyes.

Find the center of the quilt and the center of the strip. Pin these together as shown in Dia-

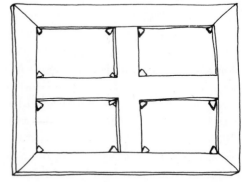

Diagram 6-15

gram 6-14, holding the pin straight and going down through the binding into the muslin. Pin the corners, then pin halfway between and halfway between again, and again, until it is all pinned. The pins should be very close together. Use stainless steel pins, as they will not rust. If you wish, you can lightly overcast the binding of the quilt to the muslin instead of pinning it. The quilt will hang loosely from this support.

Often, quilts are out of true and do not hang evenly, or they may be old and fragile, needing support. When this is the case, a more complex method of hanging is necessary. Stretchers with crossbars should be made. When measuring the quilt for the stretchers, do it as accurately as possible, erring to the small side so that you will not put unnecessary strain on the quilt while stretching it.

The stretchers, shown in Diagram 6-15, can be constructed from the lumber mentioned above or bought from an art-supply store. The assembled stretchers are covered with muslin in the following way: Lay the stretchers on the muslin, evenly centered. Pull the overlap to the back, and staple, as shown in Diagram 6-16. Check to be sure the corners are square.

Diagram 6-14

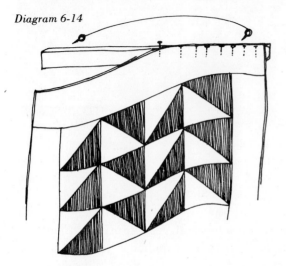

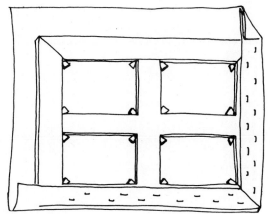

Diagram 6-16

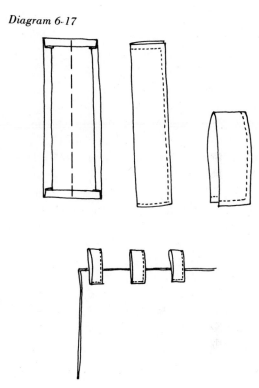

Diagram 6-17

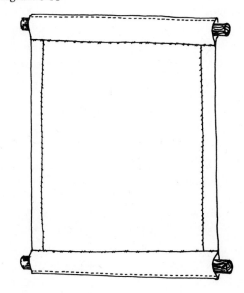

Diagram 6-18

Pin the quilt center, corners, and then the intervening spaces, to the muslin, carefully easing the fabric to keep it true. When the pinning is complete, the quilt can be overcast to the muslin.

Hanging an unquilted fabric panel: Often a wall hanging is suspended from a rod or pole. There are alternate ways of doing this.

1. Fabric strips can be attached to the top of the wall hanging to serve as loops through which a rod will be inserted. Figure the number of loops needed if spaced about 4 inches apart. Following Diagram 6-17, cut them 4 inches by 10 inches, fold ½ inch in along each edge, press, fold in half lengthwise, press, and stitch. Fold the strip in half crosswise, forming a loop. Fold in the raw edges, and attach the loop to the backing, overlapping by 1½ inches. Do the remaining strips in the same manner. We have used these measurements as an example, but the size of the loops may vary, depending on the size of the hanging.

2. A casing can be made at the top of the hanging and also at the bottom, as shown in Diagram 6-18. Rods will be inserted through these openings in the same manner as they are in

casement curtains, except that the top rod serves as hanger while the bottom one serves as a weight.

The hanging must be prepared in advance if this method is to be used. Allow 4 inches extra at the top, 4 inches extra at the bottom, and enough extra at the sides to make hems. Most hangings hang better if they are interlined and backed.

When the decoration of the hanging is complete, put it face down on the table or on the floor if it is large. Place the interlining and backing on top of it and trim them to the finished size, as shown in Diagram 6-18. Turn the side hems to the back and hem them, using a blindstitch (Diagram 6-18). Last, make the casings. Fold the fabric allowed for the casing in half and pin it to the hanging. Stitch through all three layers at the very top. Blindstitch the lower edge, as shown in Diagram 6-18. Turn the hanging around and do the same for the bottom. If you wish, drapery weights can be used at the bottom instead of a second pole.

Having the right size pole is important. It can be made of wood, brass, iron, or steel, but its diameter must be in scale with the size of the hanging. It should extend about 1½ inches beyond each side.

Rings can be sewn to the back top of a hanging, as shown in Diagram 6-19, or concealed loops can be used, as shown in Diagram 6-20. Instead of projecting above the top of the hanging, the loops are fastened to the top and also to the back of the hanging.

Mounting fabric panels: Often, smaller wall hangings are framed. If you wish to do this, you must mount it first. One-quarter-inch tempered Masonite is good to use for the mounting board. Buy it or cut it the exact size of the finished wall

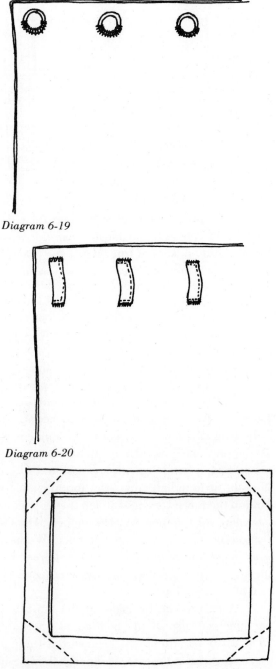

Diagram 6-19

Diagram 6-20

Diagram 6-21

210

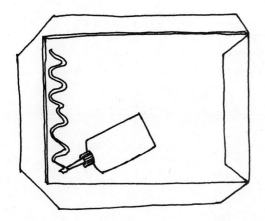

Diagram 6-22

hanging. (When making the hanging, you must
allow a margin all around it for the mounting.)
Lay the wall hanging face down on a table. As
shown in Diagram 6-21, place the Masonite,
smooth side down, on it, making sure that the
margins are even and that the sides are true to
the grain of the fabric. Clip the corners as shown
by the dotted lines. Apply white glue to the top
edge of the Masonite (Diagram 6-22), and fold
the margin down carefully into the glued area.
Miter the corners. Repeat this procedure on the
bottom, using even pressure to stretch the hanging over the edge. Do not stretch so tightly that
you cause the Masonite to bow. Continue around
the other two sides, being careful to prevent
wrinkles or extra fullness in the fabric. Frame as
soon as possible.

You can also stretch the hanging on stretchers. The same procedure as above is used except
that either staples or tacks are used for fastening. The panel must be carefully stretched, and
any small excess fullness eased out by keying
the corners with the little slot fillers provided
when you buy the stretchers.

7
Ten Quilts to Make

Ed Pryor's Birthday Quilt, designed and made by Beverly Pryor.

In the ensuing pages, we shall give measurements, diagrams, and general step-by-step procedures for making some of the quilt projects illustrated in this book. The diagrams are done to scale and can be enlarged or reduced to suit your own purposes. Many of the diagrams are self-explanatory. Since by this time, the techniques will have been mastered and the basic knowledge of quilting become second nature, we give these diagrams and instructions simply to show you how the projects were done and, perhaps, to help you to work out specific problems that may occur as you develop your own themes. Detailed instructions, such as for cutting templates and stitching together blocks, are found throughout the foregoing sections of this book. As you work, you can expect to encounter certain problems, but you will soon learn how to take them in your stride. A few general points to remember are given below.

● The diagrams show the shapes as they appear. Before cutting out the pieces, it is vital that you remember to add ¼ inch all around the shape for seam allowances.

● When cutting the fabric, cut the seam allowance accurately. When sewing, sew the seam exactly. When you are dealing with many pieces, a variation of $1/16$ of an inch, multiplied by 20, can add up to 1¼ inches extra. This is enough to throw the entire alignment of a quilt. Use particular care when sewing together pieces that have been cut on the bias, for the tendency to stretch can add unwanted inches.

● Test fabrics for shrinkage, for colorfastness, for "hand." Make detailed drawings and color plans. Buy enough fabric so that you do not run short in the middle of a quilt.

● Make a sample block first. This checks not only the accuracy of your templates but also your color scheme and your seam allowances as well. After one block has been made, cut or tear off the long strips you need for borders and lattices. Then, cut the remaining yardage into the blocks and individual pieces.

● Learn to press as you go. Seams are usually pressed to one side or the other except when three or more pieces meet at a corner. When this happens, they are pressed open.

● Be brave and uninhibited. You'll never know what you can do until you try. If you do something wrong, rip it out and do it again.

● Learn to know when a project is complete. Do not overwork and overdesign, for you will lose the spontaneity and verve you are seeking.

214

1 / LADYBUG QUILT

This is a simple quilt to make, for the appliqués are straightforward and uninvolved. The edges of the appliqué are simply turned under and machine-stitched ⅛ of an inch from the edge. The design interest is compounded by a row of neat machine-sewn quilting that outlines the design. Instructions for making matching pillowcases begin on page 275.

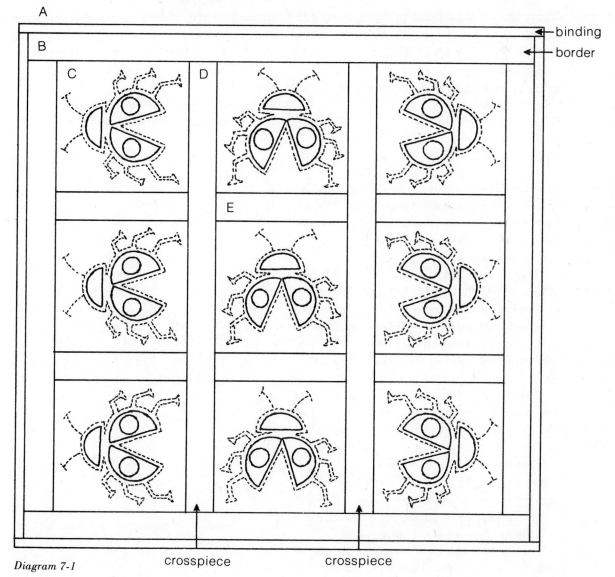

Diagram 7-1

215

Finished size: 65½ by 65½ inches

Materials:

2½ yards 36-inch-wide fabric in navy blue for binding (A on Diagram 7-1) and blocks (C on Diagram 7-1)

2 yards 36-inch-wide fabric in red for lattices (E on Diagram 7-1), borders (B on Diagram 7-1), crosspieces (D on Diagram 7-1), and appliqués

¼ yard 36-inch-wide fabric in yellow for appliqué accents

thread in red

fabric for interlining

fabric for backing

Procedure:

1. To make the blocks, cut nine 17- by 17-inch squares from the navy blue fabric, reserving the long strip at the edge for the binding. (Packaged binding may also be used.)

2. Enlarge ladybug pattern in Diagram 7-2, and cut the three body templates. Place on red fabric, and cut out 9 complete ladybug shapes (27 pieces all together). Turn under the edges ¼ inch, and machine-stitch to the individual blocks, placing them as shown in Diagram 7-1. Cut a template for the accent circle on the ladybug's body (Diagram 7-2). Using this as a pattern, cut 10 circles from the yellow fabric and 8 from the blue; appliqué them, as above, to the ladybugs, placing color as shown in Plate 84.

3. From the remaining red fabric, cut 6 strips, each measuring 4 by 65½ inches. These will be used for the four borders and the two crosspieces. Finally, cut 6 strips, each measuring 4 by 17 inches, for the short lattice strips.

4. Join the first row by sewing one completed block to a lattice strip. Then join that piece to another block, sew on a lattice strip, and complete the row with a third block. Make two more rows in the same manner, using 3 blocks and 2 lattice strips in each row.

5. Join the rows by sewing a border to the top of the first row. Then join the bottom of the row to a crosspiece (D). Add a row to that crosspiece, finish the row with the other crosspiece, join on the third row, and finish with a border strip.

6. Join the remaining two borders to the quilt top.

7. Interline, back, and bind the quilt top.

8. Using a machine stitch set at ⅛ inch, outline the appliqués as shown in Diagram 7-1.

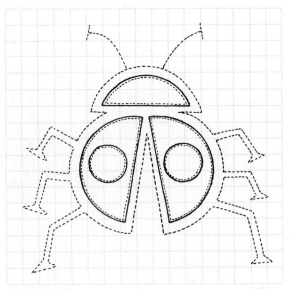

Diagram 7-2

PLATE 84: *Ladybug Quilt*, designed and made by Diane Wilson.

2 / BOW TIE QUILT (see Plate 17 on page 102)

For this quilt, 8-inch blocks are set together side by side in checkboard fashion, utilizing the directional switch of the pieced patchwork to provide variation and pop-art illusion. The bow tie design is accented by the use of prestuffed modules.

Finished size: 32 by 48 inches

Materials:
2 yards 36-inch-wide fabric in navy blue (for B areas on Diagram 7-3)
4¾ yards 36-inch-wide fabric in red (for R areas on Diagram 7-3)
Dacron batt for stuffing
thread in red
fabric for interlining
fabric for backing

Procedure:
1. Enlarge basic design pieces in one of the blocks shown in Diagram 7-3 and cut templates. These will be used to cut the foundation pieces.
2. Cut another set of templates that is ½ inch larger all around; these will be used to cut the tops of the modules (the extra fabric allows room for stuffing).
3. Using the first set of templates, cut from blue fabric those pieces designated B in Diagram 7-3. These will not be stuffed. With the same set of templates, cut those pieces designated R from red fabric. Then with larger set of templates, cut another set of red pieces (these will become the top pieces and will be stuffed).
4. Reread the section in Chapter 3 on prestuffed quilts. Then make the modules for the bow tie. When they have been stuffed and joined together, sew the single thickness (B areas) to them.
5. Join the blocks side by side, alternating the direction of the design.
6. Interline and back. Quilt by hand, outlining all the unstuffed pieces.

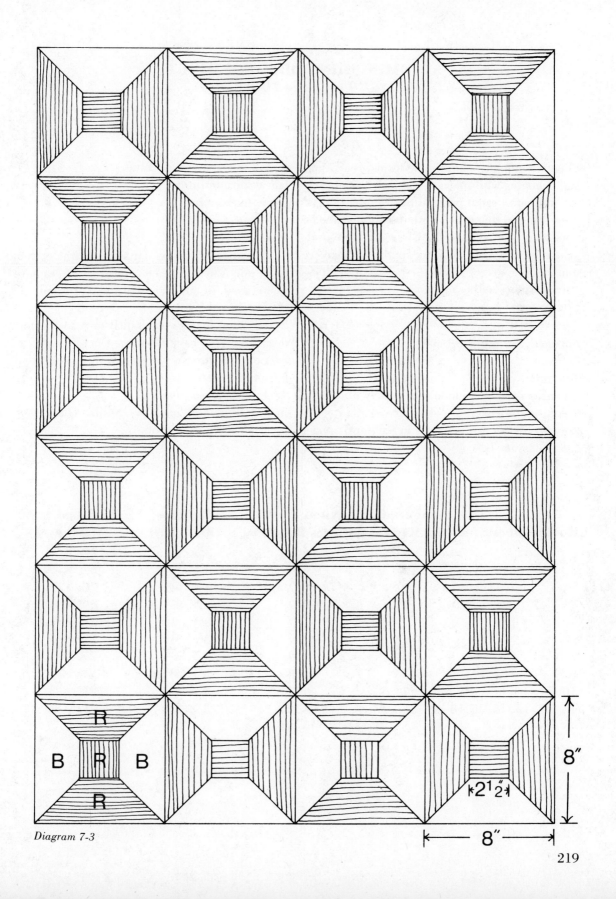

Diagram 7-3

3 / DIMINISHING OBLONGS QUILT
(see Plate 79 on page 205)

Effective graphics take simple forms, repeating and changing with staccato precision, to realize the ultimate design possibilities. Proportion is everything in this quilt; study its subtle gradations, and you will see the Greek architectural principle of entasis at work in the illusion of diminishing space. It has the power of modern supergraphics and is a stunning triumph of simplicity.

Finished size: 45 by 85 inches

Materials:
2⅓ yards 36-inch-wide fabric in navy blue (for A areas on Diagram 7-4)
2⅓ yards 36-inch-wide fabric in red (for B areas on Diagram 7-4)

thread in red and navy blue
fabric for interlining
fabric for backing

Procedure:
1. Starting with pieces for row one (the bottom row), join A to B to A, etc., until 18 pieces have been used in all. Pieces must alternate in checkerboard fashion.
2. For the second row, join B to A to B, etc., until 18 pieces have been used in all.
3. Continue to join pieces row by row until all have been used.
4. Join the rows in order.
5. Interline and back the quilt. Quilt each piece by hand in outline.

Row Number	Number of A Pieces Required	Number of B Pieces Required	Cut Size (in inches)	Finished Size (in inches)
1	9	9	3 × 11½	2½ × 11
2	9	9	3 × 10½	2½ × 10
3	9	9	3 × 9½	2½ × 9
4	9	9	3 × 8½	2½ × 8
5	9	9	3 × 7½	2½ × 7
6	9	9	3 × 6½	2½ × 6
7	9	9	3 × 5½	2½ × 5
8, 9	18	18	3 × 4½	2½ × 4
10, 11, 12	27	27	3 × 3½	2½ × 3
13, 14, 15, 16, 17, 18	54	54	3 × 2½	2½ × 2

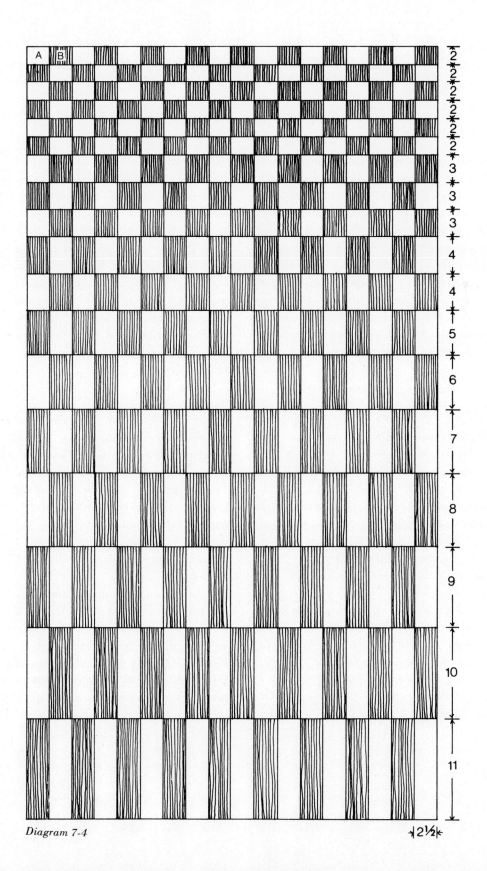

Diagram 7-4

2½

4 / ED PRYOR'S BIRTHDAY QUILT
(see Plate 61 on pages 212-13)

Look at the pattern for Storm at Sea in Chapter 3, Diagram 3-29. This quilt is an adaptation of that design, enlarging only one repeat of that pattern to full quilt size. It has been done in two different rich red prints, which contrast nicely with the black silhouettes on off-white backgrounds.

This quilt is an optical illusion pattern, for if you look at Diagram 7-5, it seems as though it is composed of curved lines. This is not the fact, as only squares, oblongs, and right-angle triangles have been cut. It is this marvelous convolute quality that gives this pattern its name.

Finished size: 72 by 84 inches

Materials:
1 yard 36-inch-wide fabric in off-white (for A areas on Diagram 7-5)
3 yards 36-inch-wide fabric in blue (for B areas on Diagram 7-5)
2 yards 36-inch-wide fabric in red print #1 (for C areas on Diagram 7-5)
1½ yards 36-inch-wide fabric in red print #2 (for D areas on Diagram 7-5)
1½ yards 36-inch-wide fabric in red (for E areas on Diagram 7-5)
1 yard 36-inch-wide fabric in black (for silhouette appliqués)
black embroidery thread (for embroidering silhouette names and tree foliage)
thread in red, black, and white
fabric for interlining
fabric for backing

Procedure:
1. From off-white fabric, cut 4 squares, each measuring 12½ by 12½ inches, and 6 squares, each measuring 6½ by 6½ inches.
2. From blue fabric, cut 10 triangles from oblongs that measure 24½ by 12½ inches and 24 right-angle triangles that have 6½-inch sides.
3. From first red print fabric, cut 24 right-angle triangles that have 4½-inch sides and 16 right-angle triangles that have 9½-inch sides.
4. From second red print fabric, cut 40 triangles whose right-angle sides are 12 inches and 6 inches.
5. From red fabric, cut 16 right-angle triangles that have 13-inch sides.
6. From black fabric, cut out silhouettes and whatever other appliqués you wish to use, and sew them to the 12½-inch squares and to the 6-inch squares (A areas on Diagram 7-5).
7. Sew the large triangles marked C and E to the large squares and the small triangles marked C and B to the small squares.
8. Assemble the 10 oblong blocks.
9. Following the pattern, sew the blocks together.
10. Interline and back; then quilt by hand. Because the pieces composing each block are so large, extra care should be taken in the quilting so that the large open areas will be held together securely. Contiguous outline quilting of each piece can be used, or more ornate quilting patterns would be effective, especially if plain fabrics were used.

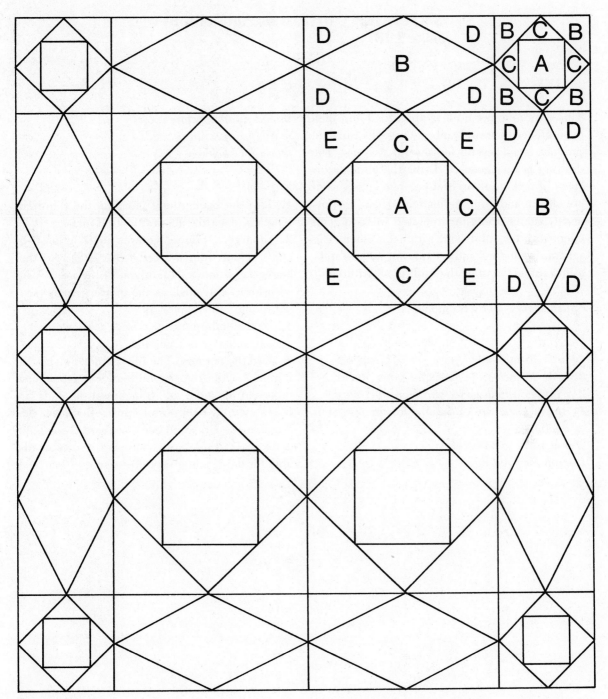

Diagram 7-5

5 / JUNGLE QUILT (see Plate 63 on page 188)

This entire picture quilt is appliquéd and then decorated with crewel embroidery. The finished product is successful for several reasons: The drawing is very good, stylizing the animals instead of making them lifelike. The colors used are offbeat and quite sophisticated, and the unusual, subtle prints incorporated work to good effect with the solids and with each other. The scheme is subdued and yet vibrant, and, in spite of the subject matter, the quilt is not childish.

Finished size: 76 by 86 inches

Materials:
4 yards 36-inch-wide fabric for background
2 yards 36-inch-wide fabric for inner border
2½ yards 36-inch-wide fabric for outer border
¼ to ½ yard 36-inch-wide fabric for each appliqué
crewel yarns in assorted colors
Dacron for padding
thread in appropriate colors
fabric for interlining
fabric for backing

Procedure:
1. Join the background fabric to the required length and width, about 60 by 68 inches.
2. Enlarge appliqué patterns in Diagram 7-6 and cut out from desired fabrics. Sew to the background fabric. Lightly stuff the areas you wish to accent, such as the giraffe's spots (see "Trapunto" in Chapter 5).
3. Do the embroidery required, as shown in the photograph and in Diagram 7-6.
4. Add the borders. The first border finishes to 2 inches wide; the second border finishes to 6 inches at the sides and 8 inches at the ends.
5. Interline, back, and quilt. Because the forms are so large and because there is so much open space, there are good opportunities available for doing some very effective quilting.

Diagram 7-6

6 / INTERACTING PYRAMIDS
QUILT (see Plate 66 on page 191)

Based upon the old Thousand Pyramids pattern, this quilt also borrows from Robbing Peter to Pay Paul (Diagram 3-48), creating additional illusion. The starkness of the black and white is very graphic; we feel that this quilt would also be attractive done in closely hued prints, spaced with white and accented in red. The design would merge and evolve with greater subtlety were the colors not in such contrast.

Finished size: 88 by 104 inches

Materials:
5 yards 36-inch-wide fabric in black (for B areas and border on Diagram 7-7)
5 yards 36-inch-wide fabric in white (for W areas on Diagram 7-7)
thread in black and white
fabric for interlining
fabric for backing

Procedure:
1. Enlarge triangle and half-circle shown in Diagram 7-7A. Cut a template for each. The

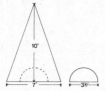

Diagram 7-7A

triangle is 7 inches at its base, and its height is 10 inches. To make the half-circle template, draw a circle whose diameter is 3½ inches. Cut it in half. Remember to add the seam allowances before cutting the fabrics.

2. Cut 120 triangles and 120 half-circles from each of the two colors.
3. Join the triangles as shown in Diagram 7-7B. You will note that you will have a half triangle at each end of each row. The triangles are joined row by row. The half-circles are appliquéd after the rows are joined together (Diagram 7-7C). This is an extremely difficult quilt to do well, even though the shapes are simple. Many of the

Diagram 7-7B

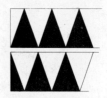

old quilt makers would have cut the circle from the base of each triangle and pieced the contrasting half circle. This can be done by hand, by an expert. Doing it by machine is almost impossible. Therefore, by appliquéing the circles after the triangles are joined, many problems in joining are eliminated.
4. Add a black 2-inch border to the quilt top. Take care not to infringe on the corners of the triangles.
5. Interline and back. Quilt by hand. Diagram 7-7D shows the completed quilt.

Diagram 7-7C

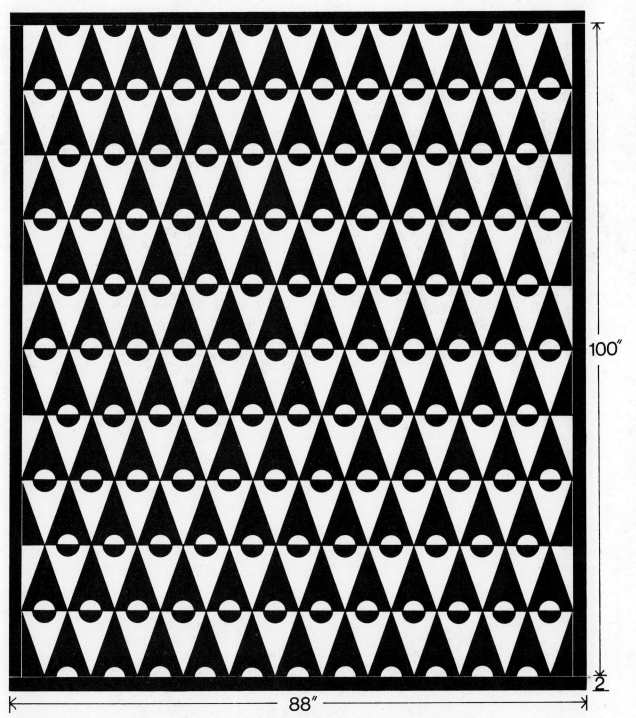

100″

2

88″

Diagram 7-7D

227

7 / KALEIDOSCOPE QUILT (see Plate 81 on page 206)

The Kaleidoscope Quilt moves and whirls in active optical illusion. Though the shapes are simple, the arrangement of color is vital, as is the quality of the color. To make it, you will need four colors, two of which must be of equal value. In this quilt, the purple and maroon are the equal-value colors. If you substitute colors, make certain that your equal-value colors are placed in the same areas as ours.

Finished size: 84 by 84 inches

Materials:
3 yards 36-inch-wide fabric in yellow (for A areas on Diagram 7-8)
3½ yards 36-inch-wide fabric in purple (for B areas on Diagram 7-8)
1½ yards 36-inch-wide fabric in light purple (for C areas on Diagram 7-8)
2½ yards 36-inch-wide fabric in maroon (for D areas on Diagram 7-8)
thread in appropriate colors
fabric for interlining
fabric for backing

Procedure:
1. Enlarge triangles in Diagram 7-8 and cut templates. Then cut 64 triangles from yellow fabric, 32 from purple fabric, 64 from light purple fabric, and 32 from maroon fabric.
2. Join the triangles for each of the 16 blocks, as shown in Diagram 7-8.
3. Setting the blocks together is a very precise operation, for if it is not done properly, the movement will stop. Study the diagram and the colored photograph, too. Set the blocks exactly as shown.
4. Make the borders from the maroon, yellow, and purple fabrics, and join.
5. Interline, back, and quilt.

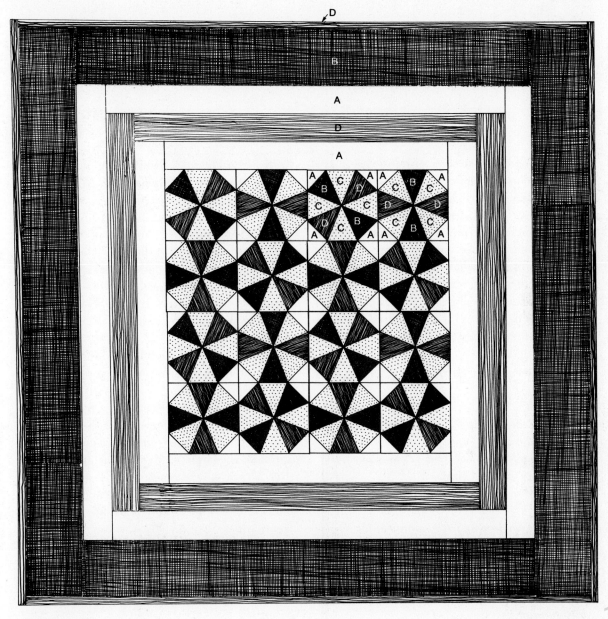

Diagram 7-8

229

8 / CLUNY WALL HANGING (see Plate 82 on page 206)

After seeing a recent show of tapestries at the Metropolitan Museum of Art in New York, we were inspired by the tender and beautifully done scenes they showed of small creatures and multihued flowers. The minute attention to detail, the busy harmony of natural forms frozen in eternal spring, brought us to this interpretation. We chose to work with felts in an effort to retain the matt, woolly feeling of the originals. Of course, we have simplified and stylized the designs, creating a mood rather than a copy.

Finished size: 41 by 71 inches

Materials:
1 yard 72-inch-wide felt (12-ounce) for foundation
1⅓ yards 72-inch-wide felt (12-ounce) for large tree and border
¾ yard 72-inch-wide felt (12-ounce) for smaller tree
⅓ yard 72-inch-wide felt (12-ounce) for dog
¼ yard 72-inch-wide felt (12-ounce) in assorted colors for other appliqués (optional)
2 yards muslin for lining
2¼ yards 44-inch-wide fabric for backing bias binding

Procedure:
1. Cut foundation to measure 36 by 66 inches. Mount it to a piece of muslin by basting all around the perimeter.

2. Refer to Plate 82 if you wish to interpret the appliqués shown in this hanging. We have not given diagrams for the appliqués, as free expression is the key to the charm of this particular work. Then from felt fabric, cut the largest appliqué shapes first; in this case, the two trees. Place them on the foundation and stitch them ⅛ of an inch from the edges. This placement will establish the design limits. Then do the machine-stitching to represent the graining of the tree trunks.

3. From felt fabric, cut birds, flowers, animals, or any other shapes you wish to appliqué. Pin them to the foundation. For greatest visual efficacy, tape the foundation to the wall before you start pinning. Do not sew down the appliqués until all the shapes are cut and each individual appliqué is complete. Many of the appliqués on this hanging are superimposed by other appliqués. All are stitched by machine so that the line of sewing becomes an integral design factor.

4. When the design is satisfactory, sew the appliqués to the foundation. Topstitch in all instances except where the line of stitching would add an unattractive element; then, blind-stitch.

5. Make a 2½-inch border, and then line the hanging. Add tabs if you wish to hang it from a pole.

9 / AMISH DIAMOND QUILT (Plate 85)

This quilt depends upon its clean proportions and atonal colors for excitement. The rococo quilting patterns embellish the plain surfaces, giving richness and texture. Instructions for matching pillowcases can be found in Chapter 8.

PLATE 85: *Amish Diamond Quilt,* concept by Audrey Heard, designed and made by Diane Wilson.

Diagram 7-9

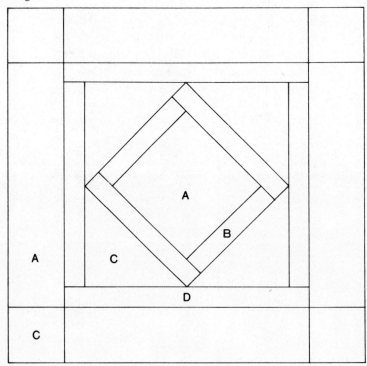

Finished size: 90 by 90 inches

Materials:
*4¼ yards 36-inch-wide fabric in purple (for A
    areas in Diagram 7-9)*
*2¼ yards 36-inch-wide fabric in orange (for B
    areas in Diagram 7-9)*
*2⅓ yards 36-inch-wide fabric in red (for C areas
    in Diagram 7-9)*
*1¼ yards 36-inch-wide fabric in green (for D
    areas in Diagram 7-9)*
thread in appropriate colors
fabric for interlining
fabric for backing

Procedure:
*(Note: ¼-inch seam allowances are included in
the following instructions)*
1. Enlarge pattern pieces in Diagram 7-9 and
cut templates. From purple fabric, cut one
28-inch square and 4 rectangles, each measuring 14 by 62 inches.
2. From orange fabric, cut 2 rectangles, each
measuring 5 by 28 inches, and 2 rectangles,
each measuring 5 by 38 inches.
3. From red fabric, cut two 26-inch squares.
Then cut each of these in half on their diagonals
to make 4 triangles. Also cut four 14-inch
squares.
4. From green fabric, cut 2 rectangles, each
measuring 5 by 52 inches, and 2 rectangles,
each measuring 5 by 62 inches.
5. Starting with the large center square, join
pieces in order, as shown in Diagram 7-9, going
toward the outside. It's a very logical,
straightforward procedure.
6. Interline, back, and quilt using the pattern
given in Diagram 7-10. Review the section on
laying out quilting patterns. You will find it
helpful if you have never done intricate quilting.

Diagram 7-10

10 / MODERN PATCHWORK
QUILT (see Plate 64 on page 189)

Although this quilt looks complicated, it is simple and straightforward, employing just two basic patterns put together by reversing the axes of the blocks as they are joined.

The interlocking effects are magnified from block to block, forming an intricate overall design.

Finished size: 84 by 84 inches

Materials:

4 yards 36-inch-wide fabric in off-white (for W areas on Diagrams 7-11A and B and for border)

2 yards 36-inch-wide fabric in brick red print (for R areas on Diagrams 7-11A and B)

2 yards 36-inch-wide fabric in indigo blue (for B areas on Diagram 7-11A and for border)

1 yard 36-inch-wide fabric in green print (for G areas on Diagrams 7-11A and B)

7½ yards 36-inch-wide fabric in green (for inner border and for backing of quilt)

fabric for interlining

Procedure:

1. For borders, cut 4 strips in off-white, each measuring 9½ by 84½ inches; 4 strips in blue, each measuring 5½ by 66½ inches; and 4 strips in green, each measuring 1½ by 56½ inches.

2. Enlarge pattern pieces for Diagrams 7-11A and B and cut templates. Then cut all required pieces in colors designated in diagram.

3. Make 12 blocks as shown in Diagram 7-11A and 24 as shown in Diagram 7-11B. Each block finishes to 9 inches square, without seam allowances.

4. Assemble the blocks as shown in Diagram 7-12. Do this row by row, finally joining row to row.

5. Join the borders.

6. Prepare the quilt for quilting with an interlining and backing.

7. Quilt the blocks in outline and the larger borders in a more elaborate pattern. We used an adaptation of the Quaker feather pattern shown in Chapter 3. The large center should also be quilted ornately.

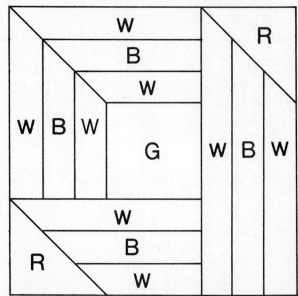

Diagram 7-11A

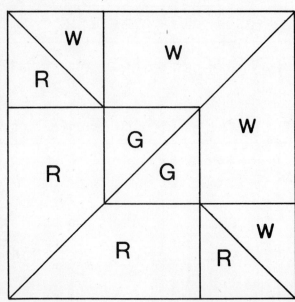

Diagram 7-11B

Diagram 7-12

8

Other Things to Make

Puff Quilt Wreath and Small Patchwork Ornaments, designed and made by Sue Knisley.
Puff Quilt Topiary Tree, designed by Audrey Heard, made by Sue Knisley.
Puff Quilt Wreath and Large Patchwork Ornaments, designed and made by Sandra Dwyer.

By utilizing the techniques you have learned in these chapters, you can make countless items for yourself, your family, and your home. Clothing, table linens, ornaments, and home furnishings accessories are just a few of the possible categories. Almost anything can be made of pieced patchwork, and appliqué is decorative wherever it is used. Quilting the result of either technique adds the final touches—body, warmth, and beauty—to anything that is made of fabric.

Remnants of old quilts can also be utilized in the making of these articles. For instance, we have used old—but sturdy—quilts to make the yo-yo skirt in Plate 86, the tie in Plate 90, the hat in Plate 92, the muffler in Plate 93, and the boat neck topper in Plate 94. We do not recommend cutting up fine old quilts to make miscellaneous articles, but when a section of a quilt is torn or worn, then we feel that the life of the quilt can be extended by making the salvageable parts into something useful and attractive. Examine the old quilt you plan to use, for often the materials will be worn or torn. Sometimes, only the patches made in one particular fabric will

have deteriorated. This happens because certain dyes have corrosive effects and, over the years, the material simply deteriorates. Browns and reds are particularly susceptible.

If the material is sound, you seldom have to worry about the stitching. We have often seen frayed fabrics hanging onto stitching as soundly as the day they were sewn.

Except for the silk and woolen quilts, which must be dry-cleaned, we have no compunctions about washing old quilts. We do not wash those that are heavily stuffed and tied, but if the quilt is made of cotton, filled with a light batt, and finely stitched, we wash it in our machine. We use cool water, a mild soap of the type used only for sweaters, and the gentle cycle on our washing machine. The dryer will not hurt the quilt. In fact, it will often help to fluff it.

Occasionally, a quilt will be yellow with age. In that case, we presoak it in a small amount of bleach added to cool water, and then we run it through the washing machine.

There are countless ways in which to use quilt remnants; we have mentioned only a few. We are sure that you will think of many more.

PLATE 86: A. *Jupon*, concept by Audrey Heard, designed and made by Helen Henry.
B. *Yo-Yo Quilt Skirt*, concept by Audrey Heard, designed and made by Helen Henry.
C. *Hawaiian Appliqué Wrap Skirt*, concept by Audrey Heard, designed and made by Diane Wilson and Helen Henry.
D. *Crazy Patch Skirt*, designed and made by Diane Wilson.

A.

B.

C.

D.

239

PLATE 88: *Flower Appliquéd Vest*, designed and made by Rieta Park.

PLATE 87: *Crazy Patch Kimono*, designed and made by Sharon McKain.

CLOTHING

Quilted clothing is an old form, for it was an excellent way to provide the wearer warmth and protection. For many centuries, jackets, skirts, hats, and trousers have been made using the cloth sandwich method—first the top, decorated or plain; next the filler, using the materials at hand; and then the backing. The layers were joined together simply or in a complicated manner, depending on the ability and the taste of the maker.

JUPON

In Brittany, many years ago, the women wore a garment called the jupon, which was a quilted petticoat. Originally, it was made of handwoven wool, of solid color, and decorated in fancy quilting stitches so that the end result resembled the whitework quilts. The decoration was created by the interaction of light on the surface, highlighting the plain surfaces and shadowing the depressions made by the sewing. Later, as they became available, printed cottons, both toiles and chintzes, were used. These petticoats were worn by the women of the Provences until after World War II, when improved communication made fashion universal. We remember when New York department stores were making jupons into tote bags and when interior designers were using them as upholstery. The jupons were charming, mainly because of the fabrics, which had the look of the toile d'Indies; they were simply quilted, either in squares or diamonds, and the articles made from them were sturdy and long-lasting.

The original jupons were extremely full, with drawstring waists. They were ankle-length, made of lightweight toiles for summer and of wool for winter. The winter ones were interlined for warmth.

We have adapted the jupon into a design for an evening skirt (Plate 86A). For it, we used handwoven Indian madras, interlined with flannel and backed with a *mille-fleur* calico. The design is realized by quilting the Amish patterns given in Chapter 3. The woman who made this skirt is an accomplished seamstress but a newcomer to quilting. We think it a major accomplishment. It took her about 250 hours to complete the work.

Materials:
2½ yards 36-inch-wide madras (washed and preshrunk) in pink for top
2½ yards 36-inch-wide best-grade outing flannel for interlining
2½ yards 36-inch-wide calico (preshrunk) for backing
thread to match the madras
7-inch skirt zipper
about 5 ounces Dacron batting
pattern for a long A-line skirt with waistband, altered to fit properly
tracing paper

Procedure:
1. Cut out one skirt front and one skirt back from each of the three fabrics you are using. Cut a waistband from the top fabric and the waistband interfacing from the flannel.
2. Baste the interlining to the wrong sides of the front and back *top*. Treating them as one piece of fabric, sew the darts and the side seams, leaving an opening on the left side for the zipper.
3. Sew the front and back *backing* together in the same manner as described above. Press all seams open.
4. Try the *top* on, and mark the hem ½ inch

longer than is required for the finished length. Try on the *backing* and mark it in the same way. Cut on marked lower edges.

5. Working on the wrong side of the *top*, turn the hem allowance up and catch-stitch it to the flannel *interlining*. Do the same to the *backing*, by basting the hem allowance. Pin and baste the *backing* to the *top* (with the *interlining*), wrong sides together. Working on a flat surface, such as the top of an ironing board, baste a center line down the entire length of both the front and the back. Then baste a line halfway between the center lines and the side seams (you will have four of these lines). Be very accurate, making sure that the seams line up perfectly. Stay-stitch around the waist.

6. Blindstitch the bottoms of the *top* and the *backing* together.

7. Check the zipper opening to be sure it is the right length, and sew the zipper in place. Attach the waistband, and finish it. Try the skirt on to be sure it fits perfectly. You are ready to quilt now, and there will be no further opportunity to adjust fit.

8. Enlarge the quilting pattern given in Diagram 8-1 and lay out on fabric in the following manner. Cut tracing paper into workable-sized strips and draw a horizontal section of the enlarged quilting pattern on each. Continue making these strips until the entire pattern is con-

tained on them. Then place each strip on the fabric area to be worked. When you are sure that the patterns work perfectly, pin them to the skirt exactly where they are to go and perforate the paper with a sharp pencil, leaving tiny pencil dots on the fabric to guide your stitching. You can do this step one band at a time, laying each out and marking it as you are ready to work on it. Then following the marked outlines, hand-stitch the patterns through all three layers.

9. When all the outline quilting has been done, fill in the large empty spaces with diagonal fillers, as shown in Diagram 8-1.

10. The bigger design elements are padded with Dacron batting to make them stand out. To do this, use a sharp instrument to make small slits in the areas to be padded. Do this through the *backing*. Then gently stuff the Dacron through the opening (see "Trapunto Quilts" in Chapter 5). When the area is full enough, overcast the slit closed.

11. This skirt can be washed and hung to dry. Do not iron it; it is not required, and if you do, you will lose the lovely puffy quality.

HAWAIIAN APPLIQUE WRAP SKIRT

We felt that the splashy decorative quality of Hawaiian appliqué would make a marvelous summer skirt. Shown in Plate 86B is the result.

Diagram 8-1

|← 2" →|

We are including our pattern for this skirt in Diagram 8-2. It is a size 8, but you can scale it up. You can, of course, use any wrap pattern, but check to see that the overlap in back is large enough. We like a very full one.

Materials:
3 yards 45-inch-wide Kettle Cloth in pink for top
4 yards 45-inch-wide Kettle Cloth in yellow for backing and appliqué
thread in pink and yellow
pattern for a long wrap skirt, altered to fit properly
tracing paper

Procedure:
1. Following skirt pattern and using pink fabric, cut out skirt *top* front (Diagram 8-2A) and two skirt back sections (Diagram 8-2B). Cut waistband 2 inches wide and as long as required. (This will finish to ¾ inch when it is folded in half and stitched with ¼-inch seam allowances.)
2. Following skirt pattern and using yellow fabric, cut out skirt *backing*—front and two back sections.
3. Join side seams of *top*. Join side seams of *backing*. Stitch darts of each separately. Try the skirt on, and mark the desired length. Make any other necessary adjustments in fit at this time. If the fit is perfect, stay-stitch around the waist of the top of each section separately, about ⅛ inch from the edge.
4. On both sections, cut off the bottom of the skirt ½ inch longer than is marked. Place the two sections together, wrong sides facing. Pin and stitch, starting at the top and going down the back seam, across the bottom, and up the other

back seam. Be sure to turn the corners squarely (see Chapter 1). Leave the waist open.
5. Trim the corners, and turn the skirt *top* and *backing* inside out. Press carefully, and sew the waist together.
6. Measure the distance across the *top* from side to side. Mark this distance on the center of the waistband. Fold the waistband in half, lengthwise, right sides together. Starting at one point marked, stitch to the end and turn the corner. Do the same on the other side. The opening is the same size as the top of the skirt. Turn the waistband inside out through the opening. Lay it on the front of the skirt, right sides together, raw edges meeting. Stitch ¼ inch from the top, on the side joining the skirt only. Press up, and blindstitch the open edge to the *backing*. Slit the left waistband at the seam line and overcast. The waistband passes through it.
7. Enlarge the pattern in Diagram 8-3, and use to cut a pattern for the appliqué. Test it on the skirt. Line it up on the center front, and be sure that the bottom corresponds exactly to the bottom of the skirt. If the pattern is short and does not come far enough around on the back overlap, lengthen it by inserting a section. To look graceful, the design should come within 3 inches of the back seam, on both sides.
8. When the appliqué pattern is satisfactorily adjusted, lay it on the yellow fabric and cut it out. It is not necessary to allow the extra ¼ inch seam allowance if you follow the procedure of sewing detailed in Chapter 4 on Hawaiian quilts. Your needle will turn in just enough fabric for the stitches to hold securely. Pin and baste the pattern to the skirt. Be sure that it's centered and comes ½ inch over the bottom edge, for you will turn this allowance under and blindstitch it to the skirt.

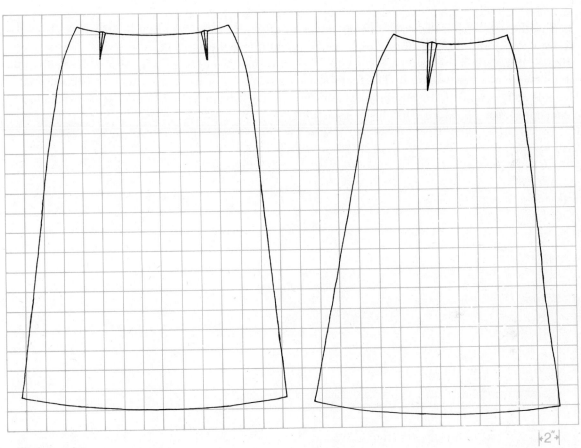

Diagram 8-2A

Diagram 8-2B

2"

9. Sew the appliqué to the skirt, turning under the raw edges and making tiny, close-together stitches. Blindstitch the bottom.

10. You are now ready to quilt. The first row is done directly outside of the appliqué. This may seem unnecessary because of its closeness to the appliqué; however, it will give a neat, puffy outline to the quilting. After doing this, measure in 1 inch from the edge of the appliqué and quilt again, following the outline. In certain areas, you will be able to do this once or twice more.

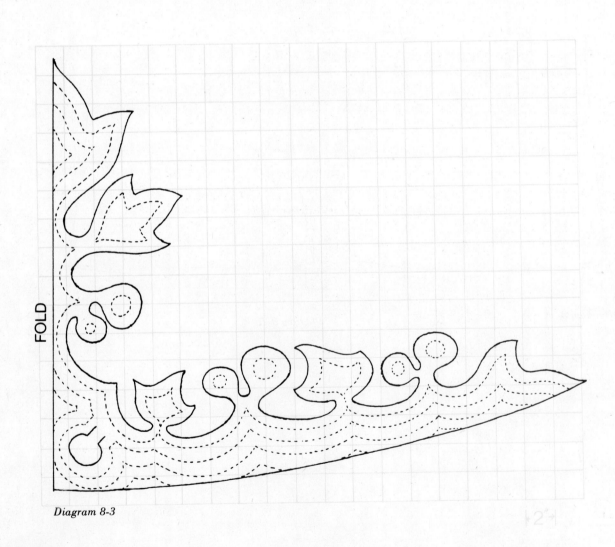

Diagram 8-3

YO-YO SKIRT

We had a marvelous yo-yo quilt from North
Carolina. It was well done, in 1930s prints, but
it didn't look good on a bed or as a wall hanging.
However, in its own way, it had charm, and we
decided to have two skirts made from it. One of
the results is shown in Plate 86C. Although they
took a tremendous amount of time to make, they
were simple to do. The woman we asked to make
the skirts first cut the quilt in half and laid a long
A-line skirt pattern over each section to get the
proper dimensions. Fortunately, the hip measurements worked out just right. Using an outside pink row of yo-yos as the bottom of the hem,
she measured up to the waist and then carefully
removed the yo-yos from the extra fabric above
the waistline. Then, she unstitched the yo-yos at
both sides of the side seams and overlapped
them to fit the curve between the waist and the
hip.

A lining of pale silklike polyester serves as a
slip. It is stitched to the top and blindstitched to
the bottom. A 7-inch skirt zipper is concealed in
the side seam. After the zipper was inserted, a
row of pink yo-yos salvaged from the extra fabric
was laid around the waist and stitched down.

We are not going to give directions for making
this skirt from scratch because it is so time-
consuming and so difficult to figure the sizes of
the yo-yos. However, Diagrams 8-4A and B
illustrate how to make yo-yos if you should want
to. Should you find a yo-yo quilt already made
up—and they seem not too difficult to find—
you might wish to make a skirt the way we did.

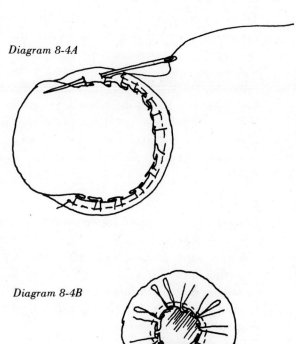

Diagram 8-4A

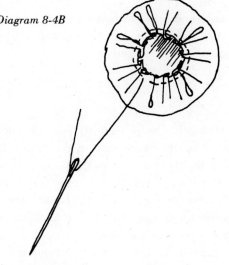

Diagram 8-4B

APPLIQUED CRAZY PATCH SKIRT

There are wonderful opportunities for creating random excitement in a crazy patch skirt. For instance, the gay party skirt shown in Plate 86D was made simply with odd-shaped pieces of taffeta and velvet, but the effect is dazzling. We will give you the basic how-tos necessary to make this skirt, but half the fun is saying your own thing in the placement of the colors, the shapes of the patches, and the whimsy of the appliqué.

Materials:
2½ yards 36-inch-wide lining fabric (we used broadcloth)
2½ to 3 yards 36-inch-wide velvet and taffeta scraps
embroidery thread in various colors
pattern for a long A-line skirt with waistband, altered to fit properly
7-inch skirt zipper

Procedure:
1. Following skirt pattern, cut out one skirt front and one skirt back in the lining fabric. Make the darts and press them to the centers.
2. Baste the lining together to check the fit. When the fit is perfect, rip the basting thread out and lay the two sections flat on a table. You are ready to cut the patches.
3. Reread the section on crazy quilts in Chapter 3 for the techniques of making a crazy quilt. Then study Diagram 8-5. Now you are ready to cut your first patch (A in Diagram 8-5). Cut it on the bias and make it large enough to accommodate the curve of the hip. You will not sew darts into the patches, for by using the fabric on the bias, you are allowing for the natural stretch.

Your second patch (B in Diagram 8-5) overlaps this but is on the same horizontal plane. The remaining patches can be cut on the straight of the goods, and their shape and placement are not important to the structure, just to the design. When you have cut enough patches to cover the lining of both the front and back sections, sew them on (see Chapter 3) and trim the outside edges to conform with the lining.
4. Do whatever embroidery or appliqué you wish.
5. With right sides together, stitch side seams and insert zipper. Following skirt pattern, make and attach waistband. Try the skirt on, adjust the hem, and cut it exactly to the desired length. Bind the bottom edge in fabric to match the waistband.

KIMONO

Plate 87 shows odd scraps of fabric combined to make a kimono. The foundation block was made first, in the required shapes: arms, back, fronts, etc. The patches were then sewn to these. Next the component pieces were joined to form the completed garment, which was then lined in the usual manner. This garment, which can be made for anyone in the family, offers a great deal of freedom in choice of fabrics, colors, and decoration. It can be made as a coat to wear outdoors or a robe to be worn at home.

Diagram 8-5

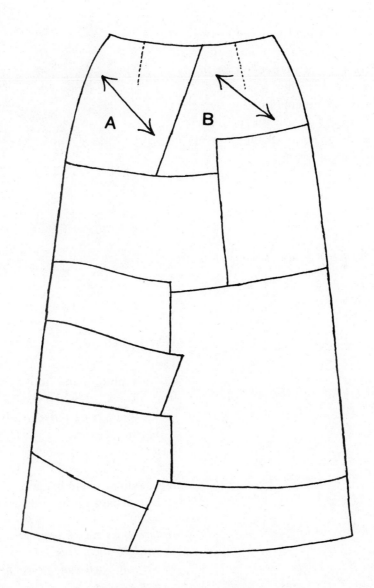

APPLIQUED VEST

The vest shown in Plate 88 was made by cutting foundation blocks in the ground color for the two fronts and the back. Use a commercial pattern for this if you wish. If darts are needed for fit, they are sewn at this point. Then whatever designs you wish are machine-appliquéd to these pieces. When the appliqués are finished, the side seams and shoulders are sewn and the vest is lined in a contrasting color.

PLATE 89: *Puff Quilt Shoulder Bag*, designed and made by Carol Hines.

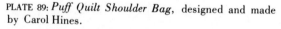

Gingham Patchwork Clutch Bag, designed by Audrey Heard, made by Ann Ross.

HANDBAGS

There are many ways of adapting pieced patchwork, appliqué, and quilting for making handbags. Totes, shoulder bags, clutches, knapsacks, drawstring purses—all can be made by using the above techniques. Either draw your own pattern on paper or use the lines from a bag you already own and like. Then translate it into the medium of quilt making. In Plate 89, we show two bags we have designed and made.

Materials for clutch bag:
½ yard 36-inch-wide fabric for outside of bag
¾ yard 36-inch-wide fabric for lining, borders, and gussets
button or snaps
½ yard pellon
thread in appropriate colors

Procedure:

1. Cut fabric for outside of bag into rectangle measuring 14 by 21½ inches.

2. Cut three lengthwise strips from lining fabric, each 2 inches wide. Reserve remainder for lining and gussets.

3. Following the instructions given in Chapter 2 for mitering corners, join the borders, going up one side, across the top, and down the other (Diagram 8-6A). Press them flat, with the seams

Diagram 8-6A

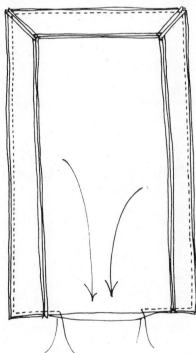

to the outer edges, and top stitch them at the inner edge.

4. Cut the lining the same size as the finished outside.

Diagram 8-6B

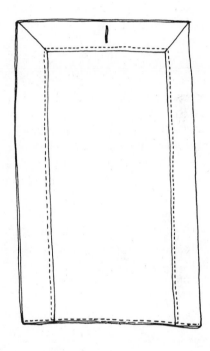

5. Cut the pellon the same size. Stay-stitch it at the outside edge.

6. With right sides together and starting 3 inches from the center of the unbordered side, sew all around to within 6 inches from where you started (Diagram 8-6A). Corners should be very square and precise. Trim seams and corners, and turn inside out. Baste opening closed (Diagram 8-6B). Topstitch the outside edge of this side.

7. Following Diagram 8-6C, cut four 2½- by 8-inch gussets from lining fabric to fit at each side. Round the bottom to fit the curve. Sew two

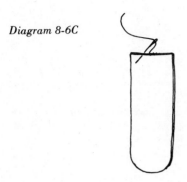

Diagram 8-6C

together for each side, right sides together, leaving an opening through which they can be turned. After turning, baste opening closed and fit them into each side carefully. Topstitch all around each side.

8. For a closure, either make a buttonhole and sew a button to the front or use snaps. Diagram 8-6D shows the finished bag.

Diagram 8-6D

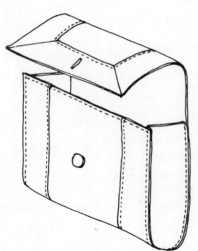

Materials for puff-quilt shoulder bag:
assorted fabric scraps for outside of bag
½ yard 36-inch-wide fabric for lining, strap,
*   and binding at top of bag*
thread in appropriate colors
Dacron batting

Procedure:
1. Review the section on puff quilting in Chapter 3, and refer to it as you approach each of the steps below.
2. From fabric scraps, cut 60 foundation blocks, each measuring 2½ by 2½ inches, to make a bag 10 by 12 inches. Then cut 60 tops, each 1½ inches larger, or 4 by 4 inches.
3. Pin the tops to the foundation blocks, taking two tucks on each of the three sides. Sew on these three sides, and stuff through the open side. Sew the opening closed.
4. Join the modules in rows of 6.
5. Join the rows: For the front, you will have 6 modules across and 5 down and the same for the back (Diagram 8-7A).

Diagram 8-7A

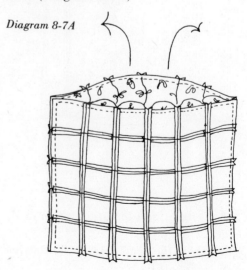

Diagram 8-7B

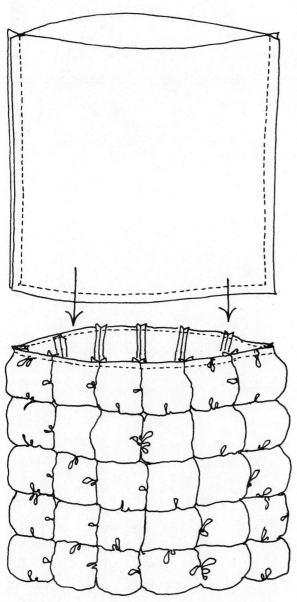

6. With right sides together, join front to back, at sides and bottom.

7. Make lining to fit (Diagram 8-7B).

8. Turn bag right side out. Insert lining, wrong side to wrong side of bag. Stitch around top.

9. Bind the top as shown in Diagram 8-7C.

10. Make strap and attach as shown in Diagram 8-7C.

Diagram 8-7C

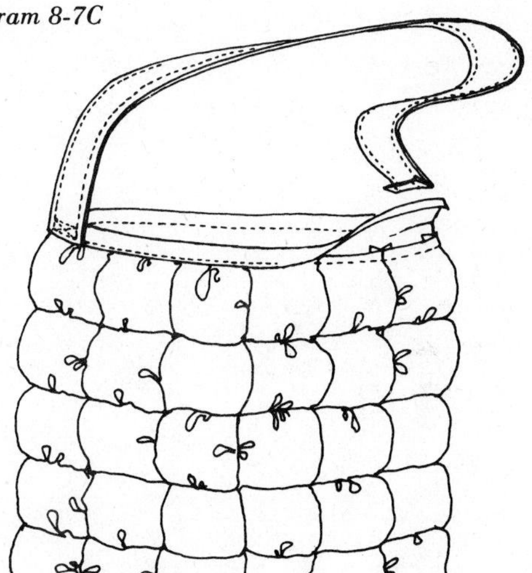

TIES

We show in Plate 90 a tie made from part of an old quilt top. To make it, buy a commercial tie pattern, lay it over pieced patchwork, and cut, being sure to center the design and seeing that it is correctly placed. Then assemble the tie according to pattern instructions.

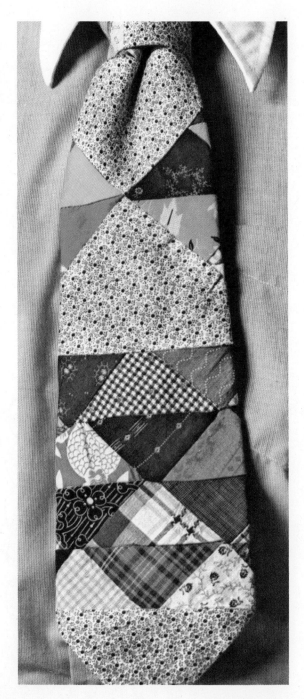

PLATE 90: *Patchwork Tie*, concept by Audrey Heard, designed and made by Ann Ross.

HATS

We designed the hat pattern shown in Diagram 8-8 and asked one of our quilters to make some hats from it. Sometimes, she uses old quilt tops for them and, other times, new fabrics. We show an example of each in Plates 91 and 92.

PLATE 91: *Slices of Calico Hat*, designed by Audrey Heard, made by Ann Ross.

PLATE 92: *Patchwork Hat*, designed by Audrey Heard, made by Ann Ross.

Materials:
½ yard 36-inch-wide fabric for brim
½ yard 36-inch-wide fabric for underbrim
¼ yard 36-inch-wide fabric for lining
assorted fabric scraps for top sections
½ yard pellon
thread in appropriate colors
⅔ yard ribbon for inner band of hat

Procedure:
1. According to Diagram 8-8A, cut 6 pie-shaped sections from assorted fabrics for top of hat and 6 from the lining fabric for the lining. Then cut 2 brim sections from the fabric for the brim, 2 for the underbrim, and 2 from the pellon.
2. Join the 6 pie-shaped pieces for the top and then the 6 for the lining. It is probably easiest to do this in threes. First join three, then the other three, and then sew together the two sections of three. Notch each seam twice, and press very carefully (Diagram 8-8B).
3. Following Diagram 8-8C, place lining in hat, wrong sides together, and stitch at the bottom edge.
4. Stitch pellon to wrong side of front and back top brim. Trim to seam line. Join front to back.
5. Join front to back of bottom brim (Diagram 8-8D).
6. With right sides together, stitch around outer edge of brim. Trim seams. Turn and press (Diagram 8-8E).
7. Topstitch 5 times around brim in even intervals (Diagram 8-8F).
8. Holding hat, crown down, pin brim to it, easing fullness. Stitch.
9. Following Diagram 8-8G, press seam up toward crown. Cut ribbon to fit head size, pin, and then sew onto the turned-up seam, covering the raw edges.

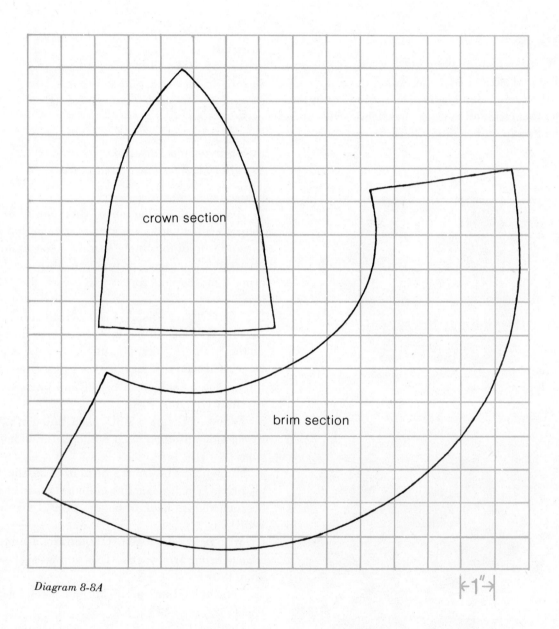

crown section

brim section

Diagram 8-8A

|←1"→|

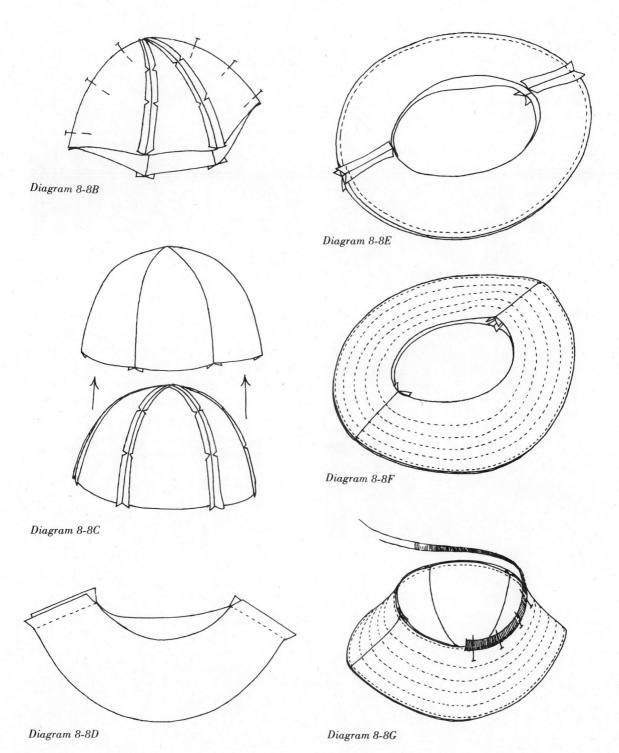

Diagram 8-8B

Diagram 8-8E

Diagram 8-8C

Diagram 8-8F

Diagram 8-8D

Diagram 8-8G

SCARVES

We made the long scarf shown in Plate 93 from the end of an old Log Cabin quilt. It was easy to cut a row, bind the raw edges, and tack fringe to the ends. Of course, if you do not have an old quilt, it is easy to piece this project yourself.

PLATE 94: *Patty's Star Topper*, designed by Audrey Heard, made by Ann Ross.

BOAT NECK TOPPER

The little boat neck topper shown in Plate 94 was also salvaged from a quilt remnant. It is composed of four pieces—a front, a back, and two sleeves. Our pattern is shown in Diagram 8-9. It is a size 12, but you can scale it up or down to fit.

To make it, cut the four pieces and join them in the usual manner. Then bind the bottom edge and the sleeves; face the neckline with bias binding. Finally, insert a 4-inch zipper on the left side to make it easier to put on.

PLATE 93: *Log Cabin Muffler*, designed by Audrey Heard, made by Ann Ross.

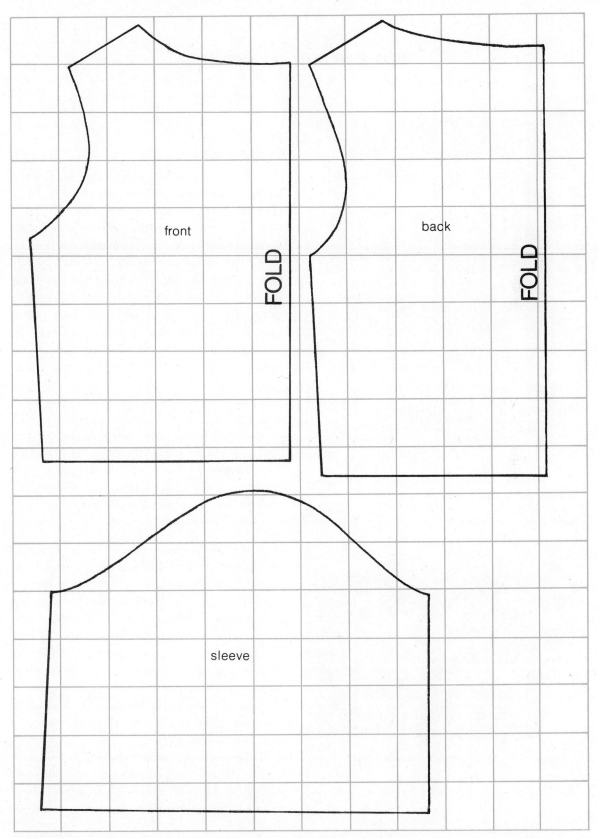

front

back

FOLD

FOLD

sleeve

Diagram 8-9

⊦2"⊣

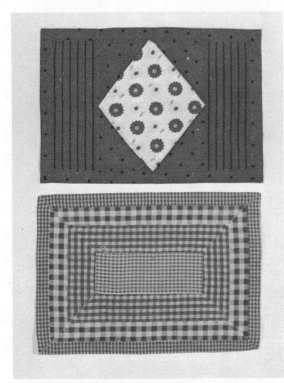

PLATE 95: *Amish Diamond Placemat,* designed by Audrey Heard, made by Ann Ross.
Log Cabin Placemat, designed by Audrey Heard, made by Rosemary Buckley.

PLATE 96: *Padded Appliqué Placemat and Napkin,* designed by Audrey Heard, made by Joyce Everett.

PLACEMATS

Pieced and appliquéd placemats are fun to make for your own home and are very special when made as shower or anniversary gifts. At Christmas, they represent a labor of love, guaranteed to delight the recipient all through the year.

We like our placemats big, at least 12 by 17 inches finished size. However, you can make them to any size that pleases you and fits your table. The shapes can vary from long oblong runners, in the Swedish manner, to hexagons, circles, and rhomboids. The techniques for making them rely on the same methods.

As a general rule, all placemats utilizing the techniques of pieced patchwork, appliqué, or quilting need to be backed; sometimes, they require interlining. The following instructions apply only to the physical mechanics of making the structure of the placemat. If you wish to decorate them with appliqué or embroidery, you must do this first before the lining, interlining (if used), and backing are joined.

To make a placemat: Do whatever piecing, appliquéing, or other decoration you wish first. Then cut the top and the interlining to the desired finished size. Next cut the backing 2½ inches larger in both the length and width. If you are making your placemats to measure 12 by 17 inches, the backing should measure 14½ by 19½ inches. Then lay the top on the backing, wrong side of top to right side of backing, sandwiching the interlining between them if one is required. Make sure that the seam allowance all around is exactly even.

Miter the corners as shown in Diagram 8-10A. All around the inner edge of the border, fold under ¼ inch. Pin it, baste if necessary, and topstitch. Blindstitch the miters closed.

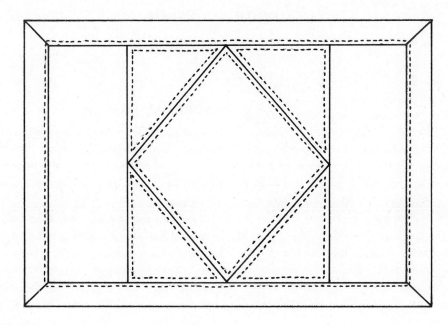

Diagram 8-10A

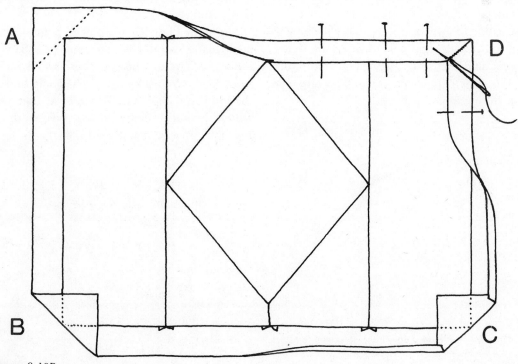

A

D

B

C

Diagram 8-10B

This is the basic technique for making placemats. Although we like the neat, decorative effect of a turned-over mitered border, you could, of course, cut the three pieces the same size and use a separate binding. Do this if it is easier for you. Diagram 8-10B shows a schematic drawing of a completed placemat.

We have designed several placemats, which are shown in Plates 95 and 96. The top one in Plate 95 is an interpretation of an Amish design and the lower one a Log Cabin arrangement of gingham checks. Plate 96 shows appliquéd padded flowers.

The center shapes of both the mats in Plate 95 are cut first. The checked gingham mat is then pieced out by adding strips one by one to the perimeter of the center piece; the Amish diamond is simply set in. The corners are then mitered.

The padded flower appliqué shows just one of the unlimited design possibilities in doing appliquéd placemats. The design on your china can serve as an inspiration, as can the wallpaper in your dining room.

TABLECLOTHS

Recently, it's been very voguish to cover round tables with floor-length cloths. Sometimes old quilts are used, with their corners pinned up or cut off, but often, these coverings are made from scratch.

If you are making a round tablecloth and wish it to come to the floor, you must first find the radius of the circle required. To do this, measure from the center of the table to the edge and down to the floor. Double this measurement to find the diameter. For example, if your table is 48 inches wide and 30 inches high, your radius will be 24 inches plus 30 inches, or 54 inches. The required diameter will be 108 inches. In order to achieve this measurement, you must join fabric 108 inches long to a width of 108 inches, plus add an allowance for hemming if required.

Shown in Plate 97 is a pieced patchwork top made to the overall measurements of 108 by 108 inches. A circle, whose radius was 54 inches, was first cut from a king-size sheet and laid over the top just completed. The top was then cut to match the sheet, which later served as the lining. The top was then placed over the lining and

PLATE 97: *Four-Patch Round Tablecloth*, designed and made by Sue Knisley.

Diagram 8-11

quilted. The edges were bound. The four corners that had been cut away were utilized in making patchwork pillows.

Any size table, whether round, square, or oblong, can be covered in this way. However, the length of the skirt must always first be determined in order to find the overall measurements.

There are other types of tablecloths that could be made using quilting techniques. For instance, pie-shaped wedges of various calicos would make an attractive round cloth. Appliqués are also good, as are many of the pieced patchwork patterns. Red, green, and white could be combined in either appliqué or pieced patchwork to make a special Christmas cloth.

We think it would be very exciting to make a Hawaiian appliqué into a tablecloth. It would be particularly beautiful done in batiste, with the appliqué done in finest white cotton. It would be as elegant as a cut-work cloth from Madeira. However, colors would be effective too, and bright green on white or navy on orange or any other two colors combined would be stunning.

Diagram 8-11 shows a cloth we have designed. For it, we adapted the breadfruit pattern, and because the cloth we designed is oblong, it shows the placement of corner appliqués. The techniques involved are all discussed in Chapter 4, in the section on Hawaiian quilting.

Tablecloths made in the Hawaiian manner can be appliquéd, interlined, backed, and quilted if you wish. But we feel that the appliqué alone, secured to the top, would be enough. The contour stitching should be used within the body of the appliqué only.

PILLOWS

Several years ago, Audrey Heard and a friend hit upon a use for those quilts in their collections that were torn or worn. They cut away the bad places and used the rest to make pillows. Their first intent was to make a few pillows, salvaging great quilts that had deteriorated, but the idea wildfired. Department store buyers saw the pillows and the orders began coming in. The original "factory" was Audrey's bedroom, and it was soon piled to the ceiling with quilts, Dacron batting, muslin, and finished pillows. The work became too much for the two of them, so a newspaper ad supplied a small army of willing sewers. A building at a shipyard in Noank, Connecticut, was rented, and production began in earnest. They called the enterprise Hands All Around, after the first quilt they used for making the pillows.

The techniques described in the following paragraphs are the ones they used, and they remain the same whether you cut the quilted squares from an old quilt or make them yourself. Plate 98 shows a number of their pillows surrounding other home accessories discussed later.

To make a boxed pillow:

1. Measure the size of the quilted piece you plan to use for the top of the pillow. Cut a backing to that size. The backing is the guide; it must be true, with square corners.
2. Tear off a 3-inch strip of backing fabric long enough to go around the perimeter of the pillow plus 3 inches for joining at the ends. This strip should be torn on the straight of the goods.
3. Measure the strip against the outside edges of the backing, and mark the corners exactly ¼

PLATE 98: *Patchwork Bench Pad*, designed by Audrey Heard, made by Jutta Chapman.
Hands All Around Pillows, designed by Audrey Heard, made by Helen Henry.
African Mask Pieced Patchwork Upholstery, designed by Audrey Heard, made by Diane Wilson.

inch in from the edge. We mark them with a tiny cut. Join the two edges to the exact dimension (Diagram 8-12A).

Diagram 8-12C

Diagram 8-12A

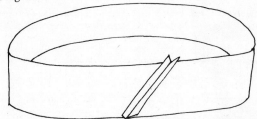

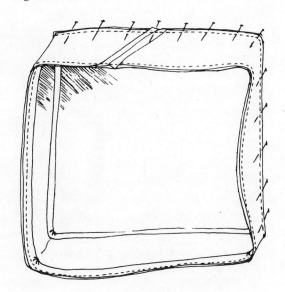

4. Using the cording or zipper foot of your machine, attach bias welting to both edges of the right side of the boxing strip (Diagram 8-12B).

Diagram 8-12B

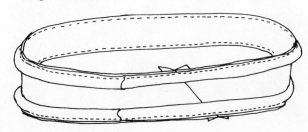

Diagram 8-12D

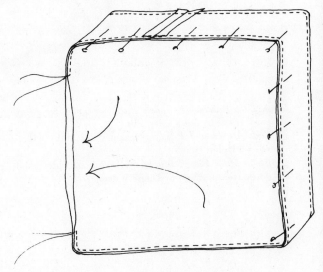

Conceal the joining by cutting back the cord in the welting and folding the edge under before fastening it over the other end.

5. Pin the boxing strip to the backing, right sides together. Pin at each side of each corner and several times across each side, as shown in Diagram 8-12C.

6. Machine-stitch, beginning about 2 inches from the corner (Diagram 8-12D). Stitch to ¼ inch from the corner, leave the needle down, and lift the presser foot. Slit the boxing to the seam line, and turn the corner, pushing the

welting from underneath with the end of a seam ripper (see Chapter 1 for instructions on turning a square corner). Pushing the welting up in this way is a little trick we learned; it gives a neat, precise little tuck, making the corner quite professional. Continue sewing to the next corner, and repeat the procedure until you have passed the last corner by 2 inches. This leaves the opening through which the pillow will be inserted.

7. The right side of the boxing is sewn to the right side of the pillow top. The preliminary pinning together must be very precise because quilted things often have excess fullness that must be gently eased to keep the top straight and true. Use as many pins as are necessary to take up the fullness. Sew the boxing to the top in exactly the same manner as you did the backing, but sew all the way around.

8. Turn the pillow inside out; poke out the corners, pinch them, and press.

9. Make a casing by cutting loosely woven muslin into a top, a bottom, and a boxing, each of which is slightly larger than the corresponding piece for the pillow—about 1 inch for a small pillow, more for a large one. Sew them together as described above, leaving an opening for the Dacron stuffing. Stuff firmly, poking the Dacron into the corners. Do not overstuff. Machine-sew the closure. (If you can find Dupont Fiberfil II, we recommend using it. It has the most resilience and the least tendency to mat and lump. It comes in sheet form; we measure about 2 inches more than the casing size, cut it in strips, and fold them to size. Two or three folds are enough for a small pillow, more for a larger one.)

10. Insert the stuffed casing into the pillowcase and blindstitch the closure. Diagram 8-12E shows the completed pillow.

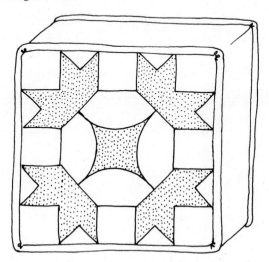

Diagram 8-12E

Diagram 8-13A

Diagram 8-13B

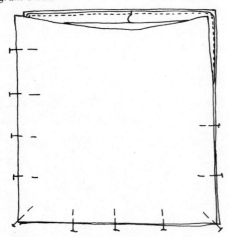

To make a knife-edge pillow:

1. Measure the size of the top you plan to use for the pillow; cut a backing to the same size. Using the technique explained in step 4 of the preceding section and with a cording foot on your sewing machine, machine-stitch welting to the right side of the backing (Diagram 8-13A).

2. Still using a cording foot and with right sides together, machine-stitch the top to the backing, leaving an opening in the center of one side through which the casing can be inserted (Diagram 8-13B).

3. Make a casing in the same way as described for boxed pillows, but make it knife-edged. Stuff it with Dacron, sew together the stuffing opening, and insert into pillowcase.

4. Blindstitch the closure of the pillowcase.

UPHOLSTERY

Also shown in Plate 98 are other quilted things made into decorative accessories for the home. This is a tremendous area for creative thinking. One of our ideas was the bench pad shown, which we designed and made from an old quilt. The woman we asked to make it up for us was very clever in piecing the borders to come to the required dimensions.

The little folding chair, also shown in Plate 98, is very attractive with its pieced seat and pillow. A seat of this type, similar to those of directors' chairs, must be able to take a lot of strain so that it is necessary to sew the pieces of patchwork directly to heavy canvas, which has been cut to the shape required. This can be done either by using the technique discussed in the section on crazy quilts in Chapter 3, where the pieces are sewn to the foundation block, or by joining the pieces to each other first and then sewing them to the canvas by topstitching on either side of every seam.

Sofas and chairs can be covered with fabric you have pieced or appliquéd and then quilted. Curtains can be made, as can Roman shades. It's also a great way to cover a valance. In fact, an entire wall or even a room could be "papered" in a quilt top you designed and made.

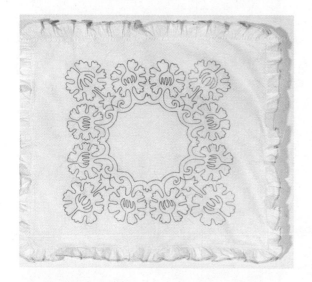

PILLOWCASES

Old quilts did not cover the pillows as our modern bedspreads do. Instead, they were used flat on the top of the mattress; the pillows were covered separately and lined up at the head of the bed. This is a look we particularly like because it is neat, precise, and decorative. It also allows the pillows to be used for naps without requiring the entire bed to be disturbed.

Sometimes, the pillows were covered with shams, which are simply oblongs of fabric made to the width of the bed by the width of the pillows. They are laid over the pillows, concealing them, and are usually made in a fabric to match the spread or quilt. They are adequate, though not terribly attractive.

Pillowcases, or pillowslips as our grandmothers called them, are a more satisfactory solution. Years ago, our grandmothers made beautiful pillowslips, embroidered with monograms or fancy designs and edged with handmade lace or ruffles. Sometimes, they would make patchwork pillowcases in patterns to match the quilts. These they would leave unquilted. Few of these have survived, which is not surprising when one considers the wear and tear put on them resulting from countless rugged washings in boiling caustics. Plate 99 shows a pillowcase made about 1880 in Ohio. The pattern, embroidered in red on homespun cotton, is reminiscent of the appliqués in vogue at that time. This style works well with many different quilts because of its scale and simplicity.

Pillowcases are divided into two categories: first, those that fit directly over the pillows and are to be used as bed linens and, second, those that will serve decoratively, covering the pillows and their cases. The latter are for show, and their construction differs from that of the first group. These basic methods of making pillowcases can be adapted to any design concept. They can be done of patchwork or appliquéd or quilted or be a combination of several techniques. The following descriptions and diagrams show you the construction of the cases. When making them, it is important to remember that all decorative work—embroidery, piecing, appliqué, or quilting—is done first. Then the pillowcase is assembled.

Making a pillowcase is a good starting project for a beginning quilter. Most important, it's small and quickly finished. It's fun to see results when you first start; instant success gives pride in accomplishment and encouragement to go on to bigger and better projects.

To make pillowcases to be used as bed linens:
1. Measure the pillow you wish to cover. The normal size is 20 by 26 inches. Cut a piece of fabric to measure 36 by 43 inches. On three sides, this allows, for seaming, 1½ inches more than the measurements of a pillow 20 by 26 inches; on the fourth side, it allows for a double 4-inch hem to hide the inserted pillow.
2. Following Diagram 8-14A, fold the fabric in half, with right sides together. Stitch ½-inch seams across the top and down one side. These

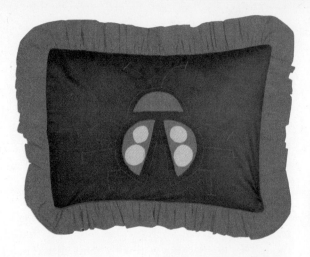

PLATE 100: *Ladybug Pillowcase with Ruffle*, front and back views, designed by Audrey Heard, made by Diane Wilson.

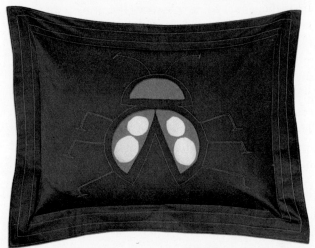

PLATE 101: *Ladybug Pillowcase with Flange*, front and back views, designed by Audrey Heard, made by Diane Wilson.

PLATE 102: *Amish Diamond and Amish Bars Pillowcases*, designed by Audrey Heard, made by Diane Wilson.

270

Diagram 8-14A

seams may be overcast to hide the raw edges. Turn the open end ½ inch to the inside and stitch all around. Measure 4 inches, fold, press, and stitch, as shown in Diagram 8-14B. This gives a generous hem. Turn inside out, and you will have made a pillowcase.

3. Pieced patchwork borders can be sewn to the hem or the body of this, or the entire case can be made of patchwork. If you choose to do this, join your patchwork to the overall measurements (36 by 43 inches) and stitch it together as described in step 2.

If you are using a patchwork border on the pillowcase, you might consider sewing another one to the turnover of the sheet. Use preshrunk fabrics, and, to be on the safe side, mount the patchwork to a muslin or percale body first so that the pieces will not fray when washed.

To make decorative pillowcases: Decorative pillowcases can be made in one of two ways—with the opening on a side seam or with it in the center of the back. A ruffle can be added, or a flange can be included. To make a side-opening pillowcase with a ruffle, as shown in Plate 100, follow the steps enumerated directly below. Following those are instructions for making a back-opening pillowcase with a flange, shown in Plate 101. Directions for making a matching quilt are given in Chapter 7.

1. To make a side-opening pillowcase with a ruffle, cut two pieces of fabric, each measuring 21½ by 27½ inches. These figures are based on a pillow that measures 20 by 26 inches, and allows 1½ inches extra all around for ease. Cut the facing 2 by 21½ inches and a strip 8 inches wide by 2½ times the perimeter of the pillow, or

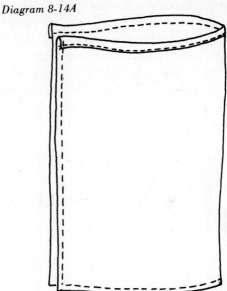

Diagram 8-14B

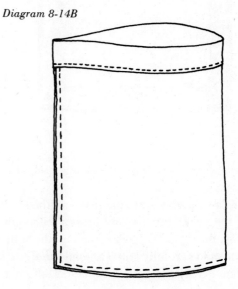

271

Diagram 8-15B

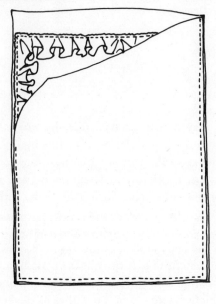

230 inches long, for the ruffle. This strip can be pieced.

2. Fold the ruffle strip in half, wrong sides together, and press. Join the ends together, keeping the seam on the inside. Using the shirring foot on your machine, gather the strip. Leave the threads long and free so that you can adjust the fullness. Distribute the fullness into equal sections and carefully pin to the top, right sides together; leave 1½ inches at the top for a turnback to hide raw edges (Diagram 8-15A). Stitch

Diagram 8-15A

4. Turn the case to the right side, and press it. Pin the facing strip to the raw edge of the top, right side up and facing the ruffle. Fold the excess at each side to the center and stitch on the seam line. Fold the facing down, turn down a ½-inch hem, and blindstitch it (Diagram 8-15C). This finishes the edge.

5. You may leave the end open if you wish, or you can insert a zipper.

all around the top, raw edges matching raw edges.

3. Turn a ½-inch hem to the inside of the short end of the back; stitch it and press. With right sides together, pin the back to the top (the ruffle is inside) and carefully stitch around three sides (Diagram 8-15B). The side hemmed is left open.

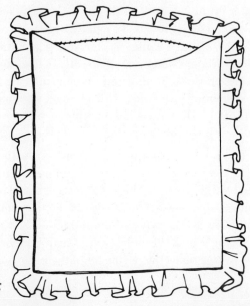

Diagram 8-15C

1. To make a back-opening pillowcase with a flange, as shown in Plate 101, cut one piece of fabric 26½ by 32½ inches (for a 20- by 26-inch pillow).

2. Cut two more pieces, each measuring 26½ by 19¼ inches. On the 26½-inch side of each piece, turn under ½ inch and press. Turn back 1¼ inches; press and stitch at this hemline and also ⅛ inch from the edge (Diagram 8-16A). When you have done this to one edge of each piece, overlap them so that the inside lines of stitching are lined up (Diagram 8-16B). This should be the center of the pillow back, and the total measurement of both pieces together should be 32½ inches. Pin them in this position, and stitch across the two of them about 4 inches from each edge (Diagram 8-16C). The two pieces can now be treated as one, forming the back.

3. Pin the back to the front, right sides together. Stitch around the entire outer edge, at least ¼ inch in. Clip the four corners, and turn inside out, through the opening in the back. Poke the corners so that they are true and sharp.

Diagram 8-16A

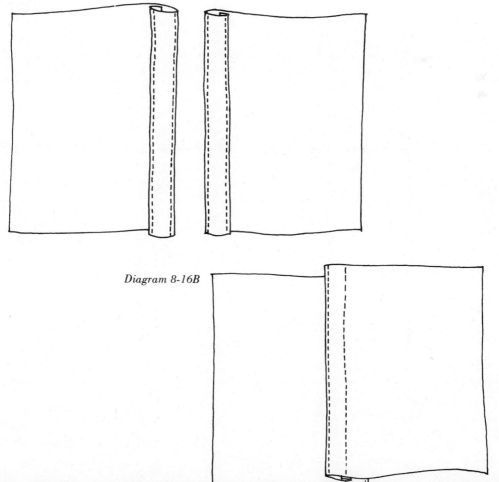

Diagram 8-16B

Diagram 8-16C

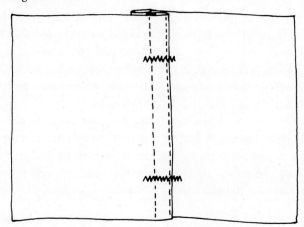

Carefully topstitch ⅛ inch in from the edge. Topstitch again 2½ inches in from this row, to form the flange (Diagram 8-16D). The pillow fits into the inside rectangle.

Diagram 8-16D

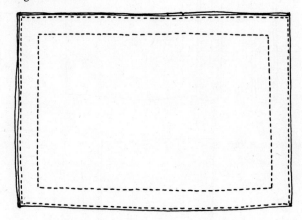

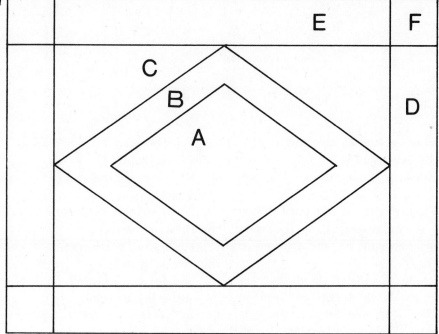

Diagram 8-17A

seam allowances must be added

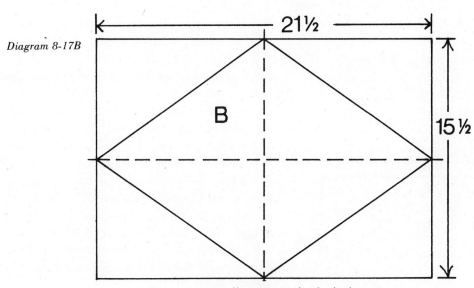

Diagram 8-17B

21½

15½

seam allowances included

Amish pillowcases: Plate 102 shows pillowcases we have designed to go with the Amish quilt shown in Plate 85. Do them in our colors or whatever colors you wish.

1. To make center diamond pillowcase, cut center diamond (A on Diagram 8-17A) from an oblong of fabric that measures 10½ inches by 14½ inches.

2. Cut middle diamond (B on Diagram 8-17A) from an oblong of fabric that measures 15½ by 21½ inches.

3. Cut two 8- by 11-inch rectangles, and then cut these on their diagonals so that you have 4 triangles (C on Diagram 8-17A).

4. Cut two strips, each measuring 3½ by 15½ inches (D on Diagram 8-17A).

5. Cut two strips, each measuring 3½ by 21½ inches (E on Diagram 8-17A).

6. Cut four 3½-inch squares (F on Diagram 8-17A).

7. Join the 4 triangles (C on Diagrams 8-17A and B) to the large diamond (B on Diagrams 8-17A and B) forming the rectangle shown in Diagram 8-17B.

8. Join one of the 4 squares (F in Diagram 8-17A) to each side of the longest strips (D in Diagram 8-17A). Then join these to the long sides of the rectangle shown in Diagram 8-17B. Join short strips to short sides of rectangle.

9. Cut center diamond (A) shown in Diagram 8-17C. Appliqué diamond to center of B diamond.

10. Interline, back, and quilt in whatever design you wish.

11. Make into pillowcase, following directions given on preceding pages.

Diagram 8-17C

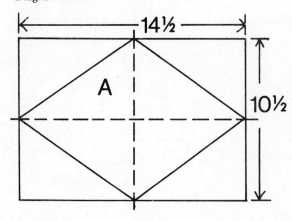

1. To make Amish Bars pillowcase, cut four 3½-inch squares for A areas in Diagram 8-18.

2. For B areas in Diagram 8-18, cut two 3½- by 15½-inch strips.

3. For C areas in Diagram 8-18, cut two 3½- by 21½-inch strips.

4. For D areas in Diagram 8-18, cut four 3½- by 15½-inch strips.

5. For E areas in Diagram 8-18, cut three 3½- by 15½-inch strips.

6. Join seven of the 3½- by 15½-inch strips, according to color plan.

7. Join corner blocks to two remaining long strips.

8. Join to top and bottom.

9. Interline, back, and quilt.

10. Make into pillowcase, following instructions given on preceding pages.

Sailboat pillowcase: You can make pillowcases to suit a variety of needs. Bed pillows, of course, are the first consideration. But how about covering a pillow with a handy washable fabric to use on the sofa in the den? It would be marvelous for naps and far more comfortable for watching TV than a little throw pillow. If you have a boat, you know that the bunk pillows are always in the way during the day. It's easy to cover them decoratively, making the pillows work full time, which will please the skipper. Plate 103 shows one we have designed for this purpose and made in Dacron sailcloth.

Materials:
¾ yard 36-inch-wide fabric in navy blue
¾ yard 36-inch-wide fabric in white
¼ yard 36-inch-wide fabric in red
thread in appropriate colors

Procedure:
1. Make templates according to Diagram 8-19.

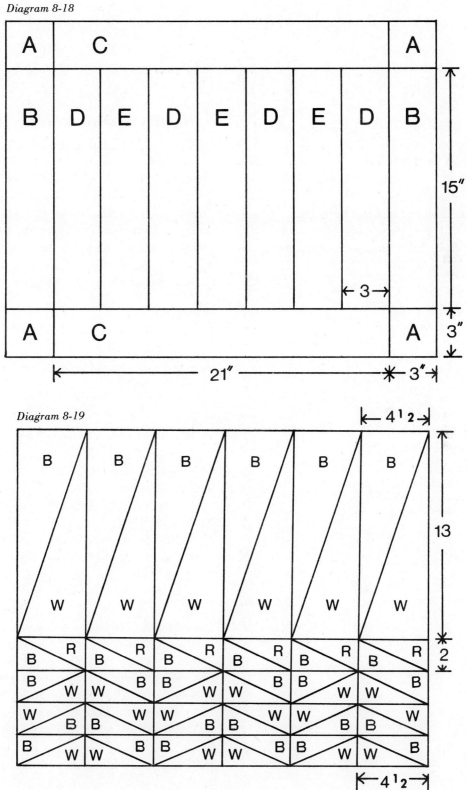

Diagram 8-18

Diagram 8-19

2. Lay them out on the fabrics, as shown in diagram, and cut. Since you are dealing with long biases for the sails, you must be very careful to cut on the straight of the goods and also not to stretch as you sew.

3. Piece as shown in Diagram 8-19.

4. When the piecing is completed, make it into a pillowcase, following instructions given on preceding pages.

ORNAMENTS AND DECORATIONS

Puff quilt wreath: Puff quilting is an intriguing decorative technique. The little "ravioli," plump and pretty, can be joined in many ways to provide decoration at Christmas time as well as throughout the year. The women who made the puff quilt Christmas wreaths shown in Plate 104 enjoyed them so much that they now keep them up all through the year. Following are instructions for making your own wreath.

Materials:
18-inch wire wreath frame
assorted scraps of fabric
thread in appropriate colors
Dacron batting

Procedure:
1. Reread section in Chapter 3 on puff quilting. Then make 45 puff modules, each with a foundation block measuring 4½ inches and a top measuring 6 inches.

2. Join them in three rows of 15 modules each.

3. Join the rows together.

4. Place over the frame, and join with stitching at the inside. It will be necessary to do this by hand, gathering as you go, in order to accommodate the decreased diameter of the inner circle.

Ornaments: Charming ornaments made from scraps of fabric decorate the Christmas tree shown in Plate 104. The small cookie-cutter shapes were made to be used on a small tree in a child's room, while the oversized fruit shapes were scaled for a giant ceiling-reaching tree.

The first were made by cutting two pieces of fabric into the desired shape and then sewing them together, with right sides together. A small opening must be left through which they can be turned. They are then stuffed with Dacron through the opening and blindstitched closed.

The others were made by machine-zigzagging the outside edges of the shapes and then sewing them ¼ inch from the edge, on the right side. An opening is left through which the stuffing is inserted, and then the opening is topstitched closed.

PLATE 104: *Puff Quilt Wreath and Small Patchwork Ornaments,* designed and made by Sue Knisley.
Puff Quilt Topiary Tree, designed by Audrey Heard, made by Sue Knisley.
Puff Quilt Wreath and Large Patchwork Ornaments, designed and made by Sandra Dwyer.

Topiary tree: We designed the topiary tree shown in Plate 104; this could be elaborated upon, however, if, for example, balls of varying sizes were used on a longer "trunk." Following are instructions for making the tree shown.

Materials:
5-inch Styrofoam ball
assorted fabric scraps
ribbon in appropriate color
thread in appropriate colors
dowel cut to desired length (for trunk)
container filled with small stones or plaster (for base of tree)

Procedure:
1. Reread section on puff quilting in Chapter 3. Then make 52 puff modules, each having a foundation block of 2 square inches and a top of 3½ square inches.
2. Join them as follows: two rows of 7 and three rows of 12. Two modules are held for the top and bottom.
3. Pin one row of 12 to the equator of the ball. Stitch the ends together. Pin and sew a row of 12 to each side. An upholsterer's curved needle makes this easy. Then add the rows of 7, and finally the single units, one at the top and one at the bottom.
4. Insert the dowel into the ball; "plant" the tree firmly into the stones or plaster in the container.
5. From a piece of fabric, make a little "boot cover" to hide the filling used in the container, if you wish.
6. Decorate your topiary tree with ribbon and anything else —garlands, a partridge, etc.

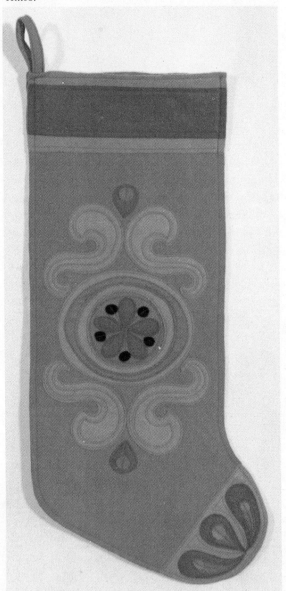

Felt appliqué stocking: The shape appliquéd for the Christmas stocking shown in Plate 105 is cut from two pieces of felt. The appliqués are then topstitched to one of them. (Follow Diagram 8-20 for the pattern.) They are then topstitched together, and a tab from which to hang them is added.

The woman who makes these stockings makes them in all sizes, from father to baby, and does them in wonderful, offbeat color combinations, such as blue with lime, turquoise and yellow, or orange with purple, pink, and maroon.

280

Diagram 8-20

|←1"→|

BIBLIOGRAPHY

Bacon, Lenice Ingram. *American Patchwork Quilts*. New York: William Morrow & Co., Inc., 1973.

Brand, Millen. *Fields of Peace*. Garden City, N.Y.: Doubleday & Company, Inc., 1970.

Carlisle, Lilian Baker. *Pieced Work and Appliqué Quilts at Shelburne Museum*. Museum Pamphlet Series, no. 2. Shelburne, Vt.: Shelburne Museum, 1967.

Colby, Averil. *Quilting*. New York: Charles Scribner's Sons, 1971.

De Dillmont, Therese. *Encyclopedia of Needlework*. France: Mulhouse.

Fennelly, Catherine. *Textiles in New England*. Old Sturbridge Village Booklet Series. Sturbridge, Mass.: Old Sturbridge Village, 1961.

Finley, Ruth E. *Old Patchwork Quilts*. Newton Centre, Mass.: Charles T. Branford Company, 1971.

French, Thomas E., and Vierck, Charles J. *Graphic Science & Design*. New York: McGraw-Hill Book Company, 1958.

Gehman, Richard. "Amish Folk." *National Geographic Magazine*, August, 1965.

Graeff, Marie Knorrs. *Pennsylvania German Quilts*. Plymouth Meeting, Mass.: Mrs. C. Naaman Keyser, 1946.

Hall, Carrie A., and Kretsinger, Rose G. *The Romance of the Patchwork Quilt in America*. Caldwell, Idaho: The Caxton Printers, Ltd., 1935.

Hinson, Dolores A. *Quilting Manual*. New York: Hearthside Press, Inc., 1970.

Hostetler, John A. *Amish Society*. Baltimore, Md.: The Johns Hopkins University Press, 1968.

Ickis, Marguerite. *The Standard Book of Quilt Making and Collecting*. New York: Dover Publications, Inc., 1949.

Inns, Helen, and Lee, Mary. *Your Own Hawaiian Quilt*. College of Agriculture Home Economics Series, no. 128. Hawaii: University of Hawaii.

Lane, Rose Wilder. *Woman's Day Book of American Needlework*. New York: Simon & Schuster, Inc., 1963.

Lichten, Frances. *The Folk Art of Rural Pennsylvania*. New York: Charles Scribner's Sons, 1946.

Lipman, Jean, and Winchester, Alice. *The Flowering of American Folk Art*. New York: The Viking Press, Inc., 1974.

McKim, Ruby Short. *One Hundred and One Patchwork Patterns*. New York: Dover Publications, Inc., 1962.

Safford, Carleton L., and Bishop, Robert. *America's Quilts and Coverlets*. New York: E. P. Dutton & Co., Inc., 1972.

Sipress, Linda. *The Metropolitan Museum of Art Bulletin*, no. 1, 1973-74. New York: The Metropolitan Museum of Art, 1974.

Timmins, Alice. *Patchwork Simplified*. New York: Arco Publishing Co., Inc., 1973.

Wellman, B. Leighton. *Technical Descriptive Geometry*. New York: McGraw-Hill Book Company, 1957.

White, Margaret. *Quilts and Counterpanes in the Newark Museum*. Newark, N.J.: Newark Museum, 1948.

Wooster, Ann-Sargent. *Quiltmaking*. New York: Drake Publishers, Inc., 1972.

Index

Italicized numbers represent photographs; bold-
face numbers represent diagrams.